Human-Computer Interaction Series

Editors-in-Chief
Desney Tan
Microsoft Research, USA

Jean Vanderdonckt
Université catholique de Louvain, Belgium

HCI is a multidisciplinary field focused on human aspects of the development of computer technology. As computer-based technology becomes increasingly pervasive—not just in developed countries, but worldwide—the need to take a human-centered approach in the design and development of this technology becomes ever more important. For roughly 30 years now, researchers and practitioners in computational and behavioral sciences have worked to identify theory and practice that influences the direction of these technologies, and this diverse work makes up the field of human-computer interaction. Broadly speaking it includes the study of what technology might be able to do for people and how people might interact with the technology. The HCI series publishes books that advance the science and technology of developing systems which are both effective and satisfying for people in a wide variety of contexts. Titles focus on theoretical perspectives (such as formal approaches drawn from a variety of behavioral sciences), practical approaches (such as the techniques for effectively integrating user needs in system development), and social issues (such as the determinants of utility, usability and acceptability).

Titles published within the Human–Computer Interaction Series are included in Thomson Reuters' Book Citation Index, The DBLP Computer Science Bibliography and The HCI Bibliography.

More information about this series at http://www.springer.com/series/6033

Jinwoo Kim

Design for Experience

Where Technology meets Design and Strategy

 Springer

Jinwoo Kim
Yonsei University, HCI Lab School
of Business
Seoul
Korea, Republic of Korea

Korean language edition: Design for our Experience by Jinwoo Kim Copyright
© Jinwoo Kim 2014 Published by Ahn Graphics Ltd

English language edition: Design For Experience by Jinwoo Kim Copyright
© Jinwoo Kim 2015 Published by Springer International Publishing AG (is part of Springer
Science+Business Media)

Additional material to this book can be downloaded from http://extras.springer.com.

ISSN 1571-5035
Human–Computer Interaction Series
ISBN 978-3-319-36495-7   ISBN 978-3-319-14304-0 (eBook)
DOI 10.1007/978-3-319-14304-0

Springer Cham Heidelberg New York Dordrecht London
© Springer International Publishing Switzerland 2015
Softcover re-print of the Hardcover 1st edition 2015

Printed on acid-free paper

Springer is a brand of Springer International Publishing
Springer International Publishing is part of Springer Science+Business Media (www.springer.com)

Preface

> We have an experience when the material experienced runs its course to
> fulfillment. Then and then only is it integrated within and demarcated
> in the general stream of experience from other experiences...
> Experience in this vital sense is defined by those situations and
> episodes that we spontaneously refer to as being "real experience;"
> those things of which we say in recalling them, "that was an
> experience." (John Dewey, Art as Experience, 1934, p. 36)

After a busy and successful life, Steve Jobs went to heaven where God asked him,

"What do you think was your greatest achievement in life?"

Jobs didn't hesitate as he proudly showed God an iPhone.

"I made this mobile phone, it's called the iPhone. I was able to transform millions of people's lives through this device by providing them with convenience and harmonious experiences. I made their lives better."

God took a look at the device and noticed how well made it was. Then God asked Jobs, "And how was the trip up to heaven?"

Jobs replied, "God, I was really glad when I finally got to see you, but the trip up to heaven was pretty terrible."

God said, "A lot of people have been saying how the way up to heaven isn't such a great experience. Since you have provided many products that have given people great experiences, I would like you to use your skills to create a great experience for the trip up to heaven. I'll provide any resources you require."

After Jobs received God's command, he went back to his house and spent the next few days and nights contemplating over a possible solution. But no matter how much he contemplated, he couldn't come up with a clear solution. Then he remembered God's promise of providing the necessary resources.

Jobs went to God and asked him, "God, when I made the iPhone, I had Jonathan Ive as my designer, Tim Cook as my strategist, and Joel Podolny as my theorist. The iPhone is a product of our collaborative effort. But these guys are all still alive, and

I don't think I'm allowed to ask you to bring them here. So I want you to provide me with the assistance of similar people already here in heaven.

Firstly, introduce me to Leonardo da Vinci. I noticed there were many bridges on the way to heaven, and I want him to design a bridge that is both convenient to cross and beautiful to look at.

Secondly, I want to meet with Sun Tzu. He's one of history's best strategists, which is especially apparent in his work 'The Art of War.' I want his strategic input on the path to heaven so that as many people can enter the gates of heaven without being led astray by the devil.

Lastly, I'd like to meet John Dewey. After all, experiences is what matters to humans and with his ideas on experiential philosophy I will not only be able to design more beautiful and practical bridges and have the best strategy in place to get people through the gates but I will do that with the humans' needs and wants in mind and make the experience as wonderful as possible."

Although this story is completely fictional, I can imagine how happy God would have been when listening to Steve Jobs' requests for those three critical aspects of designing for experience. We need to know the aspects of "understanding humans," "strategic thinking," and "concrete design" in order to provide people with great experiences.

I wrote this book to help people design really great experiences just as Steve Jobs did by using these three aspects.

Firstly, this book bases its foundation on the understanding of an experience in the perspective of both eastern and western philosophies and humanities. We constantly experience in our daily lives. Our lives feel more meaningful, valuable, and harmonious when those experiences come together. An experience is ultimately what we, as humans, perceive, think, feel and respond to. Therefore, a better appreciation of an experience, first and foremost, requires an intimate understanding of humans. This is why philosophies and humanities are a necessary prerequisite for really great experiences.

But this book is not a book about the philosophy of experiences. I am a scientist who researches Human-Computer Interaction (HCI), not a philosophical thinker of experience. I know eastern and western philosophies to a certain extent, but I am no expert. In fact, far from it. Instead, this book is a book about my own experiences. For the past 20 years, I have had valuable experiences while conducting HCI studies and projects. I have been a technical advisor to several major electronics firms, a committee member of a national research foundation, chairman of the board of directors of a major internet firm, and a strategy advisor for major mobile telecommunication companies. I am extremely thankful for these opportunities. Based on these experiences, I try to explain the abstract and complicated theories of philosophies and humanities using a concrete and personal experience of my own.

Secondly, I seek to provide a frame for strategic thinking about our experiences in this book. Experience has become a crucial strategic issue for firms because our experiences comprehensively transform our lives. People tend to naturally recognize products or services that provide really great experiences that, in turn, make their lives meaningful and valuable. Firms that provide great innovative experiences to customers are the ones that ultimately will dominate the market, and firms that do not provide those innovative experiences end up lagging behind.

Strategic thinking helps firms effectively utilize limited resources under uncertain circumstances in order to achieve the firm's goal. In this book, I explain how products or services came to achieve the position of dominant designs in their respective markets in the perspective of experience. Furthermore, I provide a frame of thinking that can help us to evaluate in which direction a firm should steer towards in order to provide real experiences in the future.

Thirdly, I present key user experience (UX) factors that are necessary for providing really great experiences. A great gap exists between knowledge of strategic thinking in the perspective of the firm, mentioned above, and designing an actual product or service. Therefore, stepping stones that can bridge this gap are required.

In this book, I present three dimensions of experience and six key experience levers that control the dimensions of an experience as the stepping stones. The dimensions of an experience I present not only apply to computers and smartphones but also general experiences in our daily lives. In this sense, this book is not about how to create a UX for digital devices. Users are people too. And users don't go through experiences that are any more special than regular people. If we can understand the fundamentals of a human experience, they can be applied to users as well. Therefore, this book is about the human experience that we, you and I, go through in our everyday lives.

Lastly, this book presents specific design features that can be used to create products and services with really great experiences. However, this book does not focus on the "how to's" of a UX design. Several books have already been published that provide specific guidelines for specific design features in order to provide optimal UXs.

The "how" of creating a product or service may be important for the present, but we need to be able to explain the "why" behind an experience in a way so that it can be applied five to ten years down the road. Even for the present, we need to be able to explain the "why:" Why is it necessary to provide a certain UX to a product or service; Why are certain design features needed in specific circumstances. By doing this, we can use the same logic to propose new design features in our ever-changing environment. Therefore does this book provide a frame of thinking that helps explains the "why" behind specific design features.

This book is divided into four parts. Part I, which comprises of Chapters 1 and 2, deals with why our experiences and designing experiences are important. I present experience in three different perspectives based on philosophies and humanities, as well as my personal experiences. Part II, which comprises of chapters 3 and 4, provides a broad frame for strategic thinking in order to understand our current experiences and predict future experiences. In Part III, which comprises of chapters 5, 6, and 7, I will explain which UX factors are important, why these factors are important, and which design features are effective for providing the UX factors. Part IV includes chapter 8 which acts as a summary to the book and provides organizational implications

Part 3 is especially based on 24 different case studies whose objectives were to deduce the UX factors and design features. However, since I can't provide every detail about every case, I have uploaded the case studies' reports to the Springer Extra Materials site (http://extras.springer.com).

This book is intended for people who are interested in the experiences behind the way we use our products and services, for example for interaction designers, visual graphics designers, service designers, students interested in pursuing HCI or design studies, or entrepreneurs in pursuit of new products or service-based startups.

One cannot design a human experience, nor should one attempt to, because a human experience is created voluntarily and subjectively through humans. This book is not focused on the attempt to design a human experience in itself but rather on designing products for a human experience and by that provide users with something that can help to make their lives more meaningful, valuable, and harmonious as well. It is important to design a product or service that can fulfill people's meaning of life. If we can design products and services that provide real experiences to users that help make their lives feel more meaningful, valuable, and harmonious, doesn't that make our lives more meaningful and valuable as well?

Acknowledgements

This book was possible only because of many people's sincere supports. I would like to thank all those who have supported me in the process of writing and publishing.

Every member of the HCI Lab in Yonsei University participated in the process. Twenty years of all the research are directly and indirectly related to the writing. During the last 2 years, members of the lab put a lot of effort in putting together the research material. I would like to thank Yoojin Lee, Sanghoo Park, Bumho Lee, and Hayang Seo for their efforts with the research in sensual experience. Their efforts allowed for the high-level sense of presence of this book. I thank Jingyu Jang, Hyunshik Shin, Hajung Eom, and Minji Kim for their efforts with the research in judgmental experience. This book is able to provide more useful values to the readers due to their help. Thanks to Sunhwa Lee, Youngsoo Shin, Chaelin Lim, and Hanna Baek for their efforts with the research on compositional experience. Because of their efforts, this book could become more harmonious with the readers. I would like to thank Youngjun Chun, Yeonjoo Kim, and Taedong Kim for their efforts with the research in the strategic aspects of experience. Due to their efforts, it was possible to incorporate strategic implications into this book. I would also like to thank Eunki Jung, who flew back from the US to review the book.

This book was published simultaneously in both Korean and English. I would like to thank Michael Sang Yun Cha and Jaimie Yejean Park for helping me with the translation. Because this book deals with the technologies and concepts from both engineering and social sciences, assistance from those who are familiar with both disciplines was essential. Michael and Jaimie are brilliant researchers who majored in fields related to HCI who can act as a bridge that connects philosophy, social sciences, management, and engineering. I also appreciate Bjarni Herrera Thorisson for his help of technically editing the entire manuscript.

I highly appreciate the help of Ahn Graphics who was in charge of publishing the Korean version of the book. I would like to thank all the affiliates—Sangsoo Ahn, Okshul Kim, Jisook Moon, Jieun Kang, and Mano Ahn—for their patience, kindness, and professionalism. I would also like to thank Hanna Baek for streamlining the publication process.

I thank Changyong Kim, the head of Samsung DMC Research Institute, for getting me started with the book. I would also like to thank those in the Next-generation Interaction Team—Yoonjae Oh, Joonwoo Kim, Byungtak Jang, Hyunseung Choo, Daeshik Kim, and Hyunseok Kim. More than two years of our valuable discussions led me to start writing the book, and my last presentation at DMC inspired me to write a good ending to the book.

Also, I would like to thank Donghoon Jang, Mijung Kim, and Jihong Jung for their constant encouragement. I appreciate their unconditional support and warm welcomes at all times. It would not have been possible to finish the book without their help.

Thank you for all those at Yonsei University. Thank you to professors Junho Choi, Soojin Jeon, Sangwon Lee, Jiyeon Lee, and Hyunjin Lee. Also, thank you to all the professors at YES_HCI in Yonsei University for all your invaluable perspectives. The experience of this book was able to breathe life due to their input.

I appreciate the advices from all my friends and colleagues. Thank you to Sehoon Choi and the board of directors at Daum Communications. Due to their help, I obtained useful insights about innovation from a firm's perspective. I would like to thank those at SBS—Seokmin Yoon, Sungchul Hong, Sanggyu Lee, and the board of directors—for their advice and experience at a broadcasting company. Thank you to Jinwoo Seo and the TFT strategic team members at SK Planet for allowing me to understand the mobile innovation. I would like to thank those at LG Electronics—President Seung-kwon Ahn, Sayoon Hong, Cheolbae Lee, Jinhae Choi– for their viewpoint on the three threads of experience. I would like to thank Hyojung Kim at Naver for her opinion and experience with the internet portals. I thank those at Hyundai MNSoft—Youngsoo Yoo, Hyunggoo Kim, and Eunsoo Kim—for their insights on driving experience of users. Thank you, Sejung Oh and the members at the Future Technology Research Team for teaching me to be in tuning with the frequency of the world.

I would like to thank those affiliated with HCI Korea Conference—Woontaek Woo, Joohyun Yoon, Jinah Kim, Kihyuk Lee, Hwanyong Lee, Kwangsoo Cho, and Hyunjin Lee. I also thank the organizers of ACM SIGCHI—Bo Begole, Gerrit van der Veer, Scooter Morris, Kori Inkpen Quinn. I could finish the book, due to their support.

Last but not least, I would like to thank my wife Mikyung Choi. Thank you for being a cooperative advisor and patient wife with me being stuck in the study room for every weekend while writing this book. Also, I thank Taehyung and Taeyoon for surviving the long summer vacation even without Dad. With my sincere gratitude and appreciation for the love and sacrifice of my family, I could finish this book.

"This work was supported by the National Research Foundation of Korea Grant funded by the government of the Republic of Korea (NRF-2010-342-B00009)."

Endorsements

This book not only shows interactive experiences between individuals in a spatial dimension in our lives, it also clearly reveals the continuity of prior and future experiences in a temporal dimension and vividly presents the development of society, which is a large thread of change."

Junyeong Park, Professor, Department of Education, KyungSung University, Busan, South Korea

"For readers who question the fundamentals of what creates value in experience and how to find such value, this book will provide the answers."

Donghoon Jang, Senior Vice President, Design Management Center, Samsung Electronics

"I assure you that this book will provide strategic thinking and foresight necessary for providing the best experience for users of your new product or service."

Seung-kwon Ahn, CTO, President, LG Electronics

"This book is a must-read for executives, managers, developers, and designers who seek fundamental values and experiential innovation that provides "where to start" and "what to consider" in a systematic and explicit way."

Jinwoo Seo, CEO, SK Planet

"Designing for experience is like the journey of life. Creating new opportunities and situations. Furthermore, actions that leave inspiration and memories to people. This book unravels the method. Experiencing that in itself is also quite enjoyable."

Sangsoo Ahn, President, Paju Typography Institute, South Korea.

Contents

Part III   UX Factors and Design Features for Real Experience

Part I
Basics of Human Experience

Chapter 1
A Real Experience

1.1 Introduction

We go through a lot of great experiences in life. And for some reason, we think our lives have become more fulfilling because of those experiences. This is especially true when we experience great products and services. The great experience lingers in our memories, and it drives us to use that product or service again and again. So when do we feel like we had a really great experience? What kind of changes take place in ourselves as a result of that experience? What are the conditions that need to be satisfied for a great experience?

1.2 Cases of Big Changes

"Professor Kim, I'm sorry to tell you that I won't be making it to our dinner gathering tonight. I was looking forward to it, and I feel terrible for not being able to come."

This was a message I received via a phone call from the design chief of the mobile design division of an electronics company in Korea in the spring of 2007. Since early 2000, I've been part of a monthly dinner gathering that brings together college professors and industry leaders who are involved in mobile phone design. The goal of this gathering wasn't grand; it was an opportunity for like-minded people to get together and talk honestly about diverse topics while eating good food.

However, on that spring day in 2007, something didn't feel right. Most of the regular attendees from the industry weren't able to come to the meeting, so it was eventually cancelled. I started wondering what was going on. I asked the design chief of the electronics company if there was some huge crisis going on.

"The situation is pretty bad. I don't remember the last time I went home. A few weeks ago, Apple released a new product called the iPhone and our executives are furious about it. This phone is something quite different, and they are pushing us to identify the iPhone's strengths and weaknesses and how we can catch up. Honestly,

© Springer International Publishing Switzerland 2015
J. Kim, *Design for Experience*, Human-Computer Interaction Series,
DOI 10.1007/978-3-319-14304-0_1

I have no idea. There's nothing to compare it to, our company is on the verge of a mental breakdown nowadays."

That same week, I heard a similar story during a technology advisory meeting at an electronics company. As someone who researches Human-Computer Interaction (HCI), I attended a monthly meeting at that electronics company as an outside expert regarding how to apply new types of technologies into their business. That month, the agenda of the meeting involved a lot of condemnation such as: How could none of you think of making a phone like the iPhone? Why didn't any of you predict that Apple was going to release a product like this? How could none of our technology advisors and engineers foresee and utilize this impactful new technology? As one of their technology advisors, I felt quite sorry and even shameful. Why couldn't I, a so called HCI expert, get a grip on the release of such a product?

It's not just physical products like the mobile phone that go through such big changes. Let's take short messaging service (SMS) as an example. Even just 4 to 5 years ago, the influence of SMS was vast. Most mobile phone users made use of SMS almost as much as phone calls. Then out of the blue, mobile instant messaging (MIM) appeared and almost instantly replaced SMS as the to-go form of service for instant communication between users. Recently, Korean firm Kakao, which offers the KakaoTalk instant messaging service, merged with Daum Communications, Korea's number two internet portal. This news caused quite a sensation since it was Kakao, a relatively new and young firm, which acquired Daum, a traditional portal giant. How could a venture firm that started out with a MIM service create so much influence as to swallow a veteran portal giant?

There are a lot of cases like this that take place so quickly that there just isn't enough time to analyze them all. But what do those cases have in common in terms of the technology they represent?

1.3   Technology Cannot Explain Everything

When we merely look at the iPhone and the KakaoTalk service in terms of their technology, they do not offer new, innovative technological breakthroughs. But this was precisely why I couldn't answer why I wasn't able to predict this new technology. Neither the iPhone nor KakaoTalk place their technology as their main feature. In fact, the iPhone wasn't evaluated very highly at all by technological experts when it first entered the market. KakaoTalk received similar evaluations. The users, however, perceived them as truly innovative.

The lack of technological innovation acts as two sides of a coin. Purely technological development can be predicted to a fair amount of accuracy, such as the speed of a semiconductor—and the semiconductor industry can build new business models based on those predictions. However, it is extremely difficult to predict future results when users perceive and experience a product or service as an innovation while there is no clear technological advancement. Professor Clayton Christensen of Harvard University coined this type of technology, that brings rapid and radical changes to people, industry, and society, as "disruptive innovation" (Christensen

1997). But disruptive innovation focuses on technological development and application. Technology itself is not enough to explain the impact of the iPhone and KakaoTalk. So how can we try to understand the phenomena of the iPhone and KakaoTalk?

1.3.1 A Weather Forecasting Stone

The anxiety that uncertainty poses to IT firms is beyond mere worry; it's better described as hysteria. The IT industry has far too often experienced the demise of a product or service that was at its peak. Top mobile manufacturers Nokia and Motorola gave way to Apple and Samsung, and heavy-weight TV manufacturers such as Sony and Mitsubishi are no longer appealing to consumers. These cases only exacerbate the anxiety that IT firms that are currently at the top of their game feel. Market research firms and the media take a jab at predicting next year's hottest trends every year partly in order to lessen the anxiety of change. Topics such as what will replace the smartphone, when the high-definition curved TV display will launch, and the rise of the Internet of Things (IoT) are frequently discussed.

I think of an image in my mind every time I hear the latest predictions: a small rock to predict the weather. (http://en.wikipedia.org/wiki/Weather_rock). This rock was tied onto a rope and hung on a tree branch. No other tools were necessary. But its weather forecast accuracy is greater than that of any supercomputer today. This rock is based on a few principles: "If the rock is wet, then it is raining. If the rock is not wet, it is not raining. If there is a shadow under the rock, the sun is shining. If the top of the rock is white, it is snowing. If the rock is shaking violently up and down, there is a hurricane or an earthquake. And if the rock has disappeared, a tornado has passed."

Isn't it extremely accurate? However, I don't need to explain why this weather rock is not useful. The weather rock merely portrays the current state of the weather; it does not predict the future. No matter how hard we try to accurately analyze what is happening in front of our eyes, there is a definitive limit to predicting the future. There is also no clear logic behind the current situation. Even firms that attempt to predict next year's hot trends and technologies possess the same problems. It is hard to predict the future, and it is even harder to logically explain the reasons behind the current situation.

1.3.2 So Close, yet so Far Away: Technology Innovation Theory

Theories such as the technology innovation theory or technology acceptance theory take a different approach in predicting technology (Schumpeter 1942). Let's take the well-known S-curve theory as an example (Henderson and Clark 1990). When a technology is first introduced into the market, its response is weak and growth is meager. But when it passes a certain point, the technology picks up dramatic growth. Then as time passes, growth stagnates. Another example is the technology acceptance theory (Rogers 2003). An innovative technology is first accepted by a few selected people, followed by a majority of people. After a certain period of time passes, even people not familiar with this technology start accepting it. At this time, the technology starts to stagnate in the market.

From when they were introduced, numerous scholars have provided evidence that support the aforementioned theories. Additional theories that support these theories have also been developed and applied in numerous different fields. These theories also provide explanations as to why certain types of phenomena take place. For example, numerous products start out with a devoted group of users but end up not being accepted by the majority of users because of a "chasm" that exists between the two groups of users, and the technology was not able to successfully bridge that chasm.

However, these theories possess problems characteristically different to the problems that market research firms' predictions possess. While it's true that generally, technology has developed based on the principles of the theories, they aren't as helpful in highlighting which specific part of the cycle a product or service is at and what kind of product or service should be made accordingly. While these theories are right in a broad perspective, it's not clear now to apply them to a specific product or service. This is why it is difficult to specifically explain the rise of innovative products or services based on these theories.

Perhaps we need something that connects the short term trend predictions of market research firms and the broad perspective of the technology innovation theory in order to make a really great product or service. This something should not only be able to explain the reasons behind the rise of a currently trending product or service, it should also be able to predict which direction that product or service is heading towards. This something should also be able to provide reasons behind its prediction of the future based on a strong theoretical foundation. And if I were to be more ambitious about the existence of this something, it should also be easily understood and used by ordinary people.

I think a method based on a person's experience can satisfy all of the above conditions. An approach based on the vivid experience of how a person feels and thinks while using a specific product or service is very concrete and specific. To add to that, theories regarding human experience provide fundamental bases on the why's of experiences. Before I get into explaining the theory and approach based on human experience, I want to introduce a brief history of HCI, a field that emphasizes UX, especially on why the recent works in HCI focus on UX.

1.4   A Short History of HCI

Studies on HCI started in the mid-1980's and the field therefore has a short history of little over 30 years now. I want to divide this history into three stages.

The first stage was when studies focused on user interface (UI); elements that you can see with your eyes, hear with your ears, and feel with your hands. During

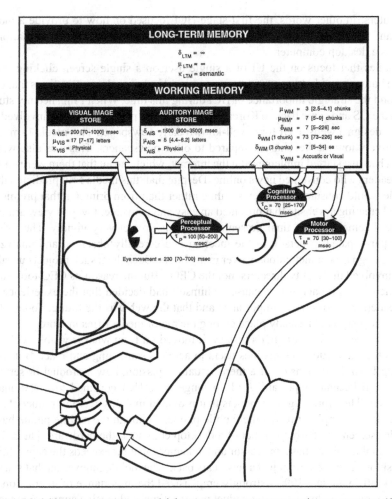

Fig. 1.1 Model human processor: a model that supports one user on a stationary computer. (Courtesy of Taylor and Francis, used with permission)

this stage, it was important to design and evaluate the UI of a computer system so that ordinary users could perform work on their computers easily and conveniently. This is when the concept of usability received a lot of attention, and usability tests became an important job for HCI professionals.

Let's think about the Model Human Processor (MHP), an important theory that represents this stage (Card et al. 1983). As Fig. 1.1 shows, there are three characteristics that define the MHP theory. Firstly, it's very concrete. For instance, the theory calculates where the eye moves from one point to another to the tenth of a second. Secondly, it involves a single user. Instead of a computing environment that includes numerous users, this theory focuses on a single user's view of the screen, touch of a button, and thought process. Thirdly, it focuses primarily on stationary computers. In other words, the first-stage HCI focused on how to provide a more easy and convenient means for a single user to use a computer on a fixed platform such as a desktop computer. Studies that focus on the UI of a single user on a single screen clicking on a single button provide a very narrow perspective. However, there were firms that understood the strategic importance of HCI during this time. When I finished my studies in the US and came back to Korea in 1994, the first project that I was involved in was to design a website UI for a well-known daily newspaper. This media firm had a relatively low market share compared to other newspapers. This was also when Korea had just started implementing the internet, which meant that there were rarely any readers who consumed news online. Despite that, this media firm predicted that people would consume more news online rather than from print. On that premise I started creating a website that provided an easy and convenient way to view articles online. I remember the final presentation of this project very vividly. The firm's CEO participated in person in the meeting and carefully observed and analyzed every design aspect meticulously over many hours. Back then, such projects usually only involved the deputy directors, not the CEOs. But the reason its CEO took such a meticulous approach was because he himself had decided that the experience of his readers were of utmost importance and that the web was the future. Today, this media firm has held a steady place among the major media firms in Korea.

In the second stage of HCI's history, it moved on from what is visible with the eye to the interaction that enables users to activate something and react to it. Departing from the dimension of a mere visual expression, how a product or service functioned became important. And no longer was HCI confined to a stationary computer. Therefore, digital products that provided mobility were introduced, and the leading example of it was the mobile phone. Although the mobile phone has a smaller screen and body than that of a desktop computer, the hardware that makes up the mobile phone has a processor and a memory that far exceeds the capabilities of desktop computers from just a few years back. The mobile innovation that started to kick off in the late 1990's strongly emphasized the importance of interaction. It became important to be able to conduct many actions and receive appropriate feedback under the constraint of a small screen and a limited number of buttons (Chae and Kim 2004).

I particularly remember a project I conducted during this interaction stage called "D-Button," as shown in Fig. 1.2 (Kim et al. 2010). Back in those days before the smartphone, numerous studies were conducted on how to use feature phones efficiently. The D-Button was a project based on the idea of tiny thumbnail-sized LCD panels that fit in place of the hard key buttons of feature phones. The concept of this project was that when a user conducted an activity on the mobile phone other than dialing a number for a phone call, the dial pad hard keys would display buttons more appropriate for the task other than the conventional zero to nine, asterisk, and sharp keys. For example, the buttons would display photos when the user entered the photo gallery, and pressing on one of them would display the photo on the main screen. By providing a change in the method of interaction, the D-Button intended to provide a more efficient mobile experience.

Fig. 1.2 The D-Button feature phone that emphasized interaction

The D-Button project received fairly good evaluations. A renowned magazine introduced the project's results, and a partner firm supported my lab with research funding and worked together on a physical prototype. However, the hype only lasted for a short period of time. While we were discussing whether to implement the D-Button in an electronic manufacturer's mobile phone, Apple's iPhone was released. Instantly, our partner firm's attitude changed. They felt that multiple LCD screens increased the risk of a faulty product, the manufacturing cost would increase, and that the design was actually pretty messy. My role was to defend this negative feedback, but in the end, an actual product never materialized despite a physical prototype being made.

There is one thing I learned from this experience: efficiency of interaction alone is not enough to make a product successful. Thinking solely in terms of efficiency, tiny LCD screens on hard keys could be more efficient than functions on a single panel like the iPhone. Nevertheless, what is the reason people favor the iPhone over the D-Button?

The reason is that people evaluate a product or service based on the entirety of their experience, not solely on interaction alone. I'm not the only person to have learned this lesson. With the release of the iPhone, HCI entered its third stage in its short history, the focus and importance of a UX.

1.5   What is User Experience (UX)?

Comparing a UX to the aforementioned UI and interaction, a UX can be explained by three characteristics. The first characteristic is its holistic nature (Wright et al. 2008). For instance, let's think about the experience of buying and using a mobile phone. When I want to buy a new mobile phone, I research by comparing products' prices and specifications and look up videos and advertisements, and finally I pay a visit to a mobile phone shop to see how the phone actually works and feels. After I buy the phone of my choice, I take it out of the box and turn the power on and start using it to get a better feeling of how it functions. As I use it over the next few days, I am filled with all sorts of thoughts and feelings. The entire process of searching, comparing, buying, and using encompasses how useful I deem my phone to be. In this sense, the International Organization for Standardization (ISO) has set forth a holistic definition for a UX. ISO defines a UX as the combined experience of what a user feels, perceives, thinks, and physically and mentally reacts to before and during the use of a product or service (ISO 9241-210:2010). Therefore, a UX encompasses a broad range that not only includes the visual, tactile, and auditory aspect of a system beyond its screen and buttons but also how the actual system functions under an appropriate usage environment or context.

There are both advantages and disadvantages to the broad range that a UX deals with. The advantage is that it contains many elements that firms think are important in influencing actual users. However, due to its broad nature, it is difficult to grasp exactly what UX attempts to convey. There are so many factors to consider that it becomes almost impossible to consider all of them simultaneously. In the end, a UX causes the side effect of a solution to a problem that changes depending on the situation rather than provide a definitive solution that can be applied.

The second characteristic of UX is that its focus is heavily tilted towards the user's perspective. As indicated in Fig. 1.3, let's place the user and computer on two ends of a spectrum and see if our concepts tilt more towards either side. UI tends to shift more towards the computer. For instance, the decision of whether

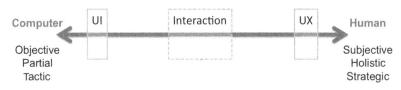

Fig. 1.3 A comparison of UI, interaction, and UX

an icon should be blue or yellow cannot be made without a computer screen and software that have been developed to suit that need. On the other hand, interaction leans relatively more towards the user compared to UI. Interaction is about how a user should manipulate the system, react to it, and in turn how the system should react appropriately while considering the user's reaction. Interaction, therefore, sits in the middle between user and computer. However, the a UX is completely tilted towards the user. How a user thinks, feels, and behaves is its focal point. Therefore, UX is a subject that is more human-centered compared to UI and interaction. While it is good that a UX is human-centered (since, after all, what and how we experience something is important), there is a disadvantage to this approach. Just as every person has their own likes and preferences, the analysis of a UX is so subjective and soft that the line between what is good and bad has become blurred. For example, a usability test can quickly and fairly accurately determine what color an icon should be that the user clicks on in a swift manner. But when it comes to evaluate whether a user had an enjoyable or a terrible experience it is extremely difficult to objectively determine because this aspect of a UX is heavily subjective. And because the UX places its focus on subjective experience, it becomes a challenge to use a UX to design industrial systems that require professional knowledge such as a control system for a nuclear power plant or commercial airliners.

The third characteristic of a UX is based on the above two characteristics. Since a UX encompasses a broad range and its effects have a direct influence on users' experiences, the quality of a UX possesses a strategic value in the perspective of a firm's development of a product or service. In the past when HCI was focused on UI and interaction, HCI professionals did not necessarily have to share their opinions with the CEO of a firm. Albeit the importance of UI, it was not a strategically decisive factor in terms of management. Going back to the UI website project I conducted for the media firm which published daily newspapers, I couldn't help but feel anxious to hear that the CEO himself was coming to see our final results. I was not sure whether the issue of changing the background color of their website to a light gray tone was important enough to explain to the CEO, who was in charge of the long term strategy and overall direction of the firm. But as the concept of UX started to pick up, this perspective started to change. CEOs began to realize that the experience of the user was a crucial aspect that determined the success or failure of firms' products and possibly the firms themselves. I recently had a chance to meet with the CEO of a major broadcasting network in Korea. We discussed for hours in detail his values and vision for the firm and actual UX strategies that can be implemented for its viewers. To emphasize the point further that CEOs and top-level executives are becoming increasingly interested in UX I give you the sample of Samsung: In November 2013 Samsung Electronics' stocks started to plunge and ended up falling by 13 % in about a month, that decrease represented about USD 28 billion of market value. One of the reasons given by market analysts and technological experts was that their newly released smartphone did not provide any new experiences to its users. UX has now become an important topic worth deep and long consideration by top executives.

1.5.1   Important Areas of UX Applications

Due to the strategic importance of UX, it is expanding to diverse fields beyond IT products and services. Let me provide three examples.

Firstly, to experience is important not only during product usage but also during the process of buying a product. The experience during the buying process is considered very important in the field of customer experience (CX). Pine and Gilmore(1988) suggested that the importance of experience during the buying process is very high and emphasized that all forms of economic activity will eventually evolve into the buying and selling of experiences rather than selling mere products or services. A good example of this is the experience that Starbucks provides its consumers. People do not only go to Starbucks to buy coffee beans and a cup of coffee; they go for the Starbucks experience, which is the experience itself of drinking a cup of coffee in the ambience Starbucks provides.

My second example is from the automobile industry. Cars are no longer chunks of metal attached to motors. Recently, Ford revealed their new car models at the Consumer Electronics Show (CES) held in Las Vegas. This may indicate that the automobile has gone through a makeover from a mode of transportation to a digital product with diverse functions. In another example, Korean automobiles have received increasingly positive reviews by consumers recently because their automobiles' functions and systems are focused on enhancing the driver's experience. Since the mid 2000's, Hyundai MN Soft, a subsidiary of Hyundai Motors that produces the Hyundai cars, has been placing priority in providing the best UX in GPS navigation systems designed for the Hyundai cars, so much so that Hyundai MN Soft has changed its name to Total Driver Experience (TDX) while continuing to focus heavily on research and development in the driving experience.

A third application of UX, which can be evidenced in the medical industry, is called patient experience (PX). This field of expertise emphasizes the quality of patients' experiences while using hospital services. I want to give you a personal example of my experience in a Korean hospital. One day, my son fainted during a physical education class in school. I didn't know why he had fainted, and I had no clue to which hospital department I needed to go. I called a general university hospital at around 10 PM, where I was connected to a consultant (not an automatic response system) who kindly recommended me to the most appropriate department and even made a reservation for me. I was even more impressed the next day when the nurse who was taking care of my son called me and explained that he needed to fast during the morning and that by conducting a few diagnostic procedures before the actual checkup, we wouldn't have to wait so long. During this experience I felt the strategic importance of a hospital service system and the patient experience and so did my son who thankfully wasn't badly injured and recovered quickly.

1.5.2   UX and Experience Design

As the importance of UX increases, there is a need to expand the concept of UX beyond IT products. A UX is important for complex products such as automobiles and watches and complex services such as coffee shops and hospital services. Therefore, it's time we go beyond the limits of UX and start thinking about general human experiences. To support this expansion in perspective, I want to introduce the concept of "design for experience." This method of thinking provides principles and methods that can provide better experiences for people in diverse circumstances. It doesn't even necessarily have to involve computing technology. What's important is the application of that technology to provide a better human experience.

As I introduced to you while explaining the characteristics of UX, the movement of designing and developing a product or service with a focus on experience possesses both advantages and disadvantages. While it's an advantage that UX deals with fundamental human experiences, it can also act as a trap because the analysis of these experiences can be subjective and deliberate. And while the effects of a well applied holistic experience can be powerful, there are so many complex elements involved that there is a danger of deducing meaningless results. UX has been receiving wide interest among executives as an important strategic issue, but it's also deemed abstract and hard to grasp tangibly. Therefore, design for experience should head towards maximizing its advantages and minimizing its disadvantages. We can do this by actively applying the many characteristics that make up the human experience. How do we apply these characteristics into design for experience?

1.5.3 Knowing the Human in Human Experience

A person is at the center of an experience, and thus the experience is very personal. Since the experience in design for experience is also very subjective and personal, we need to actively seek out and accept theories in the field of the humanities that cover these issues. Experience in the humanities is covered by western philosophies such as experientialism and eastern philosophies such as Confucianism (Dewey 1934; Li 2006). How can these philosophies benefit design for experience?

Let's look at an example. I recently planned and coordinated a seminar on eastern philosophy at the university I work at. While planning it, I expected a certain rough amount of people to be interested in attending a seminar on the philosophies of Lao-Tzu, Meng-Tzu, Confucius, and the likes. So I reserved a small lecture hall for the seminar accordingly. But when the online registration site was opened, it filled up within minutes. Immediately, I decided to move the seminar to the university's largest lecture hall. The seminar was a 14 lecture course, and over a thousand people participated in every lecture. In total, the seminar was attended by more than 10,000 people. Why were so many people interested in humanities when it wasn't exactly like a K-Pop concert? I surveyed those who attended the seminar and asked them about their interest, and the main reason for their attendance was that they saw it as a perfect opportunity to get to know themselves better. The study of humanities allows us not only to understand ourselves but humans in general. Humanities theories help guide us and deeply understand intrinsic aspects of ourselves such as motivation and desire that cannot be seen in extrinsic phenomena. For example,

Steve Jobs was actively engaged in humanities, and had an introspection about the fundamental characteristics of people through them that led him to discover users' subconscious need to listen to a lot of good quality music while on the go. This led to the creation of the iPod.

Also, the humanities allow us to develop skills for solving existing problems by thinking outside the box away from conventional methods of thinking. One of the most successful emperors in the Roman Empire was Marcus Aurelius who was also a philosopher. He was the last of the Five Good Emperors and was able to lead Rome out of turbulent times. His book, Meditations, is also one of the most widely recommended books for the middle school and high school curricula in Korea. He was not a good archer, and he did not know how to ride a horse well. Instead, he was a very meek and silent emperor who loved reading and writing. During his reign, Rome went through the peak of its golden age where the Germanic tribes did not dare look at Rome as weak. The basis of Aurelius' success laid in his insight into humanities.

Humanities can provide us with the ability of predicting the future. Because they are based on thousands of years of human history, predictions about the future can be made more probable than by using the weather rock, mentioned earlier, or similar methods that only describe the current state. This is the reason firms such as IBM and GE created departments consisting of humanities scholars to research and predict the future. In Korea, LG Electronics has established a research center called Life Soft Research (LSR) at which many humanities experts and scholars work.

1.5.4   Strategic Thinking for Human Experience

The second characteristic of an experience is that it is "strategic." Design for experience should, therefore, also possess a strategic implication. It must be able to help make critical decisions for achieving a firm's ultimate goal under limited resources and an uncertain future. I want to explain two examples related to this.

My first example is the court case between Samsung Electronics and Apple regarding their smartphones. The tech giants sued each other on the basis of patent infringements. In the Korean lawsuit, two of the patents Samsung Electronics claimed Apple infringed was "data categorization technology for distributed transfer" and "technology for informing data transfer mode." These core telecommunications technologies were ruled in favor of Samsung Electronics, and Apple was order to pay KRW (Korean Won) 20 million (around USD 20,000) per infringed patent.

Meanwhile in the US lawsuit, six claims were ruled in favor of Apple: the bounce back function in the photo gallery that shows the user that there are no more photos to show, the finger pinch interaction that enables users to zoom in and out using their thumb and second finger, the double tap interaction that enables zoom in, the rectangular size of the phone with its rounded edges, the home button and the side buttons, and finally, the grid view layout of the home screen. Samsung had to pay over USD 1 billion, or approximately USD 170 million per infringed patent.

From a quick glance, Samsung's technology seems more technology centered, while Apple's patents don't really seem like technology at all. Regardless, one patent was worth USD 20,000 while the other was worth USD 170 million. What is the reason for such a difference? The answer can be found in Samsung's response to the rulings. They claim that although the six patents Apple won may seem similar on the outside, the actual development method was completely different. Therefore, Samsung claimed that they did not infringe on Apple's patents. However, this is the point of the problem. In the eyes of the jury, it wasn't about how a technology was developed; their experiences of the technology was what mattered. Regardless of the difference in how the technology was developed, it is considered infringement if the experience is similar. Fundamentally, a user's experience is more important than a method for developing a function. Therefore, providing a new experience to people through a new product or service can be a distinguished business strategy for a firm.

Another example is Philips Ambient Experience for Healthcare (AEH) (Robert 2007). Consider CT and MRI scans. People who have gone through these scans will know well that the sound of the machine is loud and the appearance of the exterior causes even adults to be psychologically nervous. Think about how children feel about them. Due to these extrinsic tolls, the time to scan children is longer and they therefore get exposed to more radiation as a result; sometimes, children are even anaesthetized to get them through the scans. Philips identified this problem and decided to provide new experiential values to children through a new medical experience program. For example, a large MRI machine is portrayed to children as exploring a new world. Children who are waiting for checkups are provided with an atmosphere that make them feel as if they are members of an expedition force exploring space. They are given space travel passports, the ceilings are decorated with space ships, and the MRI machine is shaped like a rocket heading towards space. Philips was able to alter children's experience from something that they wanted to avoid to an exploration that they want to actively take part in. The effects of this program was vast. Scan time were reduced by 15–20%, and the use of anesthetics were reduced by 30–40%. Furthermore, exposure to radiation was reduced by 25–50%. The implication for firms like Phillips' is that hospitals are paying for these experiences rather than the medical supplies themselves. A new business model was born in the medical industry. This example shows how designing for experience can lead to new business models.

As the two examples above illustrate, if companies design for experience they can create a competitive advantage with their new experiences and make their products distinct from those of their competitors.

1.5.5   A Holistic yet Specific Thinking for Human Experience

An experience is holistic. Therefore, design for experience also has to contain a holistic characteristic. In the past, there were different methodologies for designing physical products, services, and process innovation. Based on their characteristics, methodologies that specifically suited them existed. However, distinguishing between these processes no longer becomes important when the focus shifts to experience because experience is a concept that possesses perception, thinking, emotions, and beliefs, which can be applied generally while using any type of product or service. Therefore, design for experience must be able to encompass products, services, and processes.

Simultaneously, design for experience should encompass all of the diverse elements that make up a person's experience. Let me take a project I conducted for the Korean Government with a mobile data service as an example (Choi et al. 2007). Mobile data service refers to most services on a smartphone other than voice calls. This project attempted to verify if experiencing these services can have a meaningful effect on users' quality of life. Quality of life is a concept that covers many areas in our lives. For instance, we categorized it into 13 distinct areas: cultural activities, leisure, work, education, shopping, finance, family, friends, social relationships, neighbors, and religion. For this project, we conducted a large scale survey consisting of 3,700 male participants and 2,700 female participants, a total of 6,400 people between the ages of 10 and 60. Before I conducted the survey, I honestly did not expect its results to support our expected results. Mobile data service was fairly young at the time, and I questioned whether a concept as abstract as quality of life could be influenced by a context as specific as a mobile data service. However, the results of the survey were surprising. The impact of mobile data service experience was statistically significant in all areas (with the exception of health) and showed an effect of 55 % with overall life satisfaction. Hence, we were able to find out that a product or service can indeed influence our quality of life. Design for experience should also be applicable to general areas of experience.

However, design for experience can end up becoming a very abstract story if only the holistic aspect of an experience is emphasized. Even the aforementioned strategic and theoretical characteristics of an experience endanger leading design for experience to an abstract concept. Theories like the technology innovation theory may seem to make sense when you hear them, but when it comes to actually applying them to a product or service, it's hard to grasp where to begin. So in order to prevent such side effects, design for experience needs to provide actual design features by understanding specific experiential elements that can be applied to a product or service. Furthermore, these design features need to be able to specifically explain how and why they influence certain experiences among the entire experience that people go through.

1.6 Three Principles of Experience

Let's try to understand the principles of human experience based on theories on the subject. Experientialism philosopher John Dewey proposed that human experience could be divided into three principles (Dewey 1929, 1934, 1938).

The first principle of experience is the principle of interaction. Experience is an interaction between a person (who is the organic subject of an experience) and surrounding environmental elements (which are the objects of experience). Similarly, Valera et al. (1992) claimed that humans constantly accept external stimulation through experience and live life by constantly evaluating and thinking intrinsically. For instance, my iPhone and its diverse usage contexts are the objects of my experience that I interact with. This interaction also contains actions that the human expects to perform on the objects, and also a reaction from the environment based on the initial actions. In other words, interaction is a combination of doing and undergoing. For example, on a hot summer evening, I take out my iPhone from my pant pocket to escape from my boredom as I wait at a bus station for a bus that will take me home. I turn on a podcast, and my iPhone reacts to my command and shows me the relevant contents while my screen brightness adjusts to the surrounding environment. I listen to my podcast to ease my boredom. As I conduct a series of actions and receive feedback on the results of these actions, I go through a special experience. Ultimately, my actions on the iPhone and the corresponding reactions, the other people waiting for the bus standing next to me, and the sounds I hear from my earphones and my surroundings all compile into one singular experience on a hot summer's evening at the bus station.

The second principle of experience is the principle of continuity. All experiences are influenced by past experiences while influencing experiences to come (Dewey 1938). In other words, human experience is not temporary and sensorily independent; a current experience is connected to prior experiences and future experiences. For example, my experience of listening to my podcasts resulted in me switching to an unlimited LTE (long term evolution) data service. The principle of continuity is not only emphasized in western philosophy but also in oriental philosophy as well. Let's take a look at the concept of "middle way" proposed by early Bhuddist philosopher Nagarjuna (Walser 2013). The core characteristic of the concept of middle way is that experience actually exists and the flow of time changes people's experiences, and in turn, the concept of experience changes as well. For instance, the sequence of me getting out of my house to drive to the lab in the morning and then drive back home in the evening is an actual experience that exists. However, the way I interpret my experiences may differ. If I had gone through a very busy schedule for the day, then my drive back home seems quite relaxing, while if I found out later that I had passed through a red light on the way home, the way I would interpret that day could be quite different. People live in a world full of memories about individual past experiences; these individual experiences play the role of producing more events (Dewey 1929). It is these past experiences, present experiences, and future experiences that come together to form my life (Walser 2013).

The third principle of experience is the principle of growth. Human experience does not simply connect from past to present to future; during this process, experience is constantly reorganized and developed. Development in this context means that a certain experience is not completed at some moment; it is a constant development towards the future that continues until the subject of the experience no longer exists into being. Therefore, life is development, and development is decided based on what we experience. It's been exactly 20 years since I became a university professor. One year is comprised of two semesters, and each semester consists of 16 weeks. Since, I've taught an average of three subjects per semester, I've spent an approximate total of 640 weeks with students. Each time I prepare for a course and converse with students during a lecture, I realize things I never knew and I feel like this aggregates inside me. During the 640 weeks I spent in lectures, my experience as a university professor built up and has developed my life. James Williams, a philosopher of experience, claimed that only by experience can we explain what we know and how we act, and elements other than experience must not intervene (James 1902, p. 540). His view is that the experiences we go through in life overlap and aggregate to ultimately shape our lives (1902). In other words, everything we experience becomes a part of our lives. Our experiences enable us to build up knowledge, and all knowledge is based on experience (March 2010). Even what we have not personally experienced, when imagined, becomes influenced by our past experiences. Past experiences acts as a resource required for imagination to take place. Ultimately, diverse experiences cause our imaginations to flourish (Root-Bernstein and Root-Bernstein 2013). Through experience, we imagine, think, learn, and live.

1.7 What is Real Experience?

There are two types of experiences that we need to distinguish between. The first type is experience as a process. From the moment we wake up to the time we fall asleep, we are constantly experiencing. Often times, we cannot label what those experiences are, but there is a continuous steam of experience while we interact with the surrounding environment.

The second type is experience as a result. In this case, the beginning and an end of an experience can be defined, and experience can even be named. Furthermore, this experience leads to change in our behavior and emotions. This is called "an experience."

For example, I enjoy going to an art exhibition on the weekends. My favorite time for this activity is around 10 AM when few people are there. When I lived in Boston, MA, I enjoyed the slow paced atmosphere of the Museum of Fine Arts (MFA) around 10 AM. On a sunny day, I can enjoy the warm rays of sunlight that peak through the exhibition halls. This is also the time when the café at the museum starts to make its first cups of freshly brewed coffee, and the museum fills up with its aroma. My interaction with the pieces of art inside the museum begins in this captivating atmosphere. At times I gaze closely at a painting as if looking through a magnifying glass, and at times I look at it through the side of my eyes. Sometimes, I just sit down on the floor and stare at a piece of art. My experience of perceiving, thinking, and feeling while acting the way I do at the museums builds up inside me one by one. I still remember the piece of art I saw a few weeks ago, and I look forward to going to another exhibition to see art I have not seen before. Once I'm finish and leave the exhibition around noon, the experiences of the morning holds a place deep in my heart. As these experiences pile up within me, they become a part of my life. I still clearly remember the first experience I had looking at Picasso's Les Demoiselles d'Avignon in the MFA.

Dewey defined "real experience" as something with a goal that has a clear beginning and end, and can be clearly distinguished from other experiences. Philosopher of psychology Williams explained that "pure experience" is all forms of experience that make our lives more flourishing and can be clearly distinguished by the intimate relationship between human and environment (James 1902). Heidegger coined the term "fundamental experience" as a moment as holy as meeting a god-like and absolute being (Heidegger 1963). By compiling these concepts, a "real experience" can be seen as a process that fulfills and develops our lives through the discovery of the uncommon in our daily lives and filling those moments with special meaning.

1.7.1 Three Conditions for Real Experience

So what are the conditions that are required for a real experience? Let's take an example. Where do we spend most time in our daily lives? For modern humans, it is probably school, home, the office, or inside a certain building or structure. Because of this, people have a great interest in their experiences inside architectural structures. The measurement of a person's experience after moving into a building is called a Post Occupancy Evaluation (POE) (Oseland 2007). The basics of POE is based on a Roman architect named Vitruvius who lived in the first century BC. Vitruvius claimed that architecture must satisfy three conditions in order to provide real experiences to people (http://en.wikipedia.org/wiki/Vitruvius). Those three conditions are firmitas (durable), utilitas (useful), and venustas (beautiful). These conditions describe the structural, behavioral, and expressional aspects of architecture and can be best explained using one of the most famous of Roman architecture, the Pantheon (http://en.wikipedia.org/wiki/Pantheon,_Rome) (Fig. 1.4).

Structurally, firmitas insists that a structure should be firm and should achieve harmony with its interior and surrounding structures. The Pantheon is a dome structure. It does not consist of any interior support; bricks are laid to support the structure of the dome. In order to fulfill this, each brick must achieve harmony with the surrounding bricks in order to create a stable balance. A more modern example is Frank Wright's Falling Water (http://www.fallingwater.org/). This building is not very fancy nor is it visually catchy. However, harmony with its surrounding nature is its greatest priority. The structure itself does not interfere with the nature around it, and it emphasizes natural light and ventilation while conforming to the context of the land it's built on.

Behaviorally speaking, utilitas refers to how convenient the use of the structure is. The Pantheon has been used by the Roman Catholic Church and is still a tourist site visited by a large number of tourists today. I think the fact that the structure is still used as a church illustrates how convenient this building actually is. As a more modern example, I want to mention the Museum of Modern Art (MoMA) in New York City (www.moma.org). First, the building is in the middle of Manhattan and

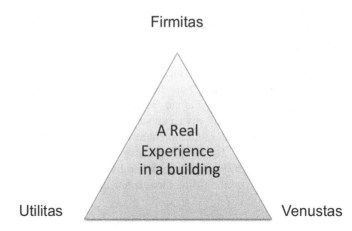

Fig. 1.4 Three conditions for real experience

is thus very accessible. The structure of the interior is very easy to understand, and each room is connected to another organically and thus enables a convenient experience when attending exhibitions.

Venustas refers to how much beauty the structure provides to people. The interior of the Pantheon is still considered a symbol of absolute beauty. From the wall closest to the floor to the hole above that shows the sky, it provides perfect beauty. A modern example of beauty can be seen in the Dongdaemun Design Plaza (DDP) (http://www.ddp.or.kr) which opened in Seoul in 2014. World renowned architect Zahar Hadid designed DDP to symbolize Korea's vision as an origin of creative design industries, and its beautiful design perfectly complements this vision.

Once structural, behavioral, and representational conditions are all met, an experience can be a real experience. Therefore, these are necessary conditions for a real experience.

These conditions do not need to be limited to architectural experiences. They can be applied to any man-made artifacts. For example, think of an internet shopping website. In terms of structure, website navigation should be clear, errors should not occur during usage, and it must be able to protect a user's private information so as to enable safe payment. Behaviorally, the process of asking users for information or payment should be easy and convenient. Finally, in terms of expression, the website should provide appropriate emotions for its users and must be visually comfortable. Based on prior research that have applied these three conditions to online shopping malls, stock exchanges, search engines, and online games, all three conditions showed statistically meaningful effects on customer satisfaction and customer loyalty (Kim et al. 2002).

1.7.2   Design for Experience

As we live our everyday lives, we go through diverse experiences, and these experiences help form our lives. A person's experience cannot and should not be artificially designed. A person's subjective and holistic experience can only be determined by that person alone because it is a product of interaction between that person and the surrounding environment that aggregates and changes over time. Design for experience does not seek to design experience for humans; it intends to design a product or service that people will interact with for long periods of time, especially its structural, behavioral, and expressional characteristics. As a result, users will be able to go through a real experience. Design for experience bases itself on theories of the humanities in order to help nurture strategic thinking in competitive situations and provide specific yet holistic guidelines. In the next chapter, I want to talk about human experience from the humanities perspective.

1.8   Summary

- The markets for products and services often reveal events inexplicable through distinction with new technology or technological development.
- The present and future of a service or a product from the user's viewpoint can only be understood through a focus on human experience.
- User experience is a holistic subjective, and strategic concept.
- Experience is created through interaction with the environment.
- Past, present, and future experiences are all connected.
- Experience continually restructures and develops itself.
- Design for experience is a principle and method that helps enable real experiences during product or service usage.
- Design for experience for a product or service should possess real experience, which can be provided through structural, behavioral, and representational characteristics.
- The principles and methods of design for experience provide specific guidelines for the structural, behavioral, and representational design of a product or a service.
- Design for experience can be applied broadly to a product, a service, and a process design.

1.9   Discussion Topics

- Think about a real experience you recently had while using a product or service.
- Why do you think the product or the service provides a real experience?

- Are there any similar products or services that exist in the market? If so, what are the differences in experience?
- What are the structural, behavioral, and representational characteristics of the product or service?

References

Card SK, Moran TP, Newell A (1983) The psychology of human-computer interaction. Taylor & Francis

Chae M, Kim J (2004) Do size and structure matter to mobile users? An empirical study of the effects of screen size, information structure, and task complexity on user activities with standard web phones. Behav Inform Tech 23(3):165–181

Choi H, Lee M, Im KS, Kim J (2007) Contribution to quality of life: a new outcome variable for mobile data service. J Assoc Inform Syst 8(12):36

Christensen C (1997) The innovator's dilemma: when new technologies cause great firms to fail. Harvard Business Review Press, Boston

Dewey J (1929) The quest for certainty. Minton, Balch and Company

Dewey J (1934) Art as experience. Minton, and Company

Dewey J (1938) Education and experience. Simon and Schuster, New York

Heidegger M (1963) Sein und Zeit (1927), vol 10. Max Niemayer, Tübingen, pp 167–170

Henderson RM, Clark KB (1990) Architectural innovation: the reconfiguration of existing product technologies and the failure of established firms. Administrative science quarterly, 9–30

James W (1902) (1985). The varieties of religious experience: a study in human nature. The modern library, Harvard University Press

Kim J, Lee J, Han K, Lee M (2002) Businesses as buildings: metrics for the architectural quality of internet businesses. Inform Syst Res 13(3):239–254

Kim S, Lee I, Lee K, Jung S, Park J, Kim YB, Kim J (2010) Mobile Web 2.0 with multi-display buttons. Commun ACM 53(1):136–141

Li C (2006) The confucian ideal of harmony. Philosophy East and West, 583–603

March JG (2011) The ambiguities of experience. Cornell University Press

Oseland N (2007) British Council for Offices guide to post-occupancy evaluation. British Council for Offices, London

Pine BJ, Gilmore JH (1988) The experience economy. Harvard Business Press

Robert G (2007) Bringing user experience to healthcare improvement: the concepts, methods and practices of experience-based design. Radcliffe Publishing, London

Rogers EM (2003) Diffusion of innovations, 5 edn. Simon and Schuster., New York

Root-Bernstein RS, Root-Bernstein MM (2013) Sparks of genius: The thirteen thinking tools of the world's most creative people. Houghton Mifflin Harcourt

Schumpeter JA (1942) Capitalism, socialism and democracy. Harper and Brothers

Rosch E, Thompson E, Varela FJ (1992) The embodied mind: cognitive science and human experience. MIT press, Cambridge

Walser J (2013) Nagarjuna in context: mahayana buddhism and early Indian culture. Columbia University Press, New York

Wright P, Wallace J, McCarthy J (2008) Aesthetics and experience-centered design. ACM Trans Comput Hum Interact (TOCHI) 15(4):1–21

Chapter 2
The Three Threads of Experience

2.1 Introduction

Our everyday experience can resemble a ball of yarn composed of multiple inter-twining threads. Experience exists, but it is hard to conceptualize in a way that is easy to grasp, and it is even more difficult to divide the concept into certain elements. However, in order to design better products or services that can provide a really great experience for users, it will be useful to identify the major elements, or 'threads,' of the experience. What are the important threads that make up our experience? What are the characteristics of each? What dimensions are important in explaining the threads?

2.2 Experience is Like an Intertwined Lump of Thread

Allotment gardening, which entails that individuals own or leas a small plot of land for non-commercial gardening, has become an increasingly popular trend over the last few years. When reading newspapers, I often run into sales advertisements on garden plots available in Seoul's suburbs. Dachas in Russia and second homes in USA are similar concepts, which are popular as well. What accounts for this recent trend among city dwellers to own or lease such garden plots?

I own a small allotment garden. About 10 years ago, my parents packed up their city life and moved to the countryside because of health issues. They built a small house and started growing plants by it. From when they moved my Sundays start at 4:30 in the morning. There is no need to set the alarm now that I'm so used to it. After getting ready, I head to the kitchen to pack what my wife had prepared last night—neat stacks of lunchboxes filled with homemade dishes for my parents. Then, I'm all set to leave. In little traffic, it takes about an hour to get to the countryside where my parents and my garden await me.

As soon as I have greeted my parents and given them their food, I change into my work clothes, pick up my tools, and head to the garden. The morning air of the countryside is always refreshing. Today, my to-do list consists of picking up dead

© Springer International Publishing Switzerland 2015
J. Kim, *Design for Experience*, Human-Computer Interaction Series,
DOI 10.1007/978-3-319-14304-0_2

leaves and trimming messy tree limbs. I also have to take care of the overgrown trees that have been growing for 10 years. I have to carefully move them to a more spacious spot. At first, when these tasks were quite unfamiliar to me they were difficult, but now I am accustomed to them and my gardening skills have improved. After the relocation of two big trees, it's already time for breakfast. The food from the lunchboxes tastes amazing as always, even better with the parents.

After breakfast, I pick two mulberry trees near the house. The berries are at their best after a period of much sunshine. I bump into the new neighbors next door who recently moved in from Seoul. We chat for a while, mostly about the cucumbers and peppers I'm planning to harvest in a couple of days. I'm quite thankful to have someone so close by to talk to in a country village in which only a handful of people live.

After a brief lunch, I reluctantly say goodbye to my parents. It's still before noon, so it takes me an hour to get home. Two hours of driving might sound like a lot, but I actually find myself spending the time to organize my otherwise disorganized thoughts. Much of the content in this book are also an outcome of those thoughts. As soon as I arrive at my home, I hand the handpicked fruits and vegetables over to my wife and by doing so I wrap up my Sunday morning.

What I saw, heard, said, and felt at the farm on this Sunday morning is all a part of my valuable experience through which I can feel more fulfilled with my life. I feel like my week is incomplete whenever I can't make the trip and experience the things I do there.

2.3   Threads of Experience: An Essential Compromise

As mentioned in Chapter 1, an experience is characterized by its holistic nature. In other words, an experience is a blend of diverse elements that cannot be easily broken down. Driving to the countryside, picking berries, having a breakfast with my parents, and talking to the neighbors all together build up my Sunday morning experience. Each part of the experience is too closely related to be separable. One part leads to another, and the whole experience cannot be fully understood if we were to try to explain only a single part of it. For instance, the two hours of driving every Sunday morning doesn't sound too pleasant was it not for the fact that the purpose of that drive was to be able to have a lovely breakfast with my 80-year old parents. Without the singing birds and sweet morning air, lifting heavy tree trunks would not make me eager to want to experience that again. All these details, as a whole, created this meaningful Sunday morning experience.

However, the story is different when trying to understand a person's experience during the process of designing a product or service that can provide a better experience. Although it is difficult to divide experience into distinct parts, it is feasible to try to understand what elements constitute an experience without overlooking the overall context or circumstances that surround it. Of course, it is impossible to draw clear boundaries between the elements because of the holistic nature of experience. What we can do is to group the pieces that are more closely related to each other and regard them as elements and analyze the relationship between the ones who are less closely related. This approach allows us to interpret human experience in a more systematic way and to provide better overall experience for users.

Experiential philosophers claim that there is no rational way of breaking down experience into elements (James 1964; Dewey 1934). This attempt to split up experience needs to be philosophically compromised, but it can be quite useful in practice if it can assist us in coming up with strategies to make our experiences more meaningful.

However, it is very dangerous to disassemble experience without any standards. If done wrong, we can end up with ambiguous elements as well as ambiguous relationships between the elements. Therefore, we need to find academically well-established standards and theories that we can refer to. Past studies on human experience suggest that an experience is like an intertwined lump of different kinds of threads (McCarthy and Wright 2004). Among them, there are three threads that are especially important and help us understand our experiences: the sensual thread, the judgmental thread, and the compositional thread.

The sensual thread of experience is concerned with what we sense through our sensory organs. The cheerful sounds of morning birds, the spectacular sunset over the countryside, the sweet and sour taste of luscious berries, and the soft walk on the garden path are all important sensory elements of the experience.

How we judge or evaluate our experience through our thoughts and feelings is referred to as the judgmental thread of experience. Pruning the branches and helping the trees to grow better by relocating them makes me feel proud of myself. I feel happy and healthy doing hard physical work out in the fresh air. My Sunday morning experience wouldn't be fully understood without these values that I appreciate.

The compositional thread of experience is the aspect concerned with relationships and interaction of oneself with others, people or things. The relationship between me and my parents and the interaction between the neighbors and me affect the harmonious experience at the farm. Also, being able to dine with the family and share the handpicked fruits and vegetables at home enriches my Sunday morning experience.

Each thread of experience—the sensual thread, the judgmental thread, and the compositional thread—can be woven (crisscrossed with each other) into different patterns. Different mixes of threads can create diverse and unique patterns that can influence human experience. It is not possible to design the experience itself, but it is worth the effort to drill down into its ingredients to see what provides the really good experience. Let us now take a closer look at how we can characterize each thread of experience.

2.4   The Sensual Thread of Experience

Have you ever been to a rock-band concert? At most such concerts the loud music is amplified to its full volume along with the screaming of the crowd. Talented performers show off their flashy dance moves in their fashionable hair and costumes.

You can feel the high temperature in the venue with a strong smell of theatrical smokes, which at some point cools down with a dry ice fog. We refer to this kind of experience as the sensual thread of experience: see, hear, touch, smell, and taste through our sensory organs (Norman 2004).

Sensual experience is very real and specific for it involves direct stimulation of our senses. It's what we naturally feel before we think deeply or make decisions. For example, at the concert, there is a moment in which we experience pure excitement, and all else is forgotten, including worries about grades or other aspects of life. At that moment you are entirely focused on the music and the performance, and this is what sensual experience is.

Sensual experience is not just about what you perceive, but also how you react to what you perceive. Swaying back and forth to the beats and singing along to the songs is a part of the sensual experience. Thus, a sensual experience is concerned not only about what we sense, but also how we naturally respond to the senses. Therefore, enjoyable interaction is also considered to be a vital part of a lively sensual experience (Steuer 1992).

Sensual experience is a critical medium through which humans can interact with the external world. If we can see but can't hear, or can hear but can't feel, then our experience would be fragmented (Dewey 1934). Through a fragmented experience, we cannot have an effective interaction with the external world, which will ultimately result in a poor quality of the experience. For a real experience, a rich sensual experience is essential. A rich sensual experience is also necessary for judgmental experience and compositional experience, which we will discuss in the following sections. It is because we can make judgments or set relationships based on what we have perceived (Hartson 2003).

2.4.1 Weaving the Sensual Thread with a Sense of Presence

Many factors affect the sensual experience of humans. Personality and current mental states of an individual as well as his/her talents and behavioral characteristics can all influence it. However, these are the factors that we cannot control by adjusting the design of products or services. With what aspects can we then strategically control a user's sensual experience through design? The answer is "a sense of presence."

A sense of presence, or simply "presence," is the sense of "being there" (Minsky 1987; Biocca 1997). In particular, presence in virtual environments has been a hot topic of interest in recent years. A virtual environment is an artificially constructed space through some sort of medium. People these days are mostly stimulated through some medium and feel its presence. Let's take a computer game for an example. We imagine ourselves being in space as we view the animated images on the computer screen and the medium engenders a sense of presence. A sense of presence in the virtual environment is also referred to as 'telepresence" (Minsky 1987).

Presence can be largely divided into three types—physical presence, social presence, and self-presence—depending on the subject that is present (Lee 2004; Lombard and Ditton 1997).

Physical presence means that objects are being felt. For example, I can feel like the physical sword I'm holding or the monster I'm fighting in an online game. They can both have a sense of physical presence. This is also known as "presence as realism."

Social presence is about feeling others that are connected to a system or network. Facebook is a good example. This presence is about whether I feel the people who I interact with on that network. Social presence is also known as "presence as social richness."

Self-presence is about being able to feel oneself in the moment. It is determined how real it is, for example how real it feels to move a medieval castle in a computer game or if I can feel like I'm truly inside a computer game as my virtual avatar. This is what we call self-presence. This is also referred to as "presence as transportation."

Users can indeed feel a high sense of presence when they can feel high physical presence, social presence, and self-presence. If I felt a great sense of presence through the online game, it means that what I saw on the screen felt like reality, that I felt close to the other gamers, and that I felt like I was actually there fighting off enemies.

2.4.2   High Presence vs. Low Presence

Modern technology is evolving in a way that could offer its users a high sense of presence. However, it's not always the best to feel high presence (IJsselsteijn et al. 2000). In case of a pop music venue I talked about earlier, you would definitely want to feel the strong sense of presence of the singers and the dancers. On the other hand, there are times where you prefer not to feel such high sense of presence. For instance, I like to listen to classical music while studying and usually keep it at a low sound-level because it helps me concentrate better. It is important to let the users feel the right level of presence, and to do so we need to fully understand the characteristics and context of products or services. A really great experience that gives users just the right amount of sense of presence—let's call it a "senseful" experience. A senseful experience can be associated with either high presence or low presence. Following are examples of each.

One example of a high-presence experience is a Klive concert (http://www.klive.co.kr/eng/). Klive is a specialized hologram performance hall where the top K-pop content is combined with cutting-edge digital technology. Audiences can watch the performance projected onto a 270° view media façade and with a 14.2 channel surround sound with lighting and special effects that allow us to a vivid sense of reality. We feel as if we are actually at a live concert sensing all that you would there.

Let's take a look at an example of a low-presence experience that is good—driving with a GPS device. The main purpose of GPS devices is to assist drivers to get to their destination quickly and safely. Therefore it is important to help the users not lose their focus on the road while providing helpful navigation during their journey. However, we can often find GPS devices that generate overly high sense of presence, mainly due to overdeveloped technology. Ostentatious 3-D graphics and endless warning sounds can be quite annoying when driving. They can even start to buzz when the driver doesn't follow the instructions. Sometimes there's can be too much distraction from the device, which can obviously be dangerous in the traffic. Steps are being taken to avoid this risk by pushing for a standardization of GPS devices (e.g. screen size, volume, displayed information) to ensure that how the devices are sensed is safe and reliable and that they are not too distracting.

2.4.3 Why is Presence Important for Sensual Experience?

A sense of presence is about being able to perceive through our senses and to react to the stimuli. Let's take Klive as an example again. Renowned singers and dancers are displayed on the screen. The sound of high fidelity singing and chorus makes the settings feel more realistic. The strong smell of theatrical smokes is provided at the right time. Dry ice fog cools down our skins. And with all of this going on we can dance to the music. All of this generates my sense of presence at the Klive.

Renowned German philosopher Immanuel Kant argued that our thoughts and behavior are heavily influenced by our mental representation that is constructed based on the sensory perceptions, and the quality of the mental representation is largely determined by the sense of presence. (Kant 2006). Presence is also related to the concept of sensory affordance, letting people see, hear, feel, and enjoy the sense of presence allows them to make the right judgments about their perception (cognitive affordance) and behave accordingly (physical affordance) (Hartson 2003).

To conclude, a sense of presence is an important factor that determines the perceived quality of our experience as shown in Fig. 2.1. Presence can be affected by the design of a product or services, thus it is regarded as a key moderating factor, with respect to sensual thread of experience (Mollen and Wilson 2010; McMahan 2003, Biocca 1997; Lombard and Ditton 1997; Lombard et al. 2000; Tamborini 2004).

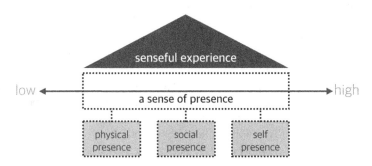

Fig. 2.1 The sensual thread of experience and a sense of presence

2.5 The Judgmental Thread of Experience

A severe drought struck my allotment garden recently, causing serious losses in fruits and vegetable crops. As a remedy, I bought a long garden hose from the near-by store to water the plants. It took me weeks until the plants came back to life, but I was happy with my achievement.

Judgmental experience is concerned with my evaluation of experience in terms of what and how I achieved or obtained from it. Was my desire to have fresh fruits on the dining table fulfilled by watering the plants using a garden hose? What impact did my decision to buy the garden hose have on my overall experience? The answers to these questions can determine my judgmental experience.

We make decisions or judgments almost every moment of our lives, and their results can spark several feelings within us, for example happiness or sadness. Thus, some people refer to judgmental experience as an emotional experience (McCarthy and Wright 2004). However, our judgments are not solely determined by our emotion, but also by our actions and the process through which we try to rationally interpret the consequences of our actions (Csikszentimihalyi and Csikzentmihaly1991). For example, I value working in my garden highly not only because of the emotional satisfaction I get from it, but also because of my rationale that the physical workout is beneficial for my health.

People in general go through the process of interpreting the external stimuli in their own way in order to understand if what they are experiencing makes sense. One thing that distinguishes judgmental experience from sensual experience is this reflexive nature of humans, also known as 'sense making.' In other words, we evaluate our experience as good or bad. My work in the garden is enjoyable to me, despite the strenuous physical effort, because I think it helps me step out of my office, get some fresh air, and stay in shape.

We constantly evaluate our experience. Evaluation can be made at the moment of our experience or even afterwards during retrospection. I can make a judgment about my gardening experience when I am there doing the work or on my way back home in my car. As such, we make judgments constantly and repeatedly in our lives, which makes the judgmental thread an important element of experience.

2.5.1 Value Judgment: is my Experience Useful?

After any experience, we tend to evaluate what value it holds, or what we get out of it. Value is related to what we want or need, and it can be viewed as the standards on which our evaluation is based. Here we introduce the two types of values that people consider most important when evaluating experiences (Sweeney and Soutar 2001; Woodruff 1997).

The first one is utilitarian value, which is related to the functional needs or goals of individuals, and it can be defined as our assessment of whether the experience was successful in terms of achieving a goal. One example would be a person searching the web for stock prices before making an investment. Another example is a traveler in a foreign country looking for directions using a smartphone. These examples illustrate the utilitarian value that we can gain from our experience.

The second one is hedonistic value, which refers to the emotional satisfaction or pleasure we get out of our experience with products or services. Hedonistic value is mostly about the positive feelings such as pleasure, excitement, satisfaction, or happiness, but sometimes it can also be associated with the negative feelings such as fear or frustration. Hedonistic value itself is a goal and a need, unlike utilitarian value. For example, we play online games because we enjoy the action of playing games, or learn a new language because of the enjoyment from the process of learning itself.

If an individual evaluates a product or a service as effective in providing his expected value, he perceives the experience as a useful one. People would like their experience to be useful, or valuable, at all times. A valuable experience can make us happy, and we look forward to a similar experience again. This explains why we tend to go back to products or services that offered us a valuable experience in the past (Venkatesh and Davis 2000), and why users' perceived usefulness is an important element of judgmental thread of experience.

2.5.2   Locus of Causality Controls the Judgmental Thread of Experience

Then which factor can alter our perceived quality of judgmental experience? What makes us appreciate our experience as a valuable and useful one? I believe it's the locus of causality.

Locus of causality is highly related to locus of control, a construct that was first introduced by an American psychologist named Julian B. Rotter. Locus of control refers to the extent to which individuals believe that they can control the events that affect them (Rotter 1966). People with an internal locus of control feel responsible for the outcomes and believe that the future is a consequence of their actions. On the contrary, those with an external locus of control tend to believe that they have very little control over what's happening and think that external factors determine their outcome. In psychology, locus of control is considered to be an important aspect of personality (Diamond and Shapiro 1973; Layton 1985). For example, lack of autonomy in the workplace is stressful for employees with an internal locus of control, while those with an external locus of control have performed better under a set of rules (Kolb 1996).

The concept of 'control' suggested by Rotter has been extended to cover two important aspects of our perception (Pettersen 1987; Wong and Sproule 1984). The first is about the perception of being able or not being able to control what is happening around us (Graybill 1983; Palenzuela 1984). For instance if a student feels that she can pull up the grades on the final exam by spending time to study, her judgment is based on the internal locus of control. If she thinks the grades will depend on the difficulty of the exam questions, her judgment is made based on the external locus of control. The second important aspect of control is concerned with causal attribution, or how we make judgments based on the cause of an event (Heider 1959; Kelley 1967). For example, if you believe you caught cold because you didn't properly take care of your body, it is based on an internal causal attribution. Thinking that it's from your colleague is a result of an external causal attribution.

The concept of control, which was traditionally valued as an important element of personality, can also be expanded to explain the aspects of experience. This is referred to as the locus of causality. Locus of causality is related to how users evaluate their experience with products or services, with respect to the process and the outcome of the experience. The concept is also associated with two other aspects: whether our judgment is based on an internal or external goal, and how much control we have during the process of experience.

2.5.3   Internal Locus of Causality
vs. External Locus of Causality

When you think you have a full control over your experience, the locus of causality is internal. An RC car, a small, self-powered model car, is one example. Unlike other toy cars, RC cars are fully customizable. It is completely up to you what motor is installed and what material is used in the body of the car. You can even choose how you want your car to be assembled. And of course the best part is driving them around the race tracks using a remote control. The entire process of shopping, assembling, and driving can be a fun experience for a user. Plus, the complete freedom of a user in customizing the car illustrates the example of an internal locus of causality.

The locus of causality is external if there's not much we, as users, can do to affect the experience. For example, a robot vacuum cleaner is often set to its default settings from the manufacturer, and there's generally not much need to change those settings. So usually we just turn on the power and the robot starts its job. There's no user involvement in the process of cleaning; the robot automatically takes a detour when it hits a wall or a threshold. It can be handy to have a robot cleaner at home, but barely anyone would feel any responsibility or enjoyment from using the device.

2.5.4   Why is Locus of Causality Important in Judgmental
Experience?

We want to be a part of a valuable experience, and it is the goal that we pursue. But the criteria of what we think is useful can change since our values may transform over time as we go through various circumstances and situations. In order to cope with such change in designing useful products or services, locus of causality is a vital factor, which needs to be understood. The reasons are as follows.

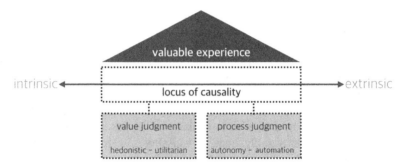

Fig. 2.2 The judgmental thread of experience and locus of causality

Judgmental experience is about the user evaluation of the usefulness of a product or a service. What people value and how they evaluate usefulness can change over time. What we value is dependent on its source, or where it comes from. It is mainly because we think that the perceived value is a consequence of the source. There can be a myriad of different sources, so it is unpredictable to rely on each and every source in understanding the users' values. Instead we need a general concept that describes the source, which can be applied in a wide range of situations. Internal and external locus of causality is a general concept that can be flexibly applied in most circumstances across diverse products or services in various contexts.

Furthermore, locus of causality doesn't favor one to another. In other words, internal locus of causality is not always preferred over the external locus of causality and vice versa. Depending on the situation, either the internal or the external can be perceived as more useful than the other.

Also, locus of causality is related to the evaluation of both the process and the outcome. For instance, locus of causality is concerned with how much control I have during the RC car buying experience. At the same time, the concept is also dependent on whether the process itself was valuable for me or if I was more interested in the outcome of the experience and how I would use the outcome for another purpose. It is a notion that deals with both process and outcome, which is directly related to our judgments from experience. In conclusion, as illustrated in (Fig. 2.2), locus of causality is a critical element of the judgmental thread of experience contributing to the meanings and values that users receive through products or services.

2.6   Compositional Thread of Experience

Back to my allotment garden in the countryside. As I mentioned before I enjoy the presence of my neighbors there, more so than in my home in the city. There are very few inhabitants where the garden is, so it's always thrilling to have new neighbors or visitors.

The compositional thread of experience is concerned with the relationship between the elements that make up an experience. Our experience is shaped by relationships among people, objects, and surroundings, and the meanings we find in an experience depend on those relationships. Without the consideration of relationships, it is not possible to fully understand an experience as a whole.

Compositional experience puts emphasis on the relationships between the parts of an experience. Unlike sensual experience and judgmental experience that try to understand an experience as a whole, compositional experience focuses on the elements of an experience and the relationships between them. Depending on what elements we are interested in, our experience can be interpreted in a whole new level. Compositional experience is largely composed of three types of relationships based on the characteristics of the elements being considered. In next three subchapters I will address those relationships.

2.6.1 Temporal Relationships: Relationships among the Past, Present and Future

One of the most important types of relationships was introduced by John Dewey: a temporal relationship between an action and its outcome (Dewey 1929). Let's say a child dipped its hand in a boiling pot of water and screamed out loud. If we perceive the incident as two independent events, the experience is not considered singular. Once we realize the relationship between the dipping and the screaming, a link is formed between the two and creates an experience of burning your finger from a hot object. With respect to the temporal aspect, an experience could be construed as a sequence of a past event, a current event, and an upcoming event. For example, watering the trees in the garden, observing them when they grow back to life, and having their fruits on a dining table are temporally related to one another. This is why compositional experience is also known as narrative structure (Wright et al. 2008). It is built upon the temporal relationships between how we act, how the environment reacts to our action, and how we react to the reaction.

2.6.2 Social Relationships: Relationships Between Me and Others

A social relationship refers to the relationship between me and others. From a social perspective, compositional experience comes from me being linked to a specific person, and that person being linked to another person who is again linked to the fourth person. For example, my experience of talking to my coworker this morning can be directly and indirectly affected by their relationships with their peers, as well as the relationships of the peers with their peers. Social relationship structures among people closely resemble those of the temporal relationship. Just like how a past event and an expected upcoming event can influence my current experience, the relationship between me and my friends as well as the relationship between my friends and their friends can all influence my experience.

I usually set my Facebook profile pictures as the ones that inspire me the most. The very first one was taken in Quebec, Canada, while I was on my summer leave. I remember I was on my way to the downtown when I took a photo of historic buildings gleaming in the sunset. A few days after I set the picture, a former graduate student of mine, now living on the other side of the globe, informed with a message that he'd also been there. We started a dialogue on my Facebook timeline, which another graduate student of mine joined who I hadn't heard from in over 20 years, and in which we reminisced about our joint projects in the past. I was delighted to hear from my former students. This was a real experience.

If I had not been emotionally tied to the students, or if the message had been from a random person who I had no emotional relationship with, my experience wouldn't have lingered in my heart for so long. This example was to illustrate that the relationship between the entities involved in an experience is significantly important.

2.6.3   Structural Relationships: Relationships Between Me and Products/Services

When we are talking about the 'relationships,' it is not just about people, but also about objects (e.g. products and services). My experience is affected by how one product or service is related to other products or services. Let's take as an example of the process of calling my wife through a smartphone. First I search for her number on the favorites list. Then I make a call but she misses the call and doesn't answer, so I end up pressing the message button to text her. The experience of searching through the favorites list and texting her are linked together, and how smoothly the two are connected can greatly influence my overall experience with the smartphone.

As illustrated, we can be interested in the relationship between different functions within a product, but we may also be interested in the relationship between multiple different products or services. A few days ago, my son asked for a picture of his grandmother. I looked for a picture on my Dropbox folder through the Dropbox application on my smartphone and attached the downloaded photo to a text message. Likewise, my experience of sharing the photo with my son was in part based on the relationship between my smartphone and the Dropbox application.

2.6.4   Harmony as the Ideal State of the Compositional Thread

In terms of the compositional point of view, what is the ideal state of an experience? The answer, based on Confucianism, is harmony, which refers to the state of balance among the elements that make up an experience (Kwan et al. 1997; Li 2006).

In the ideal world of Confucianism, all relationships are perfectly harmonious. Eastern philosophy tries to understand social relationships in terms of harmony rather than in terms of satisfaction. According to Confucianism, the concept of harmony can be explained through different levels.

Firstly, there's harmony on the individual level. An example would be the balance between one's height and weight. A balance between body and mind is important for an individual to be in a peaceful state. As discussed earlier, harmony among the past, present, and future events a person lives can together form a harmonious experience, and this harmony is also on the individual level.

Secondly, we can also think of harmony on the interpersonal level. The balance among family members, local community members, or people of different nations is an example of interpersonal harmony.

Lastly, we can find harmony in an object and its relevant surrounding. The nature around us or the IT-friendly environment can form harmony with the modern people. Being able to connect to high-speed internet service at any time through all the necessary devices is a good example of a harmonious experience among products and services.

To conclude, harmony is a broad concept that describes the balance of time, social relationships among people, and relationships between people and their surrounding environment.

2.6.5 Relational Cohesiveness: How Tight are We?

Most people always yearn for harmony in their experience, but how we evaluate harmony can vary from case to case. It's because "harmonious relationships" in our minds can transform over time, depending on the context. We need a way to control compositional experience accordingly to provide the most harmonious experience for users. In this book we propose 'relational cohesiveness' as a strategic measure that can control the compositional experience of users.

In sociology and network theory, cohesiveness measures how strongly the members of the groups are tied to each other (Moody and White 2003; Friedkin 2004). In other words, cohesiveness of a group can indicate their tendency to stick together (Wasserman 1994). The higher the cohesiveness, the more likely for the members to stay together. Likewise, the lower the cohesiveness, the higher the chance of them to leave the group (Festinger 1950).

The concept of cohesiveness is often used in an interpersonal context. The notion of 'relational cohesiveness' is adapted from the concept, and it can be used to interpret a user's experience with products or services. From a compositional perspective, an experience can be viewed as a network structure composed of its elements connected to each other. A network is composed of links that connect nodes. A simple example is a friendship network on Facebook. Each person acts as a node and a link exists between the nodes if there is a friendship relationship. A social network of a Facebook user is shaped by how its friends are connected to each other.

Let's instead think of the nodes as the elements of an experience, and draw the links whenever there is a relationship between the elements. We now have an experience network, from which we can find out the relational cohesiveness between the elements that build up an experience. For instance, we can measure the strength of relationship between Google's Gmail service and its other applications to explain a user's experience with Gmail.

2.6.6   Strong Cohesiveness vs. Weak Cohesiveness

We can think of a Korean railway station (KTX) as an example of a weak relational cohesion. Korea is a small country but we have a very well-constructed railway system; we can travel from one end of the country to the other in less than three hours. The central station in Seoul is always crammed with people, but there is barely any interaction among people. Passengers are from all over the country, and thus the probability of one person meeting another person he/she knows is very low. Therefore, it can be considered as an experience with low relational cohesiveness.

A strong relational cohesion can be observed in a faculty canteen at my university. Because I've been working at the university for the last 20 years the probability of me knowing other persons in the canteen is very high, especially given the fact that this is the only faculty canteen on the campus. In addition, those people are socially connected with others in various ways (e.g. same department, same college, etc.). Even those who I do not personally know can easily be introduced through a mutual colleague. Thus, my experience at the faculty canteen is considered an experience with a very high relational cohesiveness.

2.6.7   Why is Cohesiveness Important in the Compositional Thread of Experience?

Relational cohesiveness has several characteristics. Firstly, it does not depend on the size of a group. Just because a group has many members, doesn't mean that it's less cohesive. Similarly, small groups are not always strongly bonded. A group of three or four can be weak in cohesiveness if there isn't much interaction among its members.

Secondly, relational cohesiveness is a continuous metric. In other words, we do not say that cohesiveness exists or doesn't exist, but instead measure the strength of cohesiveness on a continuous scale (Wasserman 1994). To illustrate, a passenger service offered at the campus bus station is relatively more cohesive compared to the services offered at the railway station.

Thirdly, relational cohesiveness is dynamic (Carron and Brawley 2000). There is no absolute measure of cohesiveness, and the level of cohesiveness may change over time. When my college friends first set up a Facebook page, it was weak in cohesiveness. Over time however, I observed stronger cohesiveness as people more frequently posted pictures and status updates and participated in events they were

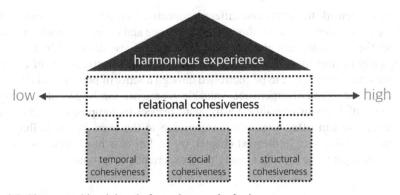

Fig. 2.3 The compositional thread of experience and cohesiveness

invited to through Facebook. These characteristics show that a group's dynamic and cohesiveness can be strategically altered. Planning a regular meet-up for team members or organizing a big gathering for the company is a part of an effort to boost the level of relational cohesiveness.

Lastly, cohesiveness can explain the structural property of a group as a whole. According to social network theory, networks can be analyzed in terms of 'connectivity' or 'distribution' (Yamagishi et al. 1988). By connectivity we mean that we are interested in one-on-one relationships between members of a group. How often I exchange messages with a friend in a Facebook group would be an example of connectivity. Distribution is a characteristic pertaining to the entire network. For instance, the Facebook group page of my high school alumni is administered by the class president, who takes charge of organizing events. We also have a vice-president and a treasurer who help the president with the planning. There is a hierarchical structure among the members of this Facebook group page, which can be viewed as a structural property of my high school alumni network. Another typical example would be a star network, where there is one central node linked to the rest of the group.

To conclude, the concept of cohesiveness (Fig. 2.3) can be used to explain temporal, social, and compositional relationships. The continuous and dynamic properties of cohesiveness can contribute to the harmonious experience of users by allowing us to be ready for the changes that occur around us. Furthermore, the fact that it does not depend on the size of a group makes it possible to easily apply the concept when interpreting diverse applications.

2.7 Unweaving Experience into the Three Threads of Experience

As mentioned in the beginning of this chapter, experience is holistic in nature, composed of closely-related parts that cannot be easily separated. However, in order to design products and service that can provide better experience for the users, an analytic framework to understand different aspects of experience is necessary. In this chapter, we identified three threads of experience and talked about what people consider the most important element in each thread. We also discussed how we can strategically control these elements. With respect to the sensual thread of experience, senseful experience can be controlled through a sense of presence. In terms of the judgmental thread of experience, valuable experience can be provided through the control of locus of causality. Lastly, with respect to compositional thread of experience, we can offer harmonious experience to the users by controlling the relational cohesiveness. In the next chapter, we will discuss how these threads are intertwined together to provide a really good experience for people.

2.8   Summary

- Human experience is holistic in nature, so we can easily miss the big picture if we focus on its parts.
- However, in order to offer users a real experience, we need to separate experience into different controllable aspects. The three threads of experience can effectively portray the aspects.
- In terms of the sensual thread of experience, it is important to allow users to feel the right amount of stimuli through their senses, which can be achieved by controlling a sense of presence.
- In terms of the judgmental thread of experience, users need to feel that an experience is valuable, which can be altered by the locus of causality.
- In terms of the compositional thread of experience, there has to be a harmony within the temporal, social, and environmental relationship among the elements that make up an experience. Harmony can be controlled through relational cohesiveness.

2.9   Discussion Topics

- With respect to the sensual thread of experience, think of the time when you felt that your experience was most senseful. Why did you feel the experience was enjoyable?
- With respect to the judgmental thread of experience, think of the time when you felt that your experience was most valuable. Why did you feel the experience was valuable?
- With respect to the compositional thread of experience, think of the time when you felt that your experience was most harmonious. Why did you feel the experience was harmonious?

- With respect to the sensual thread of experience, think of the incidents where the sense of presence was high and low. What do you think is the reason for the difference in sense of presence?
- With respect to the judgmental thread of experience, think of the incidents where the locus of causality was internal and external. What do you think is the reason for the difference in locus of causality?
- With respect to the compositional thread of experience, think of the experiences with strong and weak cohesiveness. What do you think is the reason for the difference in their levels of cohesiveness?

References

Biocca F (1997) The Cyborg's dilemma: progressive embodiment in virtual environments [1]. J Comput Med Commun 3(2):1–18. doi:10.1111/j.1083-6101.1997.tb00070.x

Carron AV, Brawley LR (2000) Cohesion conceptual and measurement issues. Small Group Res 31(1):89–106

Csikszentmihalyi M (1991) Flow, the psychology of optimal experience, vol 41. Harper&Row, New York

Diamond MJ, Shapiro JL (1973) Changes in locus of control as a function of encounter group experiences: a study and replication. J Abnorm Psychol 82(3):514–518

Dewey J (1929) The quest for certainty. Minton, Balch and Company, New York

Dewey J (1934) Art as experience. Perigee Trade. Minton, Balch

Festinger L (1950) Informal social communication. Psychol Rev 57(5):271–282

Friedkin NE (2004) Social cohesion. Annu Rev Sociol 409–425

Graybill D, Sergeant P (1983) Locus of control: perceived contingency or perceived competence? Percept Mot Skills 56(1):47–54

Hartson R (2003) Cognitive, physical, sensory, and functional affordances in interaction design. Behav Inf Technol 22(5):315–338

Heider F (1959) On Lewin's method and theory. J Soc Issues 15(S13):3–13

IJsselsteijn WA, de Ridder H, Freeman J, Avons SE (June 2000) Presence: concept, determinants, and measurement. In: Electronic imaging. International society for optics and photonics, pp 520–529

James W The varieties of religious experience: a study in human nature: a study in human nature; beeing the gifford lectures on natural religion delivered at edinburgh in 1901-1902. Mentor Book, New American Library

Kant I (2006) Kant: anthropology from a pragmatic point of view. Cambridge University Press, Cambridge

Kelley HH (1967) Attribution theory in social psychology. In: Nebraska symposium on motivation. University of Nebraska Press, Lincoln

Kolb KJ, Aiello JR (1996) The effects of electronic performance monitoring on stress: locus of control as a moderator variable. Comput Hum Behav 12(3):407–423

Kwan VS, Bond MH, Singelis TM (1997) Pancultural explanations for life satisfaction: adding relationship harmony to self-esteem. J Personal Soc Psychol 73(5):1038–1051

Layton C (1985) Note on the stability of Rotter's IE scale. Psychol Rep 57(3f):1165–1166

Lee KM (2004) Presence, explicated. Commun Theory 14(1):27–50

Li C (2006) The Confucian ideal of harmony. Philos East West 56:583–603

Lombard M, Ditton T (1997) At the heart of it all: the concept of presence. J Comput Med Commun 3(2):0–0

Lombard M, Reich RD, Grabe ME, Bracken CC, Ditton TB (2000) Presence and television. Hum Commun Res 26(1):75–98

McCarthy J, Wright P (2004) Technology as experience. Interactions 11(5):42–43

McMahan A (2003) Immersion, engagement and presence. The video game theory reader, pp 67–86

Minsky M (1980) The society of mind. The Personalist Forum, pp 19–32

Mollen A, Wilson H (2010) Engagement, telepresence and interactivity in online consumer experience: reconciling scholastic and managerial perspectives. J Bus Res 63(9):919–925

Moody J, White DR (2003) Structural cohesion and embeddedness: a hierarchical concept of social groups. Am Sociol Rev 103–127

Norman DA (2004) Emotional design: why we love (or hate) everyday things. Basic books, New York

Palenzuela DL (1984) Critical evaluation of locus of control: towards a reconceptualization of the construct and its measurement (monograph 1-V54). Psychol Rep 54(3):683–709

Pettersen N (1987) A conceptual difference between internal-external locus of control and causal attribution, Psychol Rep, 60(1):203–209

Rotter JB (1966) Generalized expectancies for internal versus external control of reinforcement. Psychol Monogr 80(1):1–28

Steuer J (1992) Defining virtual reality: dimensions determining telepresence. J Commun 42(4):73–93

Sweeney J, Soutar G (2001) Consumer perceived value: the development of a multiple item scale. J Retail 77(2):203–220

Tamborini R, Eastin MS, Skalski P, Lachlan K (2004) Violent virtual video games and hostile thoughts. J Broad Elec Media 48:335–357

Venkatesh V, Davis FD (2000) A theoretical extension of the technology acceptance model: four longitudinal field studies. Manage Sci 46(2):186–204

Wasserman S (1994) Social network analysis: methods and applications, vol 8. Cambridge University Press, Cambridge

Wong PTP, Sproule CE (1984) An attributional analysis of the locus of control construct and the trent attribution profile. In: Lefcourt HM (ed) Research with the locus of control construct: extensions and Limitations, vol 3. Academic, New York, pp 309–360

Woodruff R (1997) Customer value: the next source of competitive advantage. J Acad Mark Sci 25(2):139–153

Wright P, Wallace J, McCarthy J (2008) Aesthetics and experience-centered design. ACM Trans Comp Hum Interac (TOCHI) 15(4):18, 1–21

Yamagishi T, Gillmore MR, Cook KS (1988) Network connections and the distribution of power in exchange networks. Am J Sociol 93(4):833–851

Part II
A Strategic Framework for Experience Design

Chapter 3
The Balance of Experience

3.1 Introduction

A person's everyday experience is a complex web of sensual, judgmental, and compositional threads. This complication applies to a person using a product or service as well. Therefore, the experience of using a smartphone or a internet portal service can be approached with those same three perspectives. While understanding present experience is important in order to provide a real experience through a product or service, it is even more important to consider a more strategic approach, especially the understanding of the inevitable influences of the environment to people's experiences such as socio-cultural, economic, and technical environments. Additionally, a counter approach of analyzing how human experience influences the environment is also necessary. Real experience can be achieved only when environments and experience harmonize. Firms that produce products or services based on this real experience can acquire the possibility to secure strategic competitiveness. So what are the specific environmental elements that influence human experience while using products and services? On the other hand, how does human experience affect its environment? In addition, what is the relationship between the balance of experience and a successful products or services?

3.2 Tuning with the World's Frequency

Breakfast meetings are quite common in Korea. Usually, a breakfast meeting will start at seven in the morning and will last for around two hours. Then, a light breakfast is served and participants socialize afterwards. Perhaps this distinctive culture arose as a desperate measure to try to meet everyone's schedules while trying to avoid official working hours.

There were special breakfast meetings I attended for about five years. The meetings were held at the headquarters of Samsung Electronics. Participants included representative of the Samsung Group, executives, the members of an advisory

© Springer International Publishing Switzerland 2015
J. Kim, *Design for Experience*, Human-Computer Interaction Series,
DOI 10.1007/978-3-319-14304-0_3

committee on future technology, opinion leaders who were invited from universities and research institutes, and other key people at Samsung. At the meetings an expert in a certain field gave a lecture about its developments, which was then followed by an open debate among the attendees.

One of the things I learned at these meetings was what I call "tuning to the world's frequency." We were able to learn new things by developing diverse perspectives and getting in tune with each other through the experts' stories and debates.

One day, a lecture on the economic ripple effects of a large-scale canal project in Korea, which was hotly debated at the time, and a possible water shortage in Korea was given. One of the experts, who was seriously concerned about a possible water shortage, explained the reasons why a premium global brand like Perrier was more expensive than Samdasu, a local brand. He said that Perriers water sources were of higher quality than those of Samdasu and therefore the water they produced was more expensive.

At another meeting, flexible displays, a technology that was very new during that time in the late 2000's, were presented. We learned that the degrees of permeability and integration played a very important role in technological advancement. We took turns touching and bending a flexible display prototype while discussing potentials of how flexible display products could dramatically change our daily lives.

At yet another meeting, a very interesting discussion on socio-cultural topics took place. One professor discussed his researches on "mega trends" and gave examples of what consumers will demand and desire in the near future. His claim was that consumers integrate their self identities with the products they purchase. He had conducted a research on consumers who had bought "knock off" products, or fake products. When asked what they would do if they earned a lot of money, a majority of consumers answered that they would "purchase the real product of the knock off." His research provides an insightful aspect, that firms do not heavily engage in the crackdown of knock off manufacturers because, after all, the knock offs can act as a powerful marketing tool for leading consumers to purchase the real products.

These examples above reveal the sensitive approach of Samsung Electronics when it comes to changes in economic, technological, and socio-cultural environments. Those free discussions among decision makers in the company and with academics might have paved the way for the creation of innovative products such as the Galaxy S and the Galaxy Note series. Perhaps their spell of success was their insight into how future environments would change combined with analysis of the effects of their former successful products and services on the environment.

3.3 What Does Confucius Say About Experience?

There is a book known as "The Doctrine of the Mean" a 31 chapter compilation of the words of Confucius, who is one of the most renowned oriental scholars. This book is comprised of short aphorisms regarding rules and methods for a person to live harmoniously with other people. Confucian scholars say that The Doctrine of the Mean possesses concise yet logical oriental philosophy. Former Tokyo University professor Shizuka Shirakawa, a renowned scholar of the research of Confucianism who recently passed away, praised The Doctrine of the Mean as a realist doctrine that provides a clear path for our existence and experience of being (Shizuka 2003).

The Doctrine of the Mean is regarded as an excellent book that documents individual experience, experiences with other persons created through individual experience, and the experience of a ruler or figure of authority in constructing a society and systems. One of the most famous and symbolic passage from the book is the following:

> When joy, anger, sorrow, and pleasure have not yet arisen, it is called the Mean (中 centeredness). When they arise to their appropriate levels, it is called 'Harmony' (和 Harmony). The Mean is the great root of all-under-heaven. 'Harmony' is the penetration of the Way through all-under-heaven. When the Mean and Harmony are actualized, Heaven and Earth are in their proper positions, and the myriad things are nourished.

The Mean refers to the state of fundamental and absolute balance of the environment that surrounds humans. On the other hand, Harmony refers to the balance of a person's heart based on the elements of the mean. While the mean always exists in the natural environment, Harmony can only be achieved through the specific experiences that we, as humans, go through and how we feel about them. Once the mean and a person's Harmony meet, then a perfect balance is achieved between the human and his/her environment.

By applying the concept of mean and harmony to the three threads of experience (sensual, judgmental, and compositional threads), the mean refers to the three threads of experience before reflecting on human experience. When human experience is reflected in the threads, a person attempts to organize the three threads of experience into a harmonious state. Of course, not all experiences achieve harmony. A state of harmony for a specific experience is achieved only when the level of sensual, judgmental, and compositional threads achieve a balance based on their relative positions.

One of the points that The Doctrine of the Mean emphasizes is the point of balance among the threads of experience. Let's look at another passage from The Doctrine on the balance of experience. One day, Confucius was having a conversation with his disciple Zilu about what strength is. Confucius answered him like this:

> Do you mean the strength of the South, the strength of the North, or the strength of selfmastery? To be broadminded and gentle in teaching and not rashly punish wrong-doing is the strength of the South. The Superior Man abides in this. To be able to make a bed of weapons and armor and die without grief—this is the strength of the North. The forceful are at home in this. Therefore the Superior Man is harmonious without getting sloppy. He stands in the center without leaning to either side. How correct his strength is!

Here, Confucius claims that the Superior Man keeps his balance and does not sway to one side while maintaining the tension of balance between various elements in life. Whether issues grand or miniscule, the Superior Man always maintains balance because he is sturdy in his fundamentals and has taken this principle to heart.

Human experience can also be explained from the perspective of the balance of the Superior Man. The three threads of experience are in danger of being emphasized too much individually. The compositional thread, which emphasizes the relational aspect of experience, could easily be in danger of constant changes towards increasing connections between people and things The sensual thread has the possibility of creating powerful stimulations that lead to addictions due to its volatile reactions. The judgmental thread, by itself, will promote endless automation and externalized logic that ends up becoming a system for the system itself rather than a human-centered system. When human fundamentals are excluded, even a product built to provide users with a really great experience can degenerate into a piece of machinery. Therefore, "real experience" can be created only when a tense balance between the elements of experience can be achieved.

3.3.1   The Balance of Experience as a Three-Dimensional Model

We need to take a more integrated approach to achieve a balance between the three threads of experience. In order to look at the relationships between the threads, their external environments, and their specific experiences, the three threads need to be seen in a single integrated frame. Therefore, I want to present a three dimensional model of experience that can help explain the integrated threads of experience.

The model is divided into three axes. The y-axis indicates the sensual thread and expresses how high or low the sense of presence is in an experience. The higher the value of the y-axis, perception of sense of presence is increased due to external stimulants. On the other hand, a lower value indicates a relatively lesser degree of a sense of presence. The z-axis, or the judgmental thread, describes whether the evaluation of an experience results through internal or external locus of causality. The higher the value, the more external the value and control of human experience; the lower the value, the more internal the value and control of experience. Lastly, the x-axis refers to the compositional thread of experience. The more the value of the x-axis shifts to the right, the more cohesive a relationship is, whereas a shift to the left reveals a lesser degree of cohesiveness.

There are a number of merits in expressing our experiences of using a product or service as a point in the three dimensional space as shown in Fig. 3.1.

Firstly, experience does not exist as three different parts based on the three threads but rather exists as a single integrated point. The three dimensions must combine as a single point in order to fully and properly express the holistic nature of experience .

Secondly, the three dimensional space provides a simple way of describing human experience in using a specific product or service. Figure 3.2 shows the results of a survey on the executives of LG Electronics, a Korean electronics company. They were asked what kind of experiences consumers who had bought UHD (ultra-high definition) TVs from LG would go through. In terms of the sensual thread of experience, the results indicated that users would feel a high degree of sense of presence due to the quick reflection of a minute screen for setting changes and high

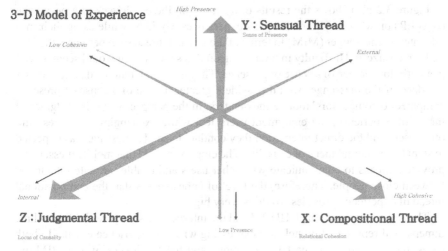

Fig. 3.1 A three dimensional model of experience

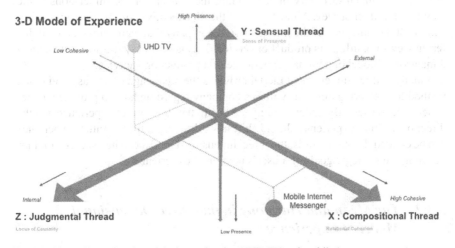

Fig. 3.2 Three-dimensional model of experiencing UHD TV and mobile internet messenger

resolution that would make them think the characters in the TV were almost real. As for the judgmental thread, the popular opinion was that users would feel a slight internal locus of causality for their experiences since the content of what they enjoy watching on the TV screens such as dramas and sports cannot be controlled. In the perspective of the compositional thread of experience, both the lack of connections between TVs and the use of a TV to communicate with other people would lead to users feeling a relatively low level of cohesiveness.

Figure 3.2 also shows the results of a survey on the employees of a portal site (NAVER) on what they think people's experiences would be while using their mobile internet messenger (MIM) In terms of the sensual thread of experience, the limited screen size and difficulty in interacting on that small screen would seem to lead to a fairly low degree of a sense of presence. They also think that the distinctive user interface of the messenger would provide a greater degree of a sense of presence compared to competitors' mobile messengers. In the perspective of the judgmental thread of experience, the enjoyment users feel while exchanging messages with other users and the direct interaction they conduct to send a message was expected to stem from internal locus of causality. The employees said that mobile messengers provide a means to communicate with other users and enable intimate interaction between close people. Therefore, the level of cohesiveness that the compositional thread of experience provides would be very high.

The two examples of the UHD TV and the internet messenger reveal that a three dimensional representation helps in expressing what an experience entails. In both cases, the executives, in the UHD example, and the employees, in the MIM example, were briefed about each dimension before they were asked to express their opinions on the product or service within the three dimensional model. Participants did not have much difficulty understanding the concept of the dimensions while they filled in their survey. Almost none of the 40 executives of the electronics firm and the 300 employees of the internet portal company that were surveyed held differing views regarding its product or service. This is how easy it is to create a three dimensional model of a human experience of a product or a service.

Finally, a three dimensional model provides the advantage of an easy and quick method for gathering opinions within a company regarding how to provide a better experience to users. By understanding the position of the current experience and the direction a future experience should shift towards, a point for the future experience can be created. In other words, the three dimensional model can be used as a tool for deciding the strategic goals of a user's next great experience.

3.3.2   The Mean and Harmony in the Three Dimensional Model of Experience

The Doctrine of the Mean is often misunderstood as a guideline towards a middle point that is neither too much nor too little. If this was true, the origin of the three dimensional model of experience should provide the best experience. However, the origin of the model is not a real experience that people can perceive. A sense of presence is neither high nor low, the locus of causality is neither internal nor external, and cohesiveness is neither strong nor weak. Basically, the origin of the graph is like food that doesn't taste like anything at all. In fact, the Doctrine of the Mean emphasizes harmony that enables an optimal balance of emotions in the human heart. When applied to products and services, harmony refers to a point that maintains and tunes itself based on the relative balance between the three threads of experience. Every product or service possesses differing degrees of experience, but harmony is achieved only when the three threads of experience meet at a single point of optimal balance.

Let's think about a middle schooler who enjoys playing the video game League of Legends. He experiences enjoyment through the desire to control every aspect of what is controllable. Therefore, its judgmental experience expresses an internal locus of causality. Also, a realistic expression of monsters and other players can provide a high degree of sensual experience. Furthermore, a stronger perception of cohesiveness with other players can provide a more harmonious compositional experience. By expressing the experience of playing League of Legend onto the three dimensional space, the point of balance will probably be somewhere on the upper left quadrant. However, if the game is neither realistic nor unrealistic, the locus of causality is neither internal nor external, and cohesiveness is neither high nor low, the gamer's experience will end up being bland.

3.4   SET: The External Environment of Human Experience

It is important to note that the dimensions of experience in using a product or service are not enough to understand the present and predict the future. In order to explain where a product or service is positioned in the three dimensional model and predict in which direction it will move, it is imperative to consider the relationship between a person's present experience and the environmental elements surrounding the person. As I mentioned in Chapter 2, experience is created through the constant interaction between a person and the environment surrounding that person. In addition, let's think from the perspective of a company that provides a product or a service. A product or a service that provides a great experience to users is constantly influenced by external factors, and vice versa. Under the same context, renowned organizational behavior scholar James March of Stanford University claimed that as the organization adjusts to the environment, the environment adjusts to the organization (March 1991). Then, what kind of external factors interact with human experience? In fact, most experiences are prone to be influenced by external environments. I want to specifically focus on three types of environments that a person or a company must confront: socio-cultural, economic, and technological (SET). SET is shown in more detail in Table 3.1.

Of course, there are other external factors that influence human experience such as political, legislative, and ecological environments. More complex systems of analysis do exist (such as PEST, SLEPT, and STEEPLED), but their influence on human experience is quite similar to SET and I decided not to include them. I want to approach the complex subject of experience in the simplest frame possible as stated in the law of parsimony.

Many studies from different fields have used SET to understand the influence of macro environments (Law 2006; Cagan and Vogel 2013). However, I believe

Table 3.1 SET elements that influence people's experiences

Socio-Cultural	Economic	Technological
✓ Lifestyle trends (e.g., family and work patterns, health issues)	✓ Home economy situation and trends	✓ Competing technology development
✓ Demographics (e.g., age distribution)	✓ Business cycles (boom and bust)	✓ Research funding
✓ Consumer attitudes and opinions	✓ Inflation	✓ Associated/dependent technologies
✓ Social mobility	✓ Employment level	✓ Replacement technology/solutions
✓ Media views (e.g., books, magazines, music)	✓ Consumer confidence	✓ Maturity of technology
✓ Law changes affecting social factors	✓ Overseas economies and trends	✓ Manufacturing maturity and capacity
✓ Brand, company, technology, image	✓ General taxation issues	✓ Information and communications technology
✓ Fashion and role models (entertainment industry patterns)	✓ Taxation specific to products/services	✓ Consumer buying mechanisms/technology
✓ Major events (e.g., sporting events) and influences	✓ Seasonality/weather issues	✓ Technology legislation
✓ Ethnic/religious factors	✓ Market and trade cycles	✓ Innovation potential
✓ Advertising and publicity	✓ Specific industry factors	✓ Technology access, licencing, patents
✓ Ecological/environmental issues	✓ Market routes and distribution trends	✓ Intellectual property issues
✓ Energy consumption	✓ Customer/enduser drivers	✓ Global communications
✓ Waste disposal	✓ Interest and exchange rates	
✓ Ethical issues	✓ International trade/monetary issues	
✓ Cultural traits	✓ Consumer buying patterns	
✓ Wars and conflicts	✓ Buying access and trends	
✓ Political stability	✓ Trading policies and tariff	
✓ Education	✓ Funding, grants and initiatives	

SET has not been applied in understanding human experience before. It is ironical that external environments have been used to analyze political policies or product development processes, but their influence on the people that need to follow the policies and processes have not been investigated yet. Let's find out how socio-cultural, economic, and technological environments influence human experience of a product or a service and vice versa.

3.4.1 The Characteristics of the Socio-Cultural Environment

The socio-cultural environment is related to the awareness and behavior of a person who uses a specific product or service. This includes population demographics, lifestyle, and miscellaneous cultural anthropological characteristics as well. Let's take the example of the cultural dimensions of different countries. Individualism and collectivism refers to whether a person within a group considers the individual's or the group's benefit as a priority (Hofstede 1980). A society with high individualistic tendencies is centered on the self, considers personal goals to be important, and individuals seek to be evaluated as such. On the other hand, a society with high collectivism considers other people's opinions to be more important than the individual's and shows high interest in how others are evaluated.

I conducted a research on the differences in individualism and collectivism among users of mobile data services in seven countries (Lee et al. 2010). The results of my research revealed that Taiwan, Korea, and Hong Kong showed high individualistic tendencies while Japan, Australia, Greece, and Denmark showed high collectivistic tendencies. Due to differences in these tendencies, I discovered that how users in each country experience a similar service differed vastly. For example, people in Hong Kong, who scored high on individualism, used personalized health services widely whereas in Japan, which scored high on collectivism, personalized health services were not widely utilized.

Companies constantly need to consider how to make a more successful product or service by adequately reflecting a target population's socio-cultural elements. A few years ago, I collaborated with Samsung Electronics that wanted to develop new mobile phones for different countries. A specialized product was created through the results of this research. One of those examples was an application with a special alarm targeted towards countries in which the population was predominantly Muslim. The application alerted the users of the times for call to prayer, showed a compass that pointed to the direction of Mecca so that users would know in which direction they should pray, and provided relevant information guiding users during a prayer.

In general, the speed of change of socio-cultural elements is relatively slow. Prior research on patterns of human reaction based on external changes to the environment reveals that awareness and attitude do not change easily (Ram and Sheth 1989). Nevertheless, there is a user category that is sensitive to the release of a product or service and seeks to spread relevant information about the product or service to other people. These people are often called opinion leaders or lead users (Von Hippel 1986). Socio-cultural elements initially tend to put a strain on new experiences, but the product or service tends to diffuse into the population rapidly once it is approved by opinion leaders and lead users. A great example of this can be found during the release of the smartphone into the market. Experts and amateurs alike in many countries, including Korea, wondered whether the smartphone would be able to effectively replace the feature phone market. However, the image of the smartphone as an intelligent and modern device spread through opinion leaders in their 20s and 30s. This change in awareness was an important element in supporting the diffusion of the smartphone into the mainstream market.

Recently, the speed of change that socio-cultural elements bring about has increased mainly due to the wide propagation of online environments and the development of social computing environments such as social networking services (SNS). Most people between ages 10 and 50 own smartphones, and so they have access to a wide variety of online environments and social computing. SNS such as Twitter and Facebook are designed to share social issues and events in real-time to as many users as possible. Since most of these people are connected to diverse SNS at all times, the rate of change that socio-cultural elements bring about is increasing at greater speeds.

3.4.2   The Socio-Cultural Environment and the Threads of Experience

Socio-cultural elements share a close relationship with the sensual, judgmental, and compositional threads of experience. First, let's take a look at the relationship between socio-cultural elements and sensual experience. Among socio-cultural elements are those that gear towards influencing the sense of presence. For instance, there is a growing demographic of single people around the developed world that possess economic power, utilize the internet well, and are not afraid to enjoy their lives. In Korea, we call them the "single-joks." The single-joks have a strong desire to live a free life and consider their freedom, rational thinking, and jobs rather than being enclosed in the traditional frame of marriage. They purchase products and services that help express their individual personalities such as cars. Several automobile models have been released to suit the demands of the single-joks and many of the automobile companies are targeting them through designs and colors that help express individual personalities. Therefore, the proliferation of the single-joks is acting as a stimulant for the release of products and services with a high sense of presence.

On the other hand, there is a socio-cultural element in society that is steering towards a low sense of presence. A good example is the rise of flat style design. Flat style design seeks to express every design element in the simplest way possible and is closely connected to minimalistic design. As products and services begin to prefer flat style design, visual stimulation has weakened in the perspective of sensual experience as designers have shifted their focus on expressing meaning through compact and implied designs. In the Apple iOS 7, it is clearly evident that they have replaced skeuomorphic elements that induce a high sense of presence with a flat UI that emphasizes typography, single color tones, and pictograms.

As socio-cultural elements are becoming more important online, especially social media, the tendency to emphasize a high sense of presence has become more concentrated. Under the context of the online environment, a product or service that cannot quickly grab the attention of a user will quickly stumble in the market.

Information that does not immediately stimulate a user's sense will end up not getting any "likes" or "views" in the vast ocean that is the internet. Therefore, the increasing intensity at which mobile phones and social media develop will cause experiences with strong, sensational stimulations.

Socio-cultural elements are also closely related to the judgmental thread of experience. Clay Shirky points out that people, who were used to passive external stimulations in the past, are now showing the desire to directly experience and control things (Shirky 2010). One good example of this is the popularity of user-generated content (UGC). While users in the past enjoyed watching video content provided by broadcasting companies or the movie industry, they now create and edit their own content and actively share it among other users. Even the behaviors in which they utilize broadcasted content show differences. For the 2014 FIFA World Cup, users were able to watch matches on multiple screens not only the default angle the broadcasting station provided but with the freedom to choose a camera angle that focused on a single player of their interest, for example. Users' utilization of social media, an element of a socio-cultural environment, shows that judgmental experience possesses an internal locus of causality.

Socio-cultural elements also heavily influence the compositional thread of experience. Recently, the desire to share information and communicate with people in different areas is growing. This means that experience is leaning towards a strong relational cohesiveness. Facebook, Twitter, Instagram, and other social networking services, as an example, provide a function often called the activity feed or dashboard that combines a real-time feed on other users' activity on the network. This function has helped these services to evolve into supporting stronger cohesiveness among users.

In the perspective of compositional experience, diverse services are heading towards providing a strong cohesive experience. As most age groups possess digital devices and utilize the internet, people are ready to use services that posess strong cohesiveness. For example, Google offers a cohesive and seamless experience for all of their services such as Google+, YouTube, Google Maps, Gmail, and many others across many device platforms such as mobile, tablet, and PC.

In a reverse perspective, the experience of using a product or service can have an effect on socio-cultural elements of the environment. A highly cohesive social computing service causes people to worry about security breaches, for example, leaking of private information. There is a growing number of people that do not use mobile messenger services like KakaoTalk because they are afraid that their information may be accessible by others. To reduce such privacy issues, messaging services have surfaced that limit the amount of time a user's message stays online until it gets deleted and cannot be accessed by the users themselves. They attempt to solve the problem of privacy leaks by setting limits to keep the level of cohesiveness to an appropriate level while maintaining social relationships. These services are examples of how users' experiences of using products or services influence the socio-cultural environment.

3.4.3   The Characteristics of the Economic Environment

Elements of the economic environment comprise of macroeconomic variables such as economic volatility, inflation, and interest rates. As the economy slows down, people spend less, i.e. consumption decreases, which leads to the reduction of "available assets," as production decreases as well. In other words, the willingness to pay for the same product has reduced. However, macroeconomic changes do not affect all people in the same way. Some people can barely afford a one-room house but at the same time own a luxury car. In an ancient oriental classic, Mencius speaks of "no stable living, no stable mind." How a person feels about his/her quality of life changes based on the state of a person's economic power and the economic environment. This leads me to assume that the quality and direction of experience is influenced by a person's willingness to pay for a product or service.

Generally, government officials in charge of economic policies reduce interest rates or expand financial policies in order to boost consumer confidence and increase consumption. However, it is questionable whether such economic policies can lead to the consumption of specific products such as digital devices. The decision to purchase products that are now a necessity in daily life such as PCs or smartphones may actually be influenced more by how much convenience they offer compared to their competitors rather than the consumption pattern of the economy. Economic variables that affect human experience tend to be influenced by artificial change, and its effects may be uncertain. Therefore, the macroeconomic environment can be changed arbitrarily with policies.

3.4.4   The Economic Environment and the Threads of Experience

Firstly, let's think about sensual experience. When people think they have a good amount of economic power, they tend to care for a high sense of presence. On the other hand, a high sense of presence may not be important for people that do not possess that level of economic power.

For instance, the economic prosperity of the United States after World War II led to the production of automobiles such as the 1957 pink Cadillac and 1959 Chevy. These automobiles entered the market when the United States reached a golden age and became the most powerful country in the world. The end of the war led people to believe that an age of suffering and depression had also ended. As the economy picked up rapid pace and economic scarcity became rare, people started to express their personalities and started to seek enjoyment in their lives. In order to meet these needs, automobile manufacturers produced models that looked different than conventional automobiles. Sensual colors such as red, pink, and green, and special exterior designs like the shark tale shape provided a high degree of sense of presence. Companies led people to believe that their automobiles reflected individual personalities and preference. On the other hand, small, fuel efficient cars were preferred during the oil crisis of the 1970s and 1980s when economic power was low. During that period, the degree of sense of presence was not very high.

The economic environment also influences judgmental experience. In the 1980s, economic depression and the effects of the oil crisis led to a continued state of economic instability. During this time, automobiles were perceived as vehicles that moved people from one point to another. Since automobiles were used for functional purposes, users were not interested in changing the exterior design or tuning the engine. They merely used the automobile in its original state. Therefore, the locus of causality was external. On the other hand, the previously mentioned 1950s was a time for expressing individual personalities as seen in the automobiles of the times; hence, the locus of causality is internal.

The economic environment also influences compositional experience. During the economic boom of the 1950s, Americans moved away from cities into suburbs and created close-knit communities. However, modern humans who feel that they lack economic power are crammed in endless rows of houses and apartments and lack relationships with their neighbors. When the economy is in a good state, people show a high degree of cohesiveness, whereas the perception of a faltering economy shows a low degree of cohesiveness in general. But interestingly enough, there are cases when cohesiveness increases amidst a dark economic situation. Let's think about the Asian financial crisis in the late 1990s. The dire economic situation actually increased the cohesiveness of the Korean society, and citizens actively participated in donating gold for the economy. In the eyes of the western world, the fact that an economy the size of Korea's received IMF help may have seemed like an exception. But an even greater exception was that people were determined to help save the economy, and so even amidst turmoil, cohesiveness among the people became stronger.

3.4.5 The Characteristics of the Technological Environment

Elements of the technological environment include everything from the maturity of a piece of technology, the potential to develop an innovative technology, the development process of a competitor technology, and complementary technologies. But while technology itself is important, there are other factors surrounding technology such as laws, policies, and intellectual property that influence human experience in significant ways. There are several characteristics of the technological environment.

Firstly, the technological environment, unlike other environmental elements, is characterized by its extremely fast-paced change. According to Moore's Law, the performance of a semiconductor will increase by two times every 18 months. Based on this law, a semiconductor 10 times faster than the semiconductor today should be developed within 6 years. Now compare that to the possible feeling if your height would double every 18 months. This is the current speed at which technology is developing.

Secondly, the technological environment is often times difficult to predict due to the inconsistency of technological changes. For instance, no meticulous analysis of the current state and future of analog film could have foreseen the emergence of the digital camera. A phenomenon, called technology discontinuity, is the source of the difficulty in explaining the influence of the technological environment on human experience.

Thirdly, the characteristic of technological elements is that it not only influences technology itself, it also has a vast influence on the experience of people using the applications of technology. CEO Joseph Fan of Taiwan Mobile once said that there are no companies that fail because of technology. What he meant was that the key is the business model that the technology creates and how the technology changes people's awareness and experiences. Therefore, the ways that technology is applied, rather than the technology itself, is how technological elements influence human experience in a large way.

3.4.6   The Technological Environment and the Threads of Experience

The influence of the technological environment on sensual experience tends to flow towards the direction of increasing immersion and sense of presence. For example, since the cathode ray tube (CRT) was first released in 1987, TV technology developed towards a larger screen and higher resolution. In the 1990s, flat screen technology developed through LCD or PDP methods, and now OLED, UHD, and curved UHD methods are being developed further. These developments are evolving towards providing higher immersion and sense of presence. In terms of audio technology, stereo systems were developed as Dolby technology in 1968. Now, audio technology focuses on getting rid of noise while enhancing sense of presence. In addition, audio technology has merged with 3D video technology, known as realistic audio technology, to predict the distance of a sound in order to further enhance immersion and the sense of presence. Furthermore, tangible technology utilizes Xinput and direct input (mobile gaming pads) to create faster reaction speeds and provide more realistic experiences to users. Game controller technology has also adopted the dual vibration motor in order to enhance the sense of presence of, for example, virtual collisions and explosions and provide more realistic experiences to users.

Changes in the technological environment themselves do not provide a clear answer to whether the locus of causality is moving toward a more internal or external direction. For instance, big data technology, which is receiving a lot of attention nowadays, weakens user's initiative and the locus of causality becomes external. Oppositely, a surgical robot arm like 'da Vinci' provides control up to degrees that humans were previously unable to manipulate on their own; user initiative is greatly strengthened and the locus of causality becomes internal. But generally, technology for many unspecified users such as automatic payment systems in banks and search functions in search engines tend to become an external locus of causality, whereas technology intended for professionals with specific objectives has the tendency to possess an internal locus of causality.

The technological environment also influences relational cohesiveness in the perspective of compositional experience. SNS such as Facebook and Twitter provide diverse methods to communicate with other people. However, the compositional relationship between products or services tends to reveal both technologies with high and low cohesiveness. This is because technologies with high cohesiveness are often times a required necessity. As technology shifts towards high cohesiveness, a product or service's functionalities increase as well as the connection between them. But many functions that are connected together in a complex way can increase users' fatigue and, in turn, weaken cohesiveness. To solve this problem, new functions are created to increase compatibility while reducing complexity, or new products or services aim to outright reduce cohesiveness. For example, the mobile phone started out with calling and texting functions. Then, the camera was added, and together with MP3 functions the mobile phone enabled greater functionalities. As functional cohesiveness increased, it led to the development of the smartphone. However, as users felt fatigue and stress from such high cohesiveness, companies have started to develop technology for products such as wearable devices that focus on a function's usefulness under specific contexts. In this way, human experience also influences the technological environment.

3.5   The Balance of Experience and a Successful Product or Service

What is the relationship between a dynamically created balance and a product that sells well? In many markets including the digital device and service markets, there is a "winner takes all" effect. A product that sells well takes the entire pie while other competitors end up in the dust. In the marketing and economics studies, this term is known as "herd behavior" (Banerjee 1992). Researchers who study herd behavior claim that by studying the diffusion or network model of how information spreads from one person to another, the origin of how it spreads can be identified. They also claim that mimicking consumption patterns of others based on word-of-mouth and reputation will naturally lead to dominance in the market. However, can herd behavior explain how a product like the iPhone dominated the market? In fact, critics said that the iPhone was basically an iPod with a phone function when it was first released. How could an iPod with a phone function succeed based on herd behavior? There seems to be something missing here, and we need to approach this phenomenon with a different perspective than that of herd behavior.

We can think about the concept of dominant design in order to explain this phenomenon from a different perspective. Dominant design refers to a general design that applies to the entire product or service group (Abernathy and Utterback 1978; Sahal 1981; Utterback and Suarez 1993a, b). In other words, it is a design generally applied by a specific field or market during certain periods. For instance, let's think about the design of the smartphone.

Whether it be Apple, Samsung, LG, or HTC, the external designs are hard to distinguish from each other when seen at a faraway distance. Furthermore, most other smartphones apart from Apple use the Android operating system, which makes their phones even harder to distinguish. From far away, they are rectangles with rounded edges. There is a screen that covers the front of the phone, and there are one or two buttons in the lower center of the front. When you turn on the power, a home screen appears with a grid view of square shaped applications. Take out your smartphone right now (this book is published in 2015) and you can see that your phone is quite similar to what I am describing. The concept of dominant design doesn't only apply to smartphones, it can be noticed in many other mature markets.

Dominant design is a crucial concept in explaining the technology life cycle theory as shown in Fig. 3.3. According to this theory, a fermentation process takes place when an innovative technology is invented. During this stage, different technologies engage in a heated competition for dominance. As time progresses, a repeated reorganization of these technologies leads to a single dominant design. Once a dominant design is formed, a time of incremental developments to the dominant design takes place without much volatility to the dominant products and services. Then when a disruptive technology is born, another round of competition, the emergence of the dominant design, and incremental improvements takes place.

Professor James Utterback of MIT refers to the automobile market of the 1900s to describe the technology life cycle theory. From the emergence of the automobile market in 1894 to numerous automobile models released throughout the early 1900s, the industry hit an important point in 1923 when a total of 75 automobile manufacturers competed in the same market. So what happened in 1923? American automobile manufacturer Dodge unveiled a design that separated the interior and exterior of the car through the frame and windows, the first of its kind at the

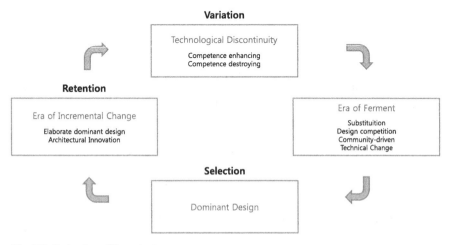

Fig. 3.3 Technology life cycle theory

time and today a standard. Two years later, 50% of all productions followed that design, and by 1926, more than 80% of manufacturers were utilizing the design. A dominant design was instated in the automobile industry. After this point, designs changed incrementally, but the same dominant design still dominates the U.S. automobile market.

3.5.1   Dominant Design and the Synchronization of Experience and Environment

Through what process is a dominant design created? Utterback and Suarez explain this process as a process of experimentation (Utterback and Suarez 1993a, b). A process of experimentation is a repetitive process in which diverse technologies in the form of different designs is presented to users and their feedback and reactions collected.

However, a design does not dominate the market simply through technological excellence. Only a design that "makes sense" to users can become a dominant design. A good example is the Hoover, a vacuum cleaner brand. As the GDP and consumption increased in the U.S. after World War II, almost every household was able to afford a Hoover. The Hoover in turn came a symbol of American wealth and a standard in every household and the word 'Hoover' replaced the term 'vacuum cleaner' for the entire product group. Other examples of brand names that replaced the relevant term for the product category were the Xerox photocopy machine and the Jeep automobile.

How do such brands get so strongly placed in people's minds? I think this is due to the synchronization of the environment and experience. People are influenced by socio-cultural, technological, and economic environments while using products or services. Oppositely, people also influence these environments through sensual, judgmental, and compositional experience. As mentioned previously, a person can have a real experience only when a point of balance is achieved between the external environment and human experience and additionally when a product or service is able to provide that point of balance to users. Basically, socio-cultural, technological, and economic environments influence human experiences of sense of presence, locus of causality, and relational cohesiveness, and vice versa. A point of balance is created through a tight relationship between experience and environment, and when this point of balance is expressed appropriately through a product or service, people are able to have a real experience. A real experience leads people to the belief that their lives have become more fulfilling. This is the point when a product or service will most likely be recognized as the dominant design.

For example, let's think about the history of Hollywood sound films. With the introduction of sound films in the 1930s, the American movie industry hit a golden age. However, the 1930s was also the period of the Great Depression. Millions of people were affected by the economy. However, the masses were partly able to heal their fatigue and devastation through the fantasy worlds shown in the movies. People watched movies through large screens. A high level of a sense of presence was important as people immersed into the movie's context and characters. Hollywood introduced the sound film method to meet the innate needs at the time and thus introduced changes to the socio-cultural and technological environments. Furthermore, the alignment of the external environment and innate experiences of people led to the recognition of the sound movies as a dominant design.

As a more recent example, let's think about the iPhone. Desktop computers that take up a lot of space on desks are fast losing their position as the main device that people use when searching for information. People today are busy and possess the need to get things done on the move, and smartphones such as the iPhone have the potential to effectively provide a solution for this need. Furthermore, the advancement of mobile processors has led to matching levels of performance with desktops. Prices of full touch LCD screens that are able to support multi-touch functions have decreased dramatically, and the combination of multiple sensors has led to the iPhone being able to take care of most of our work. This shows that a technological environment has been formed where user initiative is high and the locus of causality is internal. The iPhone was able to provide the point of balance that experience and environment created to become a dominant design.

3.5.2   The Dominance of Dominant Design

The greatest influence of a dominant design is the effect of creating a de facto standard. A de facto standard causes competitors' products and services to fall in line with the dominant design. Technically, it is not a standard, but in reality, it does possess the advantages of a standard. When a dominant design becomes the de facto standard, the providing company gains a competitive advantage that is hard for other firms to replicate. First, the scale of economy cannot be ignored. Since its product dominates the market, the relative cost of production will be lower than for other companies. Also, users will become accustomed to their product through learning effects, and their production methods and service distribution quality can all be increased quicker than their competitors'.

Intellectual property such as patents for a dominant designs can further enhance competitiveness. Let's go back to the example of the Apple vs. Samsung lawsuits, mentioned in Chapter 1. Whether it was a coincidence or not, when the U.S. court ruled that the Galaxy model of Samsung infringed upon Apple's patents, many of those elements were similar to the elements of the dominant design. What is the reason for this? When a dominant design surfaces, competitors must apply that dominant design in order to survive in the market because most users want the same experience under specific contexts. The dominant design offers that experience to users.

3.5.3 An Exception to Every Rule

In this chapter, we took a look at the relationships between human experience, external environments, and dominant design. The socio-cultural, economic, and technological environments of a specific age influence human experience. Oppositely, the sensual, judgmental, and compositional experiences of users influence external environments. The dynamic interaction between environment and experience creates a point of balance that can then be utilized to offer real experiences to users through products and services. These products and services are then recognized as dominant designs in their respective markets.

A principle is better when it can be simply applied. The simpler the principle, the wider its area of application. However, we need to discuss a few points before being able to generally apply the aforementioned principles to a wide range of products and services.

Firstly, experience is relative as mentioned in Chapter 2. The experience of a current product or service is created through comparisons with past experiences of products or services. While it is important to consider the absolute degree of sense of presence, locus of causality and relational cohesiveness to provide the experience, comparing the degrees with a prior product or service may be more important. Therefore, no matter how high a sense of presence a product provides, it needs to be higher than its prior product for people to feel a high sense of presence.

Secondly, in an age where numerous products and services are launched everyday, it becomes unclear which products and services should be compared. The most common method would be to compare a new version of a product or service with its prior version.

For instance, it's not difficult to compare the sense of presence, locus of causality, or relational cohesiveness between the experience of iOS 7 and iOS 8. But what about when we have to compare between two value systems? If a person uses a smartphone to kill time by surfing the web and watch webtoons (a Korean style webcomics), the subject of comparison in terms of relative sense of presence, locus of causality, and cohesiveness should be news apps, magazines, and games rather than the smartphone itself.

Lastly, the logic of this chapter applies to general environments and general products and services. There are instances when the same type of environment can influence the characteristics of specific products and services. Let's return to the example of the Hollywood sound film. A decrease in economic assets leads to lower consumption in general, and people are indifferent to a low degree of sensual immersion. However, the distinct characteristic of movies as a form of culture led to the preference of a high immersive experience. Although people were in a dire economic state, they sought to escape reality for a short period of time and delve into an ideal, imaginary world. This is how they wanted to relieve their stress from everyday life. Therefore, the relative comparison to a sound movie can be the settings and characters within that movie. For example, Roman Holliday, starring Audrey Hepburn, reveals a higher sense of sensual immersion through a sound movie than a silent movie, but nowhere as high as going to Rome for a date and sightseeing. But considering the context of the economic depression at the time, the film may have provided a higher sense of presence since it gave people an escape from reality (the reality in which they would never be able to afford to visit Rome) and helped them promote their imagination.

3.6   The Experiential Point of Balance

In order to successfully overcome the above constraints, a careful analysis needs to be conducted on the interaction between environment and experience of a product or service.

Firstly, deduce as many socio-cultural, economic, and technological elements that may directly or indirectly influence a product or service. However, keep in mind that elements will differ based on whether you look at a specific product or service, or a general market that includes many products or services.

Secondly, accurately measure the current levels of experiences that a product or service provides to users. What is the level of sense of presence that a product or service provides in terms of sensual experience? What is the locus of causality in terms of judgmental experience? What is the level of relational cohesiveness that the product or service provides? These questions will be able to provide answers for measuring the levels of experience. It would be more efficient to define the extreme points of each dimension and then place the product or service between the extreme points.

Thirdly, compare a product or service in order to infer people's preferences. Do people want a higher, lower, or current level of sense of presence in terms of sensual experience? Do they want an internal, external, or current level of judgmental experience? Do they want stronger, weaker, or the same level of cohesiveness in terms of compositional experience?

Fourthly, analyze the effects of each environmental element on the three threads of experience. In the case of sensual experience, will the current environmental elements lead to a higher, lower, or similar level of sensual sense of presence? In terms of judgmental experience, will the current environmental elements lead to a more external, internal, or similar level of judgmental locus of causality? In the case of compositional experience, will the current environmental elements lead to a higher, lower, or similar level of relational cohesiveness?

Lastly, find a new point of balance for the product or service where people's experiences and external environments meet. Finding a new point of balance will be discussed more meticulously in the next chapter.

3.7 Summary

- Socio-cultural, economic, and technological environments and their elements influence the three threads of experience (sensual, judgmental, and compositional) and vice versa.
- A lifestyle developed through the characteristics of the online environment has led people to prefer a high sense of presence, internal locus of causality, and strong relational cohesiveness.
- Macroeconomic environments such as a change in the economy are closely related to how people feel about how many assets they possess. When people perceive the economy to be healthy, they tend to prefer a high sense of presence, internal locus of causality, and strong relational cohesiveness.
- The development of technology tends to increase the sense of presence and strengthen relational cohesiveness, but there is no clear direction in terms of locus of causality.
- Technology geared towards the general crowd tends to have a more external locus of causality, while technology for selected professionals tends to shift more towards an internal locus of causality.
- Environmental elements and experiential elements meet to create an experiential point of balance.
- A product or service that identifies and provides a specific point of balance between experience and environment can provide users with a real experience.
- These products or services are recognized in the market as dominant designs.
- A dominant design refers to a design generally applied within a product or a service group.

3.8 Discussion Topics

- Choose a product or a service of interest and find a dominant design in the corresponding field.
- Express the levels of the threads of experience in a three dimensional graph for the dominant design.
- Express people's preferred experiences of the product or service in a three dimensional graph.
- Identify the socio-cultural, economic, and technological elements of the environment that affect people's experiences of the product or service.
- Analyze which direction each element heads towards and how much influence each element has on the threads of experience.

References

Abernathy W, Utterback J (1978) Patterns of industrial innovation. Technol Rev 80(1–8): 41–47

Banerjee AV (1992) A simple model of herd behavior. Q J Econ 107(3):797–817

Cagan J, Vogel M (2013) Creating breakthrough products: revealing the secrets that drive global innovation, 2nd edn. FT Press, Upper Saddle River

Hofstede G (1980) Culture and organizations. Int Stud Manage Organ 10(4):15–41

Law J (2006) Managing change and innovation in public service organisations. Public Adm 84:794–796. (Edited by Stephen P. Osborne and Kerry Brown.)

Lee I, Kim J, Choi B, Hong S (2010) Measurement development for cultural characteristics of mobile internet uers at the individual level. Comput Hum Behav 26(6):1355–1368

March JG (1991) Exploration and exploitation in organizational learning. Organ Sci 2(1):71–87

Ram S, Sheth JN (1989) Consumer resistance to innovations: the marketing problem and its solutions. J Consum Mark 6(2):5–14

Sahal D (1981) Alternative conceptions of technology. Res Policy 10(1):2–24

Shirky C (2010) Cognitive surplus: creativity and generosity in a connected age. Penguin UK

Shizuka S (2003) Koshi den. ChQo Koron Shinsha, Tokyo

Utterback J, Suarez F (1993a) Innovation, competition, and industry structure. Res Policy 22:1–21

Utterback J, Suarez F (1993b) Patterns of industrial evolution, dominant designs, and firm's survival, research on technolgoical innovation, management and policy, vol 6. JAI Press, Greenwich

Von Hippel E (1986) Lead users: a source of novel product concepts. Manage Sci 32(7):791–805

Chapter 4
Creative Conflicts and Dynamic Balancing

4.1 Introduction

Products and services that present a "point of balance" had dominant positions in their respective markets, and were deemed as a "dominant design." However, as is the fate of all organisms, a dominant design eventually undergoes its ups and downs over time and changes in the environment and eventually dies. Although digital products and services may evolve towards increased economic value over time, the majority of them these days are rejected and dismissed at a faster rate than ever. Until recently, a lot of studies tried to explain this phenomenon only with technological elements. But can we indeed say that such technological elements alone determine the rise and fall of a dominant design? Could a person's experience, as we have been contemplating in this book, be the answer to this question rather than technological elements? The important frame of innovation can be reclaimed as people's experiences that digest and apply this technology. So when thinking about a person's experience, why is a dominant design gradually destroyed over time? Through which principles are new dominant designs created?

4.2 There is No Eternal Winner

Sometimes I find myself observing people in crowded places. The subway in particular is an interesting place in Korea, especially during rush hour, where more than 90 % of the people repeat the same behaviors in the same positions. They stare at their smartphones, which is a scene that can also be observed while waiting for the green light at a crosswalk in Metropolitan Seoul. Studies have reported the so-called "Turtle Neck Syndrome," which occurs to people when sitting in front of a computer in the wrong posture for prolonged periods of time. This phenomenon can be found even in very young children using smartphones, and it shows just how much the smartphone is being used nowadays. The first smartphones were luxury items for businessmen and CEOs but now they have become an undeniable paradigm in

© Springer International Publishing Switzerland 2015
J. Kim, *Design for Experience*, Human-Computer Interaction Series,
DOI 10.1007/978-3-319-14304-0_4

our lives. How can we explain this rapidly changing world of digital products and services?

At this point, we need to review how digital companies create UXs and integrate it into strategic products or services. Over the past 6 years, I have been a board member of a company that owned Korea's leading internet portal site. In the beginning when discussing the agenda at a board meeting, management performance was tracked mainly through three categories: general finance, marketing, and tracking reports of users' degree of service usage. I was reported periodically on the influx of new users every month, the number of users using the portal service, and how long they stayed on it.

But one day I realized that the reports on the users were old-fashioned. In fact, the method of measuring the tracking performance itself was old-fashioned because it was done based on data that was collected by installing special equipment on a limited number of users' desktops, which created log data by tracking the order in which the services were used. By doing so, un-sampled end users were completely ignored, and with the increasing number of smartphone users, we could not examine the users connecting from mobile devices rather than desktops.

But tracking mobile device users was relatively difficult. Because the Privacy Act of Korea maintains very strict standards for such methods, it was difficult to collect sufficient information to understand the users. Within the Act, we decided to monitor the users connecting through smartphones. Only after a year or so, there was a complete reversal in the results: the number of mobile users surpassed PC-based visitors. While the curve for mobile users rose steeply, PC-based users fell gradually, showing a graph with a clear intersecting X mark.

In fact, signs of such changes had been apparent for some time. In the early 2000s, 3–4 years before the introduction of smartphones, people were purchasing feature phones in increased numbers. At this time, new service development departments of telecommunication companies were filled with countless proposals by small and medium sized companies offering additional software functions and services for mobile phones. By adding many additional services on new mobile phones and raising the price of the existing ones, the revenue from each user increased continuously in a rising curve.

During this time, I was working as a member of a future strategy group for one of the top domestic mobile carriers in Korea. One day, I had a chance to talk to the CEO who was full of insights on the developments in the IT industry. He told me, "Jinwoo, I have had terrible recurring dreams recently. Do you know how expensive the telecommunication bills per family are in Korea? A family of four pays several hundred thousand won [several hundreds of dollars] in telecommunication expenses. The situation may be better if the breadwinner earns a lot but even disregarding our average national disposable income, the fact that each family is wasting several hundred thousand won is a major social issue. The problem is—what benefits are people getting after spending so much money? They are limited to just a few minutes of phone calls and text messaging services. The companies should thoroughly reflect on whether they are returning the benefits to the consumers."

Such a confession by a CEO of a telecommunications company was a big shock to me. In fact, at the time telecommunication companies developed numerous content for the mobile phone market that were mostly unsuccessful. The only profitable business models were SMS and phone calls. But even these were not the result of solid strategies by the company, but rather a natural result due to the oligopoly state of the market. In other words, this was a result of operating in an extremely closed form of market.

But in 2009, the iPhone was introduced in Korea and the application services market became increasingly more active. An environment was created where anyone could use applications that were developed with global standards regardless of specific carriers. Meanwhile, mobile application services with immense profits emerged, weakening the telecommunication companies' influence in the mobile industry. Text messaging service, which was once a dutiful business model, had now suddenly become a neglected service, and the telecommunication companies' struggles to retain the rapidly falling profits from phone calls had begun. From PC to mobile, and from telecommunication companies to manufacturers and application markets, the landscape had changed in just a few years. Looking at this macroscopic flow of events, I became curious about where the next change would occur.

4.3 Changes of Dominant Design

Take a close look at your keyboard if you have a computer nearby. The keys on the upper left most likely spell out 'QWERTY,' which is why we call such keyboards with these layouts "QWERTY keyboards." The QWERTY layout was initially designed for mechanical typewriters in order to avoid the type bars from jamming. Almost all keyboards today come with the QWERTY layout, which is an international standard and a dominant design as well. This layout is still being used even after the transformation of computing to mobile, where no jamming bars exist. Of course, there were many other keyboard layouts that enabled faster typing and more convenience, but they were all shunned in the market.

According to INSEAD Professors Henrich Greve and Seidel, entering the market first is more important than product quality in order to secure more power (Greve and Seidel 2014). Once a company becomes the first to enter a market, the majority of people will become most familiar with its products amongst the product group. Steadily, this company's product can become the dominant design in which other companies must adapt to this company's technologies and application methods. This becomes a practical standard and a kind of norm that creates competition in a similar manner between products and services. Once a company acquires the dominant design it has greater market competitiveness and can reduce costs through economies of scale. Also, users tend to stick to what they are already familiar with, because they consider it a waste of time and money (called transaction cost) to adapt to something new unless its effect is powerful and certain.

However, once a dominant design is determined, it does not last forever, and for whatever reason, it falls out and a new dominant design emerges. Let's examine how dominant designs fall out and emerge based on the perspective of human experience. Specifically, we need to examine how the dominant design of a product or service adapts and changes regarding sensual, judgmental, and compositional elements of experience. Before we start discussing products and services, I would like to first talk about how the characteristics of a dominant design changes in the field that is easily accessible by the general public, such as art, cars, and music.

4.3.1   Sense of Presence Varies with Time

Regarding sensual experience, the sense of presence is an important variable. However, a high sense of presence does not always result in a positive experience. At times, changes in external environments lead to lessened sense of presence and sometimes the opposite happens. Let's look at this through the history of modern art.

During the Middle Ages when Christianity dominated all aspects of society, provocative and excessively immersive art was forbidden. Byzantine and Gothic paintings excluded three-dimensional effects and were painted as flat as possible. The motifs were usually biblical situations, resulting in artwork that had a low sense of presence. In the 14th century, however, after the bubonic plague and the merciless deaths of young people in religious wars, people started to realize that their current lives were more important than the afterlife. In particular, movements to revive human-centered thinking emerged. An increasing number of artists, such as Petrarca and Dante, praised the "current era" as the best times for people to live in. These ideas brought forth the Renaissance of human-centered culture.

During the Renaissance, the main subjects for painting and sculptures were all focused on people and the portrayal techniques also changed strategically. Artists like Caravaggio (1602) proposed a sensory recreation method that created a three-dimensional space through clear contrasts and hues, similar to chiaroscuro. Thus, during the Renaissance, the sense of presence of the artwork had increased.

As the Baroque style, which was centered on absolute monarchy, began to thrive after the Renaissance, art started to take a new direction. Painting styles, such as mannerism, began to show increasingly stimulating content. The most representative works are Gentileschi's "Judith Slaying Holofernes" (1614) and Tintoretto's "Last Supper" (1570). Hence, representation methods of increasing sense of presence had intensified.

However, the Rococo style, late impressionism, and the modernism era brought a change in painting patterns that were more and more understated. Simple, rustic expressions took the initiative rather than pursuing detail and extreme contrast, apparent in Hogarth's "Marriage à-la-mode" (1743–1745) and Vincent van Gogh's "Starry Night" (1889). The modernism of Matisse, which strategically selected and expressed points that were important to the painter rather than stressing the environment and individuals equally, is also a form of art that significantly lowered a sense of presence.

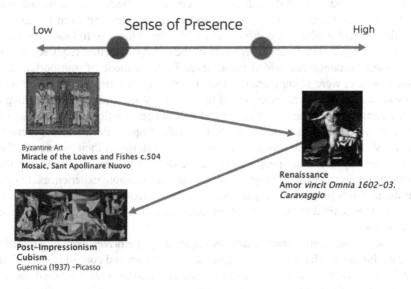

Fig. 4.1 Changes of sense of presence in art history

As shown in Fig. 4.1, the level of sense of presence in the history of modern art draws a curve similar to a sine wave, changing according to the situation and context of the time. It changes dynamically according to the era, from low presence to high presence, and from high presence to low.

4.3.2   Locus of Causality Changes with Time

We can take automobiles as an example for the change in points of locus of causality for judging what is useful according to the times and situations. The history of the automobile can be divided into three stages depending on the judgmental locus of causality: pre-World War II from 1920 to 1940 when the modern automobile first came out, post-World War II from 1940 to 1960, and during the oil crisis between the 1970s and 1990s.

From 1920 to 1940 was the time when the automobile's structure and functions were being established in order to replace the horse and carriage as the method for transportation. During this time when the automobile's functional value was emphasized, it was of utmost important to get to the desired destination quickly and safely. Also, there were no customizable options in the purchasing process that we are used to today. In those days, people utilized automobiles as a means to go from one point to another rather than enjoyed the driving process. During this time, the locus of causality was external as people put more meaning into automobiles as a mode of efficient transportation.

Between 1940 and 1960, with the development of electric ignitions and standardized braking systems, the convenience of automobiles improved to the point that the general public could drive them with ease. This was followed by paved roads and people found various reasons in their daily lives that required driving. Now, the automobile had added value beyond a mere mode of transportation. In particular, cars were being manufactured in a variety of forms as people began to view the automobile as an extension of themselves. While there are those who preferred small cars like the Mini Cooper and Volkswagen Beetle, there are those who enjoyed muscle cars like the Jaguar or Chevrolet Impala. Furthermore, there are people who completely customize the interior and exterior of their cars to suit their own tastes. By this time, people enjoyed the driving process itself and felt they controlled, to some extent, the processing of getting valuable experiences. In other words, people's judgmental experience steered towards an internal locus of causality as they started to consider options and controlled what they wanted in their automobiles.

In the 1970s, many complex actions required by the driver were automated to ease the burden on the user, for example automatic gears and control systems. During this time, roads became more complex and crowded and nations started discussing the harm of vehicle exhaust emission on the environment. Especially after the 1973 oil crisis that led to soaring oil prices, the fuel efficiency of cars emerged as an important issue. During this time, Japanese automakers received attention, as their cars were fuel-efficient, had almost no breakdowns, and had fully automated equipment. The car's functional value, its ability to move from one place to another with the lowest fuel consumption possible, was highlighted once again. In other words, the values and changes of the times shifted people's judgmental experience to an external locus of causality.

We examined how the locus of causality of judgmental experience can change according to the situation of the times. As shown in Fig. 4.2, an internal locus of causality is more relevant to people at times, whereas an external locus of causality is held in more value at other times. In addition, we saw that the locus of causality of a dominant design was not oriented to a specific direction, but rather swayed both ways.

4.3.3   Relational Cohesiveness also Changes with Time

The appropriate level of perceived relational cohesiveness can differ from person to person depending on the times. Similarly, the level of relational cohesiveness that products and services with dominant designs bring can also change, an example being the change in musical trends.

During the late sixteenth and early seventeenth century, the Medici family of Florence started what we all know as the opera (Hanskins 1990). The opera originated from the Medici family's special plays that were mixed with singing. The Medici family wanted a place to spend quality time with acquaintances and other

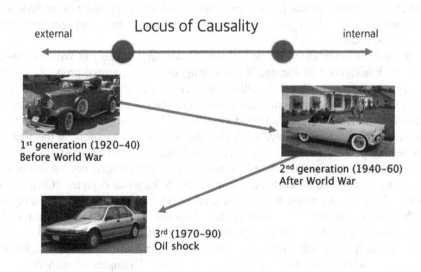

Fig. 4.2 Changes of locus of causality in automobiles history

family members and installed a small stage in the living room. Some composers were also commissioned to write songs appropriate for dining and drinking wine. This type of community was an innovative one as there were scarce opportunities to meet people with the exception of going to church. The opera needed specialized music, which led to the development of chamber music. Chamber music is usally performed for a limited audience and each part is played by a solo leader of the chamber. In chamber music, the collaborative ensemble is important without master-slave relationships between the solo and accompaniments. Chamber music was mainly played in palaces and residences of nobles or small areas such as concert halls for a small audience, who enjoyed the music with meals and refreshments. Chamber music is an example of high-level relational cohesiveness, which considers the close relationship between the audience and music important.

However, in the early nineteenth century, with the appearance of Beethoven and the advent of conductors, Western music became highly oriented to a specialized system (Horkheimer and Adorno 2001). Composers were divided into specialized categories in music, such as keyboard, strings, and vocal, while musicians were affiliated with a symphonic orchestra, a professional organization, bringing a highly structured environment. In other words, for both the music listeners and performers, the musical trends in this period changed towards lower relational cohesiveness in terms of compositional experience. Even musicians had fewer opportunities to mingle as they focused only on their own parts. Also, the audience gathered for listening to the works in theaters and halls rather than socializing like in the past. Even in Mozart's times, it was not unusual to drink coffee while seeing a performance of the "Magic Flute." However, since Beethoven, theater etiquette evolved to disapprove noise from the audience at un-appropriate times such as coughing or small talk during a performance. In this sense, symphonies have opposite characteristics to chamber music, which possesses weak relational cohesiveness between performers and the audience.

But this did not last long. There was a sharp twist in the history of Western music with the introduction of Richard Wagner. Wagner had an unusual propensity with a very short temper, and was expelled from Germany until he was 50 years old for being involved with communist ideas. However, King Ludwig of the Kingdom of Bavaria (Munich is Bavaria's largest city) built a large theater after desiring "national music", "national music," or "music that symbolizes a nation" in the area of Bayreuth, a part of Bavaria. Under this slogan, Wagner created masterpieces such as "Die Meistersinger von Nurnberg," "Tannhauser," and "Der Ring des Nibelungen," which were all based on northern European mythology that depicted "Great Germany." This was the moment when the level of relational cohesiveness rose again in the history of music. Since then, Brahms, Bruckner, and even French composers began to study the forms of expression by Wagner. Composers from nations that were not-so-friendly with Germany, such as the Czech Republic and Russia, began coming up with music that represented nationalism. Examples of such composers are Czech's Smetana and Dvorak and Russia's Rimsky-Korsakov and Borodin, who expressed the culture of their nation and people through music while escaping from the symphony orchestra's quantitative music that was centered on mechanical techniques. By using ethnic melodies and musical structures that were passed on for generations as a theme, musical content that strengthened national consciousness had begun to spread. This kind of music had a major impact on promoting social unity in times of wars and division. Thus, the change from symphony to nationalist music is an example of change from low-level to high-level relational cohesiveness from the perspective of the audience.

In summary, as seen in Fig. 4.3, the level of relational cohesiveness of a dominant design can increase and decrease depending on the external environment or the characteristics of the particular field.

We have examined how a dominant design was constantly challenged and a new dominant design was created through the perspective of human experience in the histories of art, music, and the automobile. How did dominant designs that were seemingly fixed in their dominant positions give way to other dominant designs? What is the fundamental power of such changes? Perhaps it is caused by the tension or conflict that occurs between the environment and human experience.

4.4 Conflicts and Contradictions that Power Innovation

Russian scientist G. Altshulle has an unusual past. He went into exile to Siberian camps for political reasons during the Stalin era while working at a patent office. While at the camps, he and his fellow prisoners analyzed hundreds of thousands of patents that were filed to the Russian government to find commonalities. The long Siberian winter had given him an opportunity to gather and analyze massive

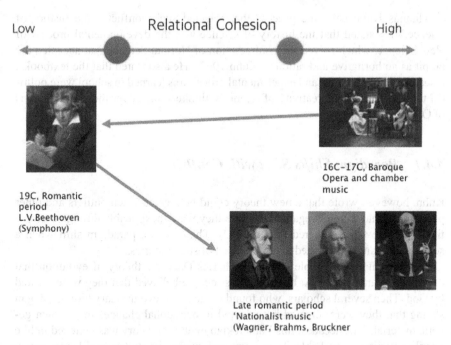

Fig. 4.3 Changes of relational cohesiveness in the generations of classical music

amounts of data. While analyzing inventions that once dominated, he discovered why and how they were made. As a result, he explained that the leading cause of new technology was conflict and the development process was the resolution of such conflicts (Kuhn 1962). In other words, he stated that the emergence of new technologies was the solution to conflicts of existing technologies. For example, the automobile was invented to help move from point A to point B. This invention was good for transportation but created a conflict by polluting the environment. We can see that, to address the conflict of air pollution, an environmentally unfriendly issue, electric car technology was created (Buchanan 1992).

In fact, many thinkers in the past had already claimed that conflict powered social changes. In his book "Leviathan," political philosopher Hobbes stated that the essence of humans was violence and conflict (Hobbes, 1928) while Hegel, who viewed the world in three stages—in itself, out of itself, and in and for itself, assumed that conflict was an inevitable element that occurred in the making of history (Hegel 2004). In "Capital," written by communist philosopher Karl Marx, human history starts a revolution to solve the past's contradictions but conceives a new contradiction in the process.

Interestingly, conflicts and contradictions also result in innovation in companies and academics. When faced with problems, people search for new ideas and methods to solve them. However, there are times when we overlook new problems in the new ideas and methods, as we are only human. As time goes by, the new ideas and methods can become authoritative by becoming the dominant design. Eventually, they become another source of new conflict.

Thomas Kuhn calls the process that rejected such conflicts "the history of science." He stated that the history of science was the developmental process of New Science, which solved the contradiction of Normal Science that accepted the pulpit as authoritative and rational (Kuhn 1962). He also stated that the textbooks, research methodologies, and experimental procedures learned in school were political tools to hinder the creativity of scientific thinkers and cover the contradictions of Old Science.

4.4.1   Paradigm Shifts Start with Conflict

Kuhn, however, wrote that a new theory could be created when outliers and other phenomena that were disregarded because they were inexplicable through conventional science were gathered (Kuhn 1962). This led to a paradigm shift when a social consensus was formed about the need of such theories.

A representative example of this is Charles Darwin's theory of evolution that overturned Lamarckism. At the time, most people believed that they were created by God. Then several scholars, who found evidence of evolutionary biology, began stating that they were 'created but adapted to occasional changes in our own genetic material.' For decades, this Lamarckian evolution theory was believed in like people believed in the Bible. Then a young British aristocrat named Darwin traveled the world, including the Galapagos Islands, and claimed that humans and other organisms did not evolve through adaptation. Rather, they evolved through natural selection, where environmental changes determined which species would survive and thrive or die out. At first, his statements were criticized by many researchers until more data was gathered and until other scholars began referring to Social Darwinism and the "survival of the fittest." This is when Darwin's theory of evolution overturned traditional science and became the new paradigm (De Beer 1963).

To conclude, the conflicts that a paradigm creates stimulate new paradigms. New paradigms have completely different characteristics than existing paradigms because they solve different problems, use different terminology, and use different solutions to explain or solve problems. So how are the conflicts and the resulting new paradigms related to the experience of using products and services?

4.4.2   Changes in the Environment Cause Cognitive Dissonance

Innovation regarding products and services can be largely approached from two positions. The first is innovation from the perspective of the person using the product or service, and the second is innovation from the perspective of the company that provides it. When considering the changes in environmental elements that affect the two perspectives, innovation can be described by the conflicts between companies, users, and the environment and the mechanism that attempts to eliminate such conflicts. Let's first look at the conflicts, from the users' point of view, and the impact they have on the emergence of innovative products and services.

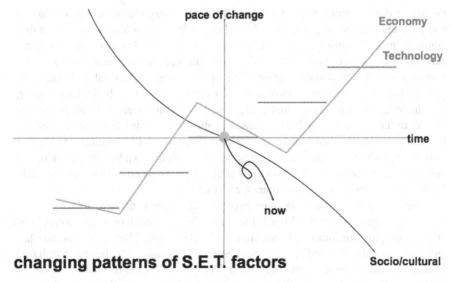

changing patterns of S.E.T. factors

Fig. 4.4 The variety in changes of the three environmental elements

In Chapter 3, we examined three external environments that affected experience: sociocultural, economic, and technological. A dominant design may last forever if these three elements and people never change. Because, in general, users do not want to change and companies that provide a dominant design do not want change either. However, the three elements do indeed change with varying patterns. The rate of change of sociocultural elements is initially very slow, but changes to a large scale once the changing rate accelerates. On the other hand, changes in economic elements are difficult to predict and are sometimes arbitrary due to policies. Changes in technological elements are very quick and tend to happen discontinuously. Thus, as shown in Fig. 4.4, the three elements have different effects on our experiences due to their varying aspects in change.

The three environmental elements can also lead to conflicts in experience. For instance, in the perspective of sensual experience, technological elements can provide a high sense of presence. But in terms of the economic environment, it may be difficult for people to appreciate a high sense of presence. If extremely stimulating technologies were abundant, then socio-culturally, products with low presence could be preferred. Regarding the perspective of judgmental experience, the sociocultural environment could drive change towards an internal locus of causaility, while the technological environment could drive a person's experience towards an external locus of causality. In the perspective of compositional experience, technology allows for a structure that supports strong relational cohesiveness, while socioculturally, such high levels of cohesiveness may be burdensome.

People feel uncomfortable as the conflicts in experience increase. This book evaluates the "uncomfortable state" between these environmental elements and a person's experience through the point of view of cognitive dissonance. Cognitive dissonance, which was first proposed in the 1960s by social psychologist Leon

Festinger, is a concept that even today is important in explaining people's behavior and psychological state (Festinger 1962). People feel psychological stress and discomfort due to cognitive dissonance in largely three cases. The first case is when a person has two or more conflicting beliefs or values at the same time. For example, you may want the new stylish smartphone in the sensual aspect but, judgmentally, you think the new smartphone would not be of much use to you. In the second case, new information is presented that conflict with existing beliefs and values. For instance, in the past you may have wanted a highly cohesive relationship with others but came across the news about the leaking of personal information online. The third case is when the behavior of a person contradicts his own beliefs and values. A good example would be when you need to study for an exam but end up sensually immersed in viewing videos of interest on YouTube.

When one reaches these states of cognitive dissonance, three main phenomena occur (Festinger et al. 1950). Firstly, the person feels a variety of negative emotions such as despair, discomfort, frustration, and even anger. That is, the person has suffered sensually. Secondly, the person begins to question whether the purchased product or used service is actually useful. The person begins to doubt in terms of judgment. Thirdly, the person becomes uncomfortable towards the purchasing process or others who have purchased the same product. Thus, the person has negative experiences in terms of compositional experience.

Therefore, when perceiving cognitive dissonance, people begin to have negative conflicts in their sensory, judgmental, and compositional experience. When they experience such negative conflicts, they gain the desire to solve them, because people have the internal desire to resolve the conflicts that they experience in their daily lives. These desires eventually provide the power to the entire process of developing a new paradigm that can understand people's lives and solve their conflicts (March 2010).

4.4.3   Conflict is a Golden Opportunity for New Experiences

The driving force of innovative changes that alter paradigms cannot be solely explained with cognitive dissonance as there need to be companies that take advantage of such cognitive dissonance to create new technologies and products. As argued by economist Schumpeter (Schumpter 1976), we need creative entrepreneurs and companies that expand their capacities by strategically using these conflicts to find out problems of existing products. Thus, such conflicts are rather good opportunities for those creative companies and entrepreneurs. An important concept here is the aspiration level (Cyert 1963; March and Simon 1958). In growing organizations, an aspiration level exists that aims towards something different than the current self. Here, change and innovation occur during the conflict between aspiration and current levels.

Network theorist and strategic researcher, Professor Joe Labianca of the University of Kentucky, introduced the concept of "discrepancy" that upgraded the conventional definition of aspiration (Labianca 2009). Professor Labianca called "competitive discrepancy" the difference between the performance of similar organizations and the performance of one's own organization. He also labeled the difference between the performance levels of the ideal organization and one's own organization as "striving discrepancy."

Competitive discrepancy is a trendy concept because it is related to competitor trends inside the same industry. Most companies try to capture competing technology trends. Therefore, although it is difficult to understand the confidential content of the technology itself, it is possible to judge which kinds of experiences are provided to the users. Here, companies that feel the discrepancy between themselves and competitors attempt to overcome the differences through continuous technology investments and incremental innovations.

On the other hand, striving discrepancy refers to the difference between a company's utopia in the distant future and the current state. Environmental changes and users' potential desires create future-oriented company's utopia. And these companies try to overcome such striving discrepancies through basic R&D departments and radical innovations.

4.5 Two Kinds of Very Different Innovations

There are concepts of innovation that are closely associated with competitive or striving discrepancy. These are sustaining innovation and disruptive innovation, proposed by Professor Christensen of Harvard University (Christensen et al. 2006). Sustaining innovation is innovation that caters to people's needs by gradually improving existing products and services. A prime example of sustaining innovation is the semiconductor, that becomes smaller and faster at a predictable speed, mentioned in Chapter 3 as an example of technological life cycle. Despite these developments, people still want smaller and faster semiconductors. We can say that a sustaining innovation is the gradual innovation that happens after a dominant design is formed.

On the other hand, a disruptive innovation is an innovation that destroys existing markets and creates new ones. An example of disruptive innovation is Japan's car manufacturers' requisition of the American market. Japanese companies first entered the compact car market with cheap and reliable cars that had good fuel economy. American car manufacturers at the time were not interested in the compact car market because of the small market size and revenue. Thus, they focused on large sedans and SUVs, which were larger, more luxurious, and provided more profits. They did therefore not intervene when the Japanese manufacturers entered the compact car market. However, the Japanese manufacturers' market penetration that started with the compact car market soon encroached mid-sized and large-sized sedans, and eventually the SUV market. A case such as this is also an example of a paradigm shift described by Kuhn, because it defined and solved the problem from a completely different perspective than what was intended by the existing paradigm.

These theories of technological innovations explain new products or services that change paradigms from the perspective of companies. But it does not explain the shifts in paradigms from the perspectives of users of those products and services. Then, when do sustaining innovations and disruptive innovations occur from the UX point of view? And in which directions do these innovations lead users' experience?

4.6   The Dynamic Balance of Experience

Let's explain the change in dominant design by sustaining innovation and disruptive innovation using the individual's cognitive dissonance and the discrepancy level of a company. The changes in sociocultural, economic, and technological elements affect the three aspects of people's experience in different directions and speeds. When this is the case, people experience cognitive dissonance while companies experience competitive discrepancy within the extent of the dominant design and progressively change it in a particular direction to lower the discrepancy.

However, these gradual changes do not meet all the challenges caused by the various environments. While the sociocultural, economic, and technological environments cause differing levels of influence to the three threads of human experience, a movement to retain the dominant design also affects human experience, thereby skewing human experience to one direction. Therefore, as incremental innovation progresses continuously, companies attempt to overcome competitive discrepancy within the frame of the existing dominant design. These efforts lead to a discrepancy between a user's desired experience and the experience provided by companies and the user's cognitive dissonance increases accordingly. When this happens continuously, after a certain point due to increased cognitive dissonance, it is not possible to solve people's conflicts with existing dominant designs.

At this moment, a new product or service is introduced by companies that recognize striving discrepancies. These products or services operate on people's experiences in a complete new direction from existing dominant designs and solve problems that are entirely different than the experiences, which were gradually changing within the existing dominant designs. In other words, a paradigm shift occurs that resolves the accumulated cognitive dissonance due to continuous innovation in a new way, which eventually results in a disruptive innovation.

The above can be difficult to understand because it is conceptual and abstract. To complement this, let's examine examples of sustaining innovation from the three aspects of experience and take a look at the patterns of a disruptive innovation similarly.

4.6.1   Sustaining Innovation from the Perspective of Sensual Experience

Consider the case of Ultra High Definition (UHD) TVs, which feature life-like vivid pictures with extremely high resolutions that are clearer than those of Full HD

TVs (1920×1080). Compared to HD TVs, UHD TVs have more than 4 to 16 times the number of pixels. In HD TVs, the pores of the skin can be seen faintly, while it is possible to see the fine soft hairs on a persons's skin in UHD TVs. In addition, UHD TVs have improved color reproduction that provides a more three-dimensional display. The audio of UHD TVs have also improved, implementing channels ranging from 10.1 up to 22.2 channels and providing three-dimensional sounds from various directions. Thus, compared to people watching HD TVs, the experience of people watching UHD has evolved to experiencing a clearer sense of presence towards what is displayed on the TV.

A similar trend can be seen in portable gaming devices. Existing gaming devices, such as the Nintendo DS or Tamagotchi devices, had low resolutions and lacked three-dimensionality, making it difficult to feel a high sense of presence. The games themselves provided immersion, but it's hard to say that this immersion was due to a high sense of presence. In contrast, let's take a look at virtual reality gaming devices, such as the Oculus Rift. The headset detects the user's head movements in real-time and updates the visual display accordingly. In addition, the concave lenses provide a panoramic display. Head tracking technology and displays on both eyes create the illusion that the user is actually inside the game. We can say that portable gaming devices have been developed for a long time to provide a higher sense of presence to its users.

From the perspective of sensual experience, as shown in the two examples above, there is a trend for products and services to continuously change towards providing a higher sense of presence to users. This also matches with the changes in the technological or sociocultural environments mentioned earlier in Chapter 3. That is, it becomes possible to receive immediate feedback that is more sensory and lively as technology advances. Especially, people tend to prefer stimuli that provide a higher sense of presence as they become familiar to online environments (Fig. 4.5).

4.6.2 Sustaining Innovation from the Perspective of Judgmental Experience

Let's consider automobile GPS navigation devices as an example of moving toward an external locus of causality in the perspective of judgmental experience. GPS navigation devices were developed to search for routes in order to provide a convenient way of reaching a destination. However, early GPS navigation products were not popularized because they had to be constantly operated manually by the driver, which was a significant safety risk. So navigation devices evolved in the direction of developing automated technology. For example, with the sharing of GPS satellite data by the U.S. in 2000, navigation devices that used satellite signals were born, which automatically transmitted the driver's precise location. Afterwards, a number of automatic functions were added to navigation devices, an example being the automatic calculation of the quickest route that takes into account real-time traffic. This function reduces the cognitive burden on the driving user, and instead, is carried out by the device automatically. In other words, people's judgmental experience of GPS navigation devices shifted towards an external locus of causality.

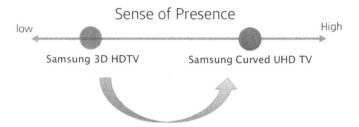

Fig. 4.5 An example of sustaining innovation in the sensual thread of experience

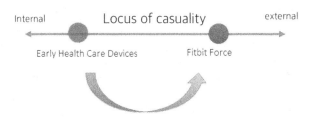

Fig. 4.6 An example of sustaining innovation in the judgmental thread of experience

Another example of a shift of judgmental experience towards an external locus of causality is personal healthcare devices. The early healthcare devices required manual input. However, recent smart healthcare systems that work with wearable devices have advanced towards doing tasks that people consider troublesome. For example, the Fitbit Force provides automated health management program by measuring and displaying daily activities such as accumulated travel distance, accumulated steps, consumed calories, and active hours. Not only does it collect sport data, but when switched to sleep mode, it also automatically measures total sleep time, number of wakes, time of wakes, and duration of wakes to analyze sleep efficiency and patterns. With this data, it finds the optimal time for the user to wake up and works as an alarm using vibrations. Therefore, personal healthcare devices have shifted people's judgmental experience towards an external locus of causality.

As shown in the previous two examples, the continuous change in terms of judgmental experience tends to shift towards an external locus of causality. This is because once a dominant design is established, people do not want to be bothered; they seek more automated devices. This is also consistent with the technological environment mentioned in Chap. 3 (Fig. 4.6).

4.6.3 Sustaining Innovation from the Perspective of Compositional Experience

Let's take a look into SNS as an example of sustaining innovation in the compositional thread of experience. SNS services have developed in a relatively short

Fig. 4.7 An example of
sustaining innovation in
the compositional thread of
experience

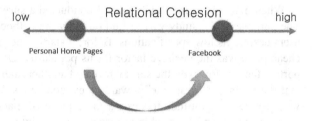

amount of time from personal home pages and blogs to today's form of Facebook, Twitter, and Instagram. In addition, the development of SNS has led to an easier means of communication between users such as personal updates and the sharing of real-time information through the diffusion of smartphones, tablets, and data/Wi-Fi. Sharing real-time events and activities allowed the formation of an environment where, not just friends, but people with common interests can form relationships with each other. In this way, people's compositional experiences are changing towards stronger relational cohesiveness.

This is also commonly apparent in the relationship between products and services that people use. For instance, let's think about the services that Google offers. In order to meet the demands of users who seek to get work done anywhere and anytime, Google has increased the degree of relational cohesiveness between its services by integrating them together. Furthermore, their services are connected with other third-party services like Dropbox, thereby strengthening cohesiveness between services.

As the above two examples illustrate, sustaining change leans towards the direction of strong relational cohesiveness in the perspective of compositional experience. Once the dominant design is set, a stronger cohesiveness is created incrementally through more connections with other experiences. This is similar to the direction of technological evolution and socio-cultural change mentioned in Chap. 3 (Fig. 4.7).

4.6.4   Disruptive Innovation from the Perspective of Sensual Experience

Disruptive innovation in the perspective of sensual experience can be explained through the example of the once-popular netbook during the mid-2000s. The netbook is a combination of "the internet" and "a Notebook" that provides basic capabilities for internet-related activities such as surfing the internet, writing e-mails, and chatting. Furthermore, it was cheap and was light in terms of weight. The netbook was a personal computer that was small enough to carry around more conveniently than conventional laptops. However, its specifications were low enough that tasks that require a lot of resources such as 3D rendering would be difficult to perform. Laptops during those times raised the level of presence by offering faster processors, larger screens, and more realistic sound quality. On the contrary, netbooks provided lower levels of presence while keeping prices down.

When netbooks were widely used, I conducted a survey on 410 netbook users. The purpose of the study was to find out why the netbook was so popular among users despite its low specifications. Before I started the study, I suspected that the cheap price was the decisive factor for its popularity. Of course, price was an important factor. However, the survey revealed another unexpected important reason, that the users felt "gratitude" towards their notebooks. I was quite suspicious of why people felt gratitude towards a mere piece of machinery. A closer analysis was conducted, and I was able to discover a very interesting fact. Netbooks were light and mobile; internet access was available anytime and anywhere, and it was easy to use due to its more simple structure compared to conventional laptops. Furthermore, the netbook empowered users with the confidence that it could be used without much effort or hassle. These elements allowed users to feel gratitude towards their netbooks. The benefits that netbooks provided were passed down to the next generation of tablet devices such as the iPad and the Galaxy Tab. The reason for the popularity of tablets nowadays can be explained in a similar manner as the netbook's; it was a disruptive innovation in the perspective of sensual experience.

Another example of a disruptive innovation is the minimalist design put forth by Apple products. Recently, smartphones and other electronic devices have developed incrementally towards providing higher sense of presence. Screen size, resolution, and sound quality have all risen towards more realistic presence. On the other hand, the design concept of Apple products is based on minimizing decorative elements. Minimalism radically reduces artistic technique and expresses the fundamental being of an object. As the discrepancy between reality and artwork is minimized, the reality of the artwork is expressed with high fidelity. Apple has applied minimalism in the design of its iPhone, iPad, and other devices as well. Through minimalism, Apple devices are differentiated and create a new market of products. By emphasizing simple and modern presence rather than fancy and clear presence, Apple is providing disruptive innovation in terms of sensual experience.

A product or service, in the perspective of sensual experience, tends to incrementally move towards a higher sense of presence. By doing this, products appear to provide a much higher sense of presence than users seek. People feel cognitive conflicts about products or services that offer a much higher sense of presence than they desire socio-culturally or expect to purchase economically. These conflicts end up leading to anxiety or dissatisfaction, and greater conflicts lead to a higher possibility that a disruptive innovation emerges. These disruptive innovations then steer towards dramatically lowering the already-too-high sense of presence (Fig. 4.8).

4.6.5   Disruptive Innovation from the Perspective of Judgmental Experience

A good example of a disruptive innovation in terms of judgmental experience is user-generated content (UGC). UGC is user-inspired and user-created online con-

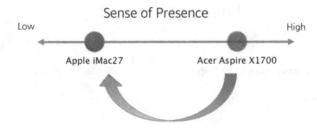

Fig. 4.8 An example of disruptive innovation in the sensual thread of experience

tent that is shared with other users (Seo et al. 2007). Prior to UGC, most online content was provided through content distributors such as broadcasters, newspapers, or other professional companies. However, the rise of UGC has enabled common users to actively participate in creating and sharing content. For instance, users write personal opinions or experiences on web pages or blogs and upload pictures or videos taken by themselves. This shows that the paradigm of the internet shifted from a one-way to a two-way interaction (Levy and Stone 2006). Whereas professional creators and distributors were responsible for producing content online in the past, UGC has enabled more diverse content types and paths of distribution through the participation of users in content creation (Jung et al. 2009).

I conducted a survey and experiment to find out the motivations behind the creation of UGC on 130 participants who actively created and shared UGC (Kim 2010). The results were very intriguing. The most powerful motivation that influenced active UGC usage was intrinsic motivation such as that UGC creation and sharing itself was very valuable to users. Also, users possessed a high degree of freedom in being able to create and edit the content they wanted. On the other hand, extrinsic motivations such as monetary reward and fame were not influential. What's intriguing is that UGC content created through intrinsic motivation were evaluated as more well-made and creative. The locus of causality shifted from external to internal: from the one-way method of prior times such as broadcasting networks and newspapers to the opposite direction of being able to create, share, and consume what users want. I think that although UGC may lack the professional look as that of broadcasting networks for example, UGC may receive far more interest and can take over the market of web based content.

A more recent example is the Phillips Hue smart light bulb. Until now, the light bulb remained very functional. The important functional factors of a light bulb are how much power it uses, how long its light lasts, and how bright the light is. Of course, there are light bulbs of different colors that are used by designers to emphasize emotional aspects, but such a market is very small. However, smart light bulbs are steering towards providing intrinsic values to people. It provides more enjoyment than conventional light bulbs. For instance, Hue can be controlled through a smartphone application. The color board of the application enables control of the desired color and hue of the light bulb. The Hue World Cup application enabled users at home to express diverse emotions through its light bulb during FIFA World Cup matches in Brazil in 2014. You could even select the country you're rooting

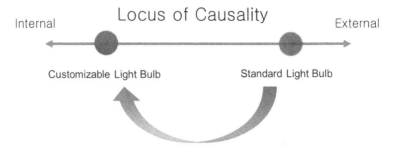

Fig. 4.9 An example of disruptive innovation in the judgmental thread of experience

for, and the colors will change accordingly to the national flag's colors. A user could also have the colors of the light bulb change to the beat of a certain national anthem. The Phillips Hue takes something as functional as a light bulb, which has an external locus of causality, and has transformed it into a product that emphasizes an internal locus of causality.

As the two examples above illustrate, it is common for an external locus of causality to shift to internal. Once the dominant design is established, the law of inertia leads the product or service towards a more external direction. Then at a certain point, it exceeds the level that people desire socio-culturally. This is when a conflict surfaces between the dominant design and what people want. When this new conflict exceeds a certain level, the likelihood increases that a new disruptive innovation that changes the course of direction emerges (Fig. 4.9).

4.6.6   Disruptive Innovation from the Perspective of Compositional Experience

The emergence of wearable devices provides a good example of disruptive innovation in the perspective of compositional experience. The dominant design of a mobile device is the smartphone, which is a convergent device that combines many functions into one device. A strong relational cohesiveness among the functions of a smartphone enables better connections between the functions where many tasks can be conveniently conducted through a single device. However, the complexity of a system inevitably increases as relational cohesiveness increases. A higher complexity of a system requires faster processors and larger memory to effectively complete tasks, and by providing that will lead to an increase in the price of the device. Furthermore, the complexity of completing tasks increases; the products become difficult for people to use easily. But recently, wearable devices provide simple structures that concentrate only on a few functions. Wearable devices have greatly reduced the relational cohesion among functions and have thereby become a disruptive innovation in terms of compositional experience.

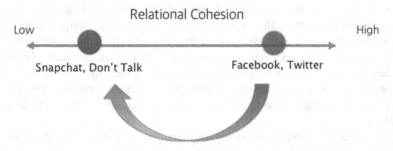

Fig. 4.10 An example of disruptive innovation in the compositional thread of experience

Another example of disruptive innovation in the perspective of composition-al experience is 'constrained SNS.' Services such as Facebook and Twitter have consistently evolved to strengthen relational cohesiveness such as better functions and services to connect new people and enhance already established friendships. However, due to such strong levels of relational cohesiveness, many side effects have surfaced. For instance, too much information sharing between people has caused a cognitive overload of information. Furthermore, privacy has become a critical issue; users have become more sensitive about sharing private information and think twice about expanding their relationships through SNS. In order to solve these problems, constrained SNSs have emerged such as Snapchat and DonTalk, both of which provide time constraints to their services. Snapchat takes advantage of people's psychology behind sharing and cultural trends by providing ephemeral messaging so that data is not saved eternally while still providing a platform for the act of sharing. Opposite from prior SNS where posts and content is recorded and kept on a timeline or profile, Snapchat messages, or "snaps," disappear automati-cally. Hence, users do not need to be concerned about what content was shared and do not have to feel the obligation to reply to a message.

Generally, a product or service tends to lean towards strengthening relational cohesiveness in the perspective of compositional experience. However, relational cohesiveness that is too strong makes it difficult for people to accept the product or service socio-culturally, and it exceeds the economic amount that users can af-ford to purchase. The further this discrepancy, the more people feel conflicted, and ultimately, a high degree of conflict raises the probability of a disruptive innovation that weakens relational cohesiveness (Fig. 4.10).

4.7   Using 'Design for Experience' for Innovation

We saw that sustaining and disruptive innovations exist in the perspective of peo-ple's experiences of technology, not just in the perspective of technology. Such in-novations are created within the interaction between three aspects, namely: changes in the socio-cultural, technological, and economic environments; the state of the person that receives this change; and the firm that utilizes this change. When a dominant design is established, companies seek continuous change through one-way, sustaining innovations. But when it exceeds a certain level, sustaining innovation incites cognitive dissonance among users. When this dissonance heightens to a degree that the dominant degree cannot resolve, other firms that seek to solve this problem come up with disruptive innovations that steer towards the opposite direction of the dominant design. Through this process, a new dominant design is established.

Usability tests of the past focused on incremental change. They attempted to find out the usability issues of a product or service, and companies utilized them to provide new interfaces or interactions that resolved the usability issues. This is why incremental innovation is claimed to be more appropriate to human-centered design methodology (Norman 2013; Norman and Verganti 2014).

On the other hand, there aren't many cases that deal with disruptive innovation in the eyes of a person's experience. This is because both the frequency of disruptive innovation is low and its success rate is not very high either. However, the reason we should pay attention to disruptive innovation is because disruptive innovation is a golden opportunity to overcome the dominant design of the market and create a new one.

Nonetheless, it is not recommended to provide a disruptive innovation too quickly, while people do not feel cognitively dissonant enough and the current dominant design still provides satisfaction. In that case companies must focus on sustaining innovations that can close the competitive discrepancy with other companies within the boundaries of the dominant design. In other words, firms must focus on the current dominant design and come up with new yet incremental ways to enhance the design of a product or service. However, once the conflict is heightened enough and the discrepancy between human experience and dominant design is high enough, firms no longer need to rely on the dominant design. They must actively come up with a product or service that can act as a disruptive innovation. But to do this, there are a few prerequisite conditions.

Firstly, a company must understand the current dominant design in the perspective of human experience. They must meticulously investigate what characteristics the dominant design possesses in terms of sense of presence, locus of causality, and relational cohesiveness. To do this, it would be helpful to compose a three dimensional model of experience as covered in Chapter 3 of this book.

Secondly, a company must understand the degree of change and direction of sustaining innovation after a dominant design has been settled. We must analyze the directional changes of the sense of presence, locus of causality, and relational cohesiveness during the sustaining innovation period. Previously, I mentioned that while a sense of presence heightens, the locus of causality shifts towards the external, and relational cohesiveness strengthens. However, this is only a general pattern; based on the specific type of product or service, change may occur in a different direction.

Thirdly, companies must measure the degree of cognitive dissonance that people feel towards the current dominant design. There are two ways to do this: the first is to analyze the difference between what the dominant design offers and the degree of what people desire in terms of sense of presence, locus of causality, and relational cohesion for each of the threads of experience. Cognitive dissonance can only be high when the differences between people's striving aspirations and the dominant design are large. Another method is to measure the negative symptoms that arise due to cognitive dissonance. As previously mentioned, cognitive dissonance can be measured by three kinds of aspects: (1) despair and irritation in the sensual aspect, (2) doubt about one's own judgment in the judgmental aspect, and (3) dissatisfaction about the purchasing process or towards others involved in the purchasing process in the compositional aspect.

After deducing new experiential points of balance through the above methods, the next step is to find an effective method to provide a balanced experience to people. Think about what important experience elements can raise or lower the sense of presence, externalize or internalize the locus of causality, and raise or lower relational cohesiveness. Then, consider what design features are needed to express these experience elements in an actual product or service. Let's address these issues in the following three chapters.

4.8 Summary

- A dominant design changes with time. There is no eternal dominant design.
- These changes are influenced by changes in the macro environment, people's cognitive dissonance, and the striving aspiration of the firm.
- In the beginning stages of a dominant design, a firm seeks to engage in sustaining innovation that gives it an edge against its competitors within the boundaries of the dominant design.
- Sustaining innovation generally increases the sense of presence, considers the external locus of causality as important, and strengthens relational cohesiveness.
- However, the longer the sustaining innovation lasts, people feel cognitive dissonance with the dominant design, and the striving aspirations of the firm increases.
- A firm that understands this discrepancy in striving aspirations establishes a new dominant design; this is called a disruptive innovation.
- A disruptive innovation creates a new paradigm that shifts the direction of experience of the sustaining innovation towards the opposite way.

4.9 Discussion Topics

- Think of a dominant design in a product or service group of interest. Compose a three-dimensional experience model of this dominant design.
- Analyze which towards direction the sustaining innovation has shifted and how much it has shifted.

- Analyze the possible changes in the environment that can influence the dominant design based on the SET frame.
- Analyze the degree of cognitive dissonance that people feel towards the dominant design.
- Analyze the aspirational and competitive discrepancies that the company possesses regarding the dominant design.
- Predict towards which direction a new dominant design will head based on changes in the macro environment of the dominant design, the level of people's cognitive dissonance, and the aspirational or competitive discrepancies of the company.
- Based on these aspects, predict how fast towards each direction the disruptive innovation will move.

References

Buchanan, R (1992) Wicked problems in design thinking. Des Issues 8(2):5–21
Christensen CM, Baumann H, Ruggles R, Sadtler TM (2006) Disruptive innovation for social change. Harv Bus Rev 84(12):94–101
Cyert RM, March JG (1963) A behavioural theoryofithe firm. Prentice-Hall, Englewood Cliffs
De Beer SG (1963) Charles Darwin: evolution by natural selection. T Nelson, London, p 166
Festinger L (1950) Social pressures in informal groups: a study of human elements in housing, (No. 3). Stanford University Press, London
Festinger L (1962) A theory of cognitive dissonance, vol 2. Stanford University Press, London
Greve H, Seidel MD (2014) Defend your research: being early beats being better. Harvard Business Review, Boston, June 30–31
Hanskins J (1990) Cosimo de'Medici and the'Platonic academy. J Warbg Courtauld Institut 144–162
Hegel GW (2004) The phenomenology of spirit (The phenomenology of mind). Digireads.com Publishing
Hobbes T (1928) Leviathan, or the matter, forme and power of a commonwealth ecclesiasticall and civil [1651]. Oxford: Basil Blackwell.HobbesLeviathan, Or the Matter, Forme, and Power of Commonwealth Ecclesiastical and, 155(1651), 1928. Yale University Press, New Haven
Horkheimer M, Adorno TW (2001) The culture industry: enlightenment as mass deception. Media Cult Stud Keyworks 41–72
Jung S, Lee K, Lee I, Kim J (2009) A qualitative study on the facilitation of user created contents: focused on folklore theories. Asian Pac J Inf Syst 19(2):43–72
Kim J, Yang S, Lim S, Lee I (2010) An empirical study on motivation elements and reward structure for user's createve contents generation: focusing on the mediating effect of commitment. Asian Pac J Inf Syst 20(1):141–170
Kuhn TS (1962) The structure of scientific revolution. University of Chicago press, Chicago
Labianca G, Fairbank JF, Andrevski G, Parzen M (2009) Striving toward the future: aspiration—performance discrepancies and planned organizational change. Strateg Organ 7(4):433–466
Levy S, Stone B (3 April 2006) The new wisdom of the web. Newsweek
March JG (2010) Rediscovering institutions. Simon and Schuster
March JG, Simon HA (1958) Organizations. Wiley-Blackwell
Norman DA (2013) The design of everyday things. Basic books, New York
Norman DA, Verganti R (2014) Incremental and radical innovation: design research vs. technology and meaning change. Des Issues 30(1):78–96
Schumpeter J (1942) Capitalism, socialism and democracy. Harper and Brothers
Seo H, Ahn J, Yang J (2007) Continued usage of hedonic information system: focused on UCC. Asian Pac J Inf Syst 17(3):25–53

Part III
UX Factors and Design Features for Real Experience

Chapter 5
Design for Senseful Experience

5.1 Introduction

Some people are very "senseful." They are active when they need to be, and they are
patient when they need to wait. They know how to fulfill their roles perfectly. Similarly, a senseful experience refers to the experience of using a product or service that
is neither too excessive nor lacking. The dimension of experience that can account
for this is the sense of presence. This refers to how clearly a person has perceived
the existence of a product or service. Presence can help control people's sensual
experiences according to changes in the external effectively. If so, what levers can
control the sense of presence? What user experience (UX) factors must we offer to
users in order to provide levers for the sense of presence? What are the necessary
system design features that can provide users with these UX factors?

5.2 Virtual Golf Simulator

I don't play a lot of golf. I learned the basics in the U.S. during my sabbatical for a
few months, but I haven't been to a golf course since I came back to Korea. I don't
really have the time to spare to engage in this time consuming sport and the green
fees are also rather expensive in Korea.

But in the few recent years I've been able to observe an interesting fact about
golf. I taught an executive MBA course and in every semester a team of students
chose the virtual golf simulator, as an example of a product or service that provided
innovative experience. The virtual golf simulator is an indoor simulation game that
comprises of a large screen representing the course on which people can play 18
holes of golf. The simulator's advantage is that it's less costly and less time consuming for players. But I couldn't really imagine what was so great about swinging a
golf club and staring at a screen in an enclosed space. But after this recurring topic

The online version of this chapter (doi: 10.1007/978-3-319-14304-0_5) contains supplementary
material.

J. Kim, *Design for Experience*, Human-Computer Interaction Series,
DOI 10.1007/978-3-319-14304-0_5

in my classes I decided to give it a go and visit a "screen golf hall," as they are called in Korea. My perception of the simulator changed 180°.

The first thing that struck me was the screen resolution. Each room had a large screen that provided crisp, realistic graphics. The occasional sounds of birds chirping made me feel like the air conditioning was a natural breeze from the scenery.

I needed to select a golf course to play on. There were both Korean and overseas golf courses and I selected a golf course I had played on before. I was startled by how similar the virtual field was to the actual one.

As I would do on a real golf course, I chose a club that fitted for each play. First, I used the driver to swing far, the sand wedge to get the ball out of the bunker, and the putter for the final stroke. Real golf clubs and golf balls were used as you would use on a real course.

What I was most surprised about was that the slope and height of the floor I was standing on synchronized with the view from my position on the screen. Considering you have to change swings based on the slope on a real golf course, I could see that the people who made the virtual golf simulator put in a considerable effort when creating a similar experience.

Another thing that impressed me was the accuracy of the sensors. The ball must be correctly positioned on top of the mat in order for the sensor to activate so that I can proceed to hitting the ball. The sensors measure the paths of the ball and club. When I swung, I could tell that the simulator calculated the distance of my swing quite accurately. To a certain extent, I felt as though I was playing a round of real golf. The fact that I was able to think that I was outdoors, regardless of the enclosed urban structure I was in, made me understand why my MBA students would bring the virtual golf simulator as a case of innovative experience every semester.

5.3   Sense of Presence

As I mentioned in Chapter 2, the sensual thread of experience is the specific experience of seeing and touching. Also, sensual experience provides a basis for judgmental and compositional experiences. Therefore, it not only includes what we perceive, it also includes our reactions and behaviors to what we perceive. For instance, in the case of the virtual golf simulator, the chirping of birds, the soft wind, and the slopes are all sensual experiences. During this process, an important strategic control factor that determines the quality of our sensual experience is the sense of presence. As I went through in Chapter 2, the sense of presence refers to the psychological state of "being there" (Biocca 1997). A high presence of a person experiencing a product or service refers to being there to see and feel the objects of interaction and other people connected through the system. For instance, a high presence experience of a virtual golf simulator refers to the virtual golf course feeling like a real golf course, feeling as if I am actually there. In this sense, I can say that my experience was one of very high presence as shown, in Fig. 5.1, in the three-dimensional experience model analysis I conducted on my virtual golfing experience.

Levers that control the sense of presence can be divided into two: perceptual and behavioral. The perceptual lever refers to how real we perceive the simulations

3-D Model of Experience

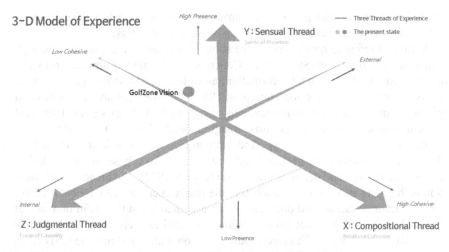

Fig. 5.1 A three-dimensional experience model of a virtual golf simulator

through our five senses. For instance, a painting that resembles an actual figure is said to have a higher presence. An extreme example of this may be the painting of a pine tree in an acient temple during the Shilla dynasty (an ancient kingdom of Korea) that was said to be so vivid that birds would hit the wall while trying to land on the painted pine tree's branches (http://koreanart21.com/review/conference/view?id=2052).

On the other hand, the behavioral lever refers to what actions we can take and how real the reactions to those actions are (Welch et al. 1996). For instance, a virtual golf simulation system that allows a continuously smooth gaming experience has a higher presence than a system that constantly halts during the game (Weghorst and Billinghurst 1993).

If so, what are the perceptual and behavioral levers that influence the sense of presence in people's experiences? Based on prior research on presence, I chose "vividness" and "interactivity" as perceptual and behavioral levers, respectively (Steuer 1992; Laurel 1993; Rheingold 1991). Let's take a closer look at them.

5.3.1   Vividness: A Key Perceptual Lever of Sensual Experience

It's easy to spot 4D movies in movie theaters nowadays. 4D films add extra physical effects to 3D films. For example, a fight scene between robots will release the smell of gunpowder, or a cold winter scene will release cold air. 4D films provide enhanced vividness through the stimulation of touch and smell in addition to enhanced video resolution.

On the other hand, let's take an example of the lounge music heard in hotel lobbies and hospital waiting rooms. Lounge music is calm and subtle and does not catch the attention of the person in the space and aims to provide a relaxing atmosphere. This type of music can be said to possess low vividness.

Vividness refers to how abundant the stimulation itself that is provided through a medium to a person is (Steur 1992). Concrete and detailed information provides more vividness than abstract information, and pictures and videos provide more vividness than text (Taylor and Thompson 1982). Websites that are said to be vivid provide abundant sensory content utilizing visual and/or auditory senses. This vivid content stimulate our senses and instill imagination (Nisbett and Ross 1980).

In the past, vividness was expressed through the characteristics of the medium that delivers stimulation to people. Therefore, vividness was based on two technical factors: the breadth and depth of stimulation (Biocca 1992). The breadth of stimulation is the types of sensory channels that the medium can provide (Gibson 1996). Visual, auditory, tactile, and olfactory senses are included in this definition, and at times, the sense of physical balance is also included as a channel. While lounge music has a narrow breadth since it only relies on auditory stimulation, 4D films have a relatively wide breadth due to the utilization of visual, auditory, tactile, and olfactory senses. The second factor of vividness is the depth of stimulation. Depth is the quality of the perception of the stimulation. Generally, it is determined by the amount of encoded data of a certain stimulus or the bandwidth of the channel. For example, lounge music doesn't need to have high quality sound, so the size of the music file is relatively small. On the other hand, the video file of a 4D film is large due to its high resolution.

What is the relationship between vividness of a stimulus and the sense of presence? Both the number of channels and fidelity of a stimulus are related to presence (Zeltzer 1992). First, let's take a look at the number of channels. For example, providing multiple stimuli results in a higher presence than providing a single stimulus (Short et al. 1976). For example, the addition of body movements and tactile information in a 4D film has a higher presence than TV, which in turn has relatively higher presence than radio.

The depth of a stimulus also influences presence. A high resolution and large visual stimulus within a shorter distance will enhance presence. Also, a photo or a video has a higher presence than a sketch or an animation. Vividness is comprised of the breadth and depth of a stimulus, which affects presence. Therefore, a more vivid stimulation will increase the sense of presence.

5.3.2 Interactivity: A Key Behavioral Lever of Sensual Experience

There is an application on iOS called GarageBand. Both amateurs and professionals can compose music through this application. The application offers keyboards, guitars, drums, percussions, and even vocals that enables a high degree of freedom to compose new music. I can choose the instruments I want, and the application expresses my music on a score. I can play my composition on an instrument and revise the parts that I want in real-time. I can change detailed aspects of sounds such as the bending of a guitar string, and I can check my revisions in real-time.

On the other hand, let's think about a broadcast program or a news article. They are mostly created by professional producers, anchors, and reporters. Therefore, users rarely have the chance to participate in creating the content. And there is almost no way to revise a program or an article that has already been released.

Interactivity refers to how much a user can change an object of interaction. The degree of change can be divided into three factors. The first factor is speed, which is the interaction or reaction speed. The fastest speed is to respond in real-time. If a person can change in real-time either the form or contents the content of a system in a virtual environment, the system possesses high interactivity. For example, GarageBand enables real-time revisions to music compositions. Therefore, its level of interactivity is high. The second factor is the range of interaction. This refers to how much and diversely a property can be changed. For instance, a newspaper article does not provide the possibility to be changed. A person can write a reader's opinion, but that's about all there is to it. Therefore, the range of interactivity of a newspaper article is low. The third factor is the mapping of interaction. This refers to how much the actions within the system match that of real actions. A racing game that provides a physical wheel that a person can steer left to go left and steer right to go right provides a high level of mapping. On the other hand, left-clicking the mouse to accelerate and right-clicking to brake offers a low level of mapping. Whether between human and system or human and human, the speed, range, and mapping of an interaction determine the level of interactivity.

So what is the relationship between interactivity and the sense of presence? To put it simply, the higher the interactivity with a certain object, the higher the sense of presence. Of course, the sense of presence can be felt by staring at an object. However, a higher sense of presence can be felt if I can manipulate the object in some way. For example, there is a limit to how much presence you can feel by listening to music that someone else composed. However, being able to revise music while listening to it can provide a higher sense of presence. If I can control the key or tempo and check the results right away, or if the system is designed as if I am manipulating a physical composition tool, then the sense of presence of that music will increase. In this way, a higher interactivity with the object of interaction provides a high sense of presence as well.

5.3.3 Vividness and Interactivity

Let's go back to the virtual golf simulator experience. If I can't play an actual game of golf and merely watch others play, then it will be hard to imagine that I am on the golf course no matter how real the virtual golf course appears on the screen.

Think about playing golf with mouse and keyboard controls while receiving visual feedback through text and numbers. The sense of presence I feel would be drastically lowered.

Therefore, both vividness (in terms of perception) and interactivity (in terms of behavior) need to be increased in order to enhance the sense of presence. On the other hand, presence may need to be lowered intentionally by lowering both vividness and interactivity as in the case of the lounge music. In addition, a middle level of presence would require more vividness and less interactivity, or vice versa. In order to effectively control the sense of presence, there needs to be a method to individually control vividness and interactivity.

A point I want to emphasize is that the vividness and interactivity people feel is more important than the stimuli themselves. This is because presence is ultimately what people experience sensually. Therefore, in order to provide high vividness for people through a product or service, we need to understand the experiential elements that are directly related to vividness. Then, the design features that enable the development of the product or system in which people will experience vividness need to be understood. In addition, what are the UX elements closely related to interactivity, and what are the design features that provide the UX elements related to interactivity?

5.4   Eight Case Studies on Vividness and Interactivity

In order to deduce the UX factors and design features that influence vividness and interactivity, I chose eight products and services that offer a combination of both high and low vividness and high and low interactivity as shown in Table 5.1. These eight cases are currently or have been dominant designs respective markets. They are cases that provide real experiences to people while possessing clear characteristics in terms of vividness and interactivity.

By meticulously analyzing these cases, we can figure out which UX factors are important and what design features the product or service is comprised of. Each case and its study method are available on this book's website (http://extras.springer.com). Here, I will go through a brief explanation of why each case is relevant.

Table 5.1 Eight cases used in the case study

	Vividness HIGH	Vividness LOW
Interactivity HIGH	Product: GolfZon Service: Su Norebang	Product: Nintendo WII Service: Gorilla Radio
Interactivity LOW	Product: UHDTV Service: Klive	Product: eBook Service: BGM

5.4.1 Golfzon Vision

A product case of high vividness and high interactivity. (http://www.golfzon.com/)

The virtual golf simulator, which was mentioned in the introduction to this chapter, considers the motion of swinging a golf club towards the screen and the ball following a natural trajectory within the screen as a prerequisite for a natural interaction. Golfzon's most recent simulator, called Golfzon Vision, utilizes cutting edge technology to enhance the feeling of being in an actual golfing experience through an accurate portrayal of ball movement and the installation of rough mats and bunker mats. Golfzon Vision provides accurate data analysis through its sensor technology to increase the interaction between the user and the system. Furthermore, the development of sensing technology enables users to feel high vividness by checking the direction and speed of a shot on the screen. The system even vividly expresses tree graphics. Therefore, Golfzon Vision is a product that possesses both high vividness and high interactivity.

5.4.2 Su Norebang

A service case of high vividness and high interactivity. (http://www.skysu.com)

Su Norebang (norebang refers to a Korean-style karaoke establishment) provides diverse services for its customers through its bright and refreshing image that allows customers to enjoy diverse activities related to singing. They provide high quality soundtracks for songs that were used in the actual recording of the songs rather than the machine tunes that prior karaoke machines provide. They match the songs that customers sing with videos that express the song well, and fancy stage lights, surround sound, and combined with quality video equipment provides high vividness. In the perspective of interactivity, Su Norebang provides services for a wide range of tasks such as after mixing, recording, and soundtrack controls. The results can be checked speedily, and customers can save these works on their USB memory sticks. Lastly, the interior design of the room includes a standing microphone on top of a mini-stage and lights to map the experience of performing in an actual concert or recording studio, thereby enhancing interactivity.

5.4.3 UHD TV

A product case of high vividness and low interactivity. (http://www.samsung.com/sec/consumer/tv-video/tv/)

A UHD TV provides a vast array of detailed visual information that fills in the sensory information that gets lost while displaying real objects through a TV. Because humans possess a high dependency on visual information when it comes to recognizing objects, the strengthening of visual information allows us to draw the images in our minds more clearly. Therefore, the UHD TV provides high vividness.

However, the UHD TV does not provide very high interactivity. Of course, the introduction of smart TVs has enabled more interactivity than prior TV products. However, most people do not actively use the smart functions of a TV. Most of the time they watch the TV or tune in to radio programs. Therefore, despite the potential of the UHD TV, the perceived interactivity of the product is low.

5.4.4 Klive

A service case of high vividness and low interactivity. (www.klive.co.kr)

Klive, a K-Pop hologram concert hall, is a convergent cultural technology project that combines K-Pop content and hologram technology. Diverse audio-visual devices are used to show hologram concerts of famous K-Pop singers such as Psy, Girls' Generation, and EXO. In terms of providing diverse stimuli that comprise the concert, Klive offers many different types of audio-visual stimuli. Sensory stimuli such as hologram effects, panorama media façade videos, lasers, and fancy lighting provide visually deep and abundant stimuli. At the same time, multi-channel sound effects offer people diverse types of sensory stimuli. In these ways, Klive offers high vividness. However, the level of interactivityy is very low. Klive audiences are only allowed to accept one-way stimuli throughout the concert. There are no interactions that influence and change the content of the concert. In this manner, the interactivity of Klive is low.

5.4.5 Nintendo Wii

A product case of low vividness and high interactivity. (www.nintendo.co.kr/Wii/main.php)

The Nintendo Wii, with more than 100 million devices being sold worldwide by 2013 after its release before Christmas 2006, has been a huge hit. In the perspective of vividness, the Wii does not support high vividness. Although the breadth of stimulation is not narrow as the Wii supports visual, auditory, and tactile stimuli, the depth of stimulation is quite meager. Compared to competitor products such as the Sony PlayStation and the Microsoft Xbox 360, the Wii's video resolution and sound quality are much lower. Due to this, the game characters in a Wii game may seem simple and, at times, crude. However, the interactivity of the Wii is considered to be quite high because the speed of feedback from user movements is very fast. Also, its range is wide because users are able to move freely in three dimensions to manipulate game characters. Furthermore, the game carefully maps the movements of users within the game. Because the Wii provides high levels of speed, range, and mapping, it is considered to provide high interactivity.

5.4.6   Internet Radio Application

A service case of low vividness and high interactivity. (http://gorealra.sbs.co.kr)

Internet radio applications allow people to tune in to the radio through the internet. Its vividness is not very high, especially when compared to video broadcasting services that provide high levels of auditory and visual stimuli. The vividness of internet radio applications are intentionally low in order to prevent lagging and to provide the optimal amount of data to be transferred through the internet. Therefore, the vividness of internet radio is obviously much lower than high definition TVs or movie-related services. Nevertheless, the reason there are so many fans of internet radio is because of its high interactivity. Internet radio possesses a number of functions that allow people to interact with the broadcast. For instance, "visual radio" shows the studio where the broadcast is being recorded, and song lists and broadcast information are provided to users in real-time. Through this user-friendly approach, users are able to add comments and chat so that the broadcast can receive user feedback in real-time and reflect it in the broadcast. Compared to conventional radio, internet radio has a much higher level of interactivity.

5.4.7   eBook

A product case of low vividness and low interactivity. (digital.kyobobook.co.kr)

In the past, much existing content was moved to eBook formats. But recently, new content solely for eBooks has increased dramatically. eBook devices try to mimic reading paper books by lowering eye fatigue, and their vividness and interactivity are lowered so that people can immerse in the act of reading itself. An eBook mostly offers text to users, and illustrations at times. Not only is it focused on visual stimulation, the stimulus itself is mostly black and white which may at times seem tacky. Also, interactivity is included in the eBooks, for example, highlighting, underlining, and dictionaries, but usage of these functions is infrequent and quite limited compared to other devices. By lowering vividness and interactivity, the eBook tries to maintain the integrity of conventional paper books in order to retain a high level of immersion for users.

5.4.8   Background Music

A service case of low vividness and low interactivity.

It is almost unavoidable to go to a place without background music (BGM) in our daily lives, whether we go to the mart or a shopping mall. The goal of BGM is not to catch people's attention; rather, it is to create the atmosphere of a certain environment. Therefore, vividness is intentionally lowered for BGM. In addition, the place, time, and goal of BGM is often used to influence people's behaviors or utilized as a marketing tool. In this way, there is some interactivity involved in BGM, but it is provided subtly and naturally; hence, its interactivity is low.

5.5   UX Factors and Design Features for Vividness

By analyzing the above eight cases, I was able to find out that there are three UX factors that enhance vividness: narrativity, concreteness, and media richness. Below, I want to explain in detail these UX factors and specific design features that help express these UX factors.

5.5.1   Narrativity

Going back to the golf simulator discussed previously in this chapter. When you first start a game, there is a practice mode. In this mode the system checks your swing speed, trajectory, and ball quality. It is similar to practicing at a golf range before actually playing on a real golf course. The next step is the first hole. I take the tee shot with my driver, and continue with my fairway shot with a wood club and send the ball towards the green. I then use my wedge to place the ball on the green, and finally aim for the hole using my putter. Once I finish all 18 holes, the game ends and my score card is calculated. The process from practice to the end of the game follows a continual, connected stream. This type of causal relationship between many situations through the flow of time is called narrativity (Graesser et al. 1980).

From the perspective of experience, narrativity can be seen as content that people consume and how they react to, rather than what content a system is comprised of (Mar and Oatley, 2008). There are many experiences rich with narrativity without necessarily following the traditional form of narrativity, such as novels and movies. A treadmill in a gym offers a running course to users, and that is an example of narrativity. The course is appropriately distributed between flat land and hill. A fair distribution between these two types of courses helps provide a connecting story for a single run. Narrativity is not just limited to formats such as books or movies; it can apply to any context where a person's mental representation is formed. For example, the causal relationship of playing a round of golf on the simulator from the warm up swings in the practice mode to seeing the final scorecards is the narrativity of events pictured through my mental representation (Ryan 2002).

Therefore, narrativity is a person's mental representation of temporal causal relationships. Mental representation is divided into four components. The setting, which is the worldview or environment that a person recognizes, the characters within that setting, events and plots about the characters, and the temporal dimension that connects them all. For example, the people playing with me, situations that arise on each hole, and the flow of time from the first shot to the 18th hole are all combined to form a narrativity of my experience of the virtual golf simulator.

Narrativity can be seen as a UX factor that is expressed in degrees rather than through its status of existence. It is the degree of how clear the causal relationship between events can be drawn out during an experience of provided stimuli or content. In other words, it refers to the degree of being able to understand the relationship between specific actions and behaviors and why something happens, what happens after, and how that affects future events, all based on the flow of time.

So how does narrativity influence vividness? Expressing experience through a story provides higher vividness than simple statistics Taylor and Thompson 1982. For instance, statistics on how many times I swung on each hole throughout the 18 holes does not provide me with much vividness. On the other hand, "you hit a tee shot in the eighth hole, but unfortunately it splashed into the pond" is a story that provides more vividness to a person who hears it because the story contains both specific facts and enables more imagination. This is called mental simulation (Escalas 2004).

Mental simulation is the sequential process of behaviors, the resulting reactions of those behaviors, and behaviors that follow suit while thinking of the self as the main character. The higher the narrativity of an experience, the more appreciation one feels for the characters that appear in the experience and the causal relationship between the sequences of events. The more specific the causal relationships of the sequence of events, the more active our mental simulations can be; therefore, high narrativity helps perform mental simulations more actively. Also, more active mental simulations lead to more content to imagine. This leads to more abundant emotions that raise the level of vividness.

When the narrativity of a stimulus is high, then the stimulus can create more perceived stimulation through the imagination even though the depth of stimulation from external factors is not very high. This is because a strong internal model of causal relationships between events has been established. Also, some experiences that we have not directly felt can still be predicted based on stimuli and causal relationships that we already know beforehand. Therefore, a higher narrativity leads to a more vivid experience.

A good example of how narrativity enhances vividness can be seen in advertising. Many advertisements nowadays try to deliver an inspirational or an emotional story to people within 30–60 seconds. For example, the KIA Soul advertisement features three hamsters wearing colorful clothes getting off the Soul, amidst a colorless robot battle scene, and heading to a party while dancing the shuffle dance which was quite popular back in 2012 (http://www.youtube.com/watch?v=f2xDiXhrLPc). Although the stimuli provided are only auditory and visual and the visual resolution was low, the cute hamsters, the popular music, and the contrast they provided to the battle scene all contributed to the advertisement being evaluated as one of the best advertisements of that year.

There are three types of design features that enhance narrativity: metaphor-based symbol interaface, metaphor-based interaction, and narrative based information architecture.

5.5.1.1 Metaphor-Based Symbol Interface

A metaphor is commonly referred to something that connects a concept from one domain to another (Lakoff and Johnson 1986). A metaphor design connects two different domains known as the source domain and the target domain (Ryan 2002). The source domain is a domain that people are familiar with. For instance, the concept of a music concert is something we are familiar with because we have ex-

Fig. 5.2 A case of symbolic interface based on metaphors: Klive time machine (courtesy of KLIVE, used with permission)

perienced it over a long period of time. The target domain, on the other hand, is a domain that people are not familiar with. For instance, a holographic concert such as Klive is not something many people are familiar with yet. Symbol design based on metaphors refers to the interface design of products or services using narrative concepts such as characters or backgrounds (Ryan 2002). For example, in Klive, the audience travels through time to concerts in the past or in the future. The concert hall is symbolized as a metaphor for a giant time machine.

Like the above example, characters or environments of a narrative can be used as metaphors to make symbols. These symbols can be expressed as information or functions that increase narrativity that the user feels, and this contributes in raising the level of vividness. This is because the context of the story follows the metaphor so that when it is expressed in a product or service, then users are able to imagine and feel more (Fig. 5.2).

5.5.1.2   Metaphor-Based Interaction

Metaphors can be used to provide interaction methods for products and services (Laurel 1997). This refers to the product or the system providing the real world-like reactions for actions that help users think that they are doing it in the context of the real world. For example, the virtual golf simulator allows swinging a golf club as if in the real world and also provides ball quality and trajectory as if playing in the real world. In this way, the simulator provides metaphors for actions within the system. Also, the system enhances narrativity by providing slopes on the floor equivalent to the slope in the virtual golf course. Furthermore, narrativity is enhanced when the ball trajectory reflects that of when hit on a slope. As seen in Fig. 5.3, many actions of the system are provided based on metaphors to enhance narrativity and ultimately increase the level of vividness.

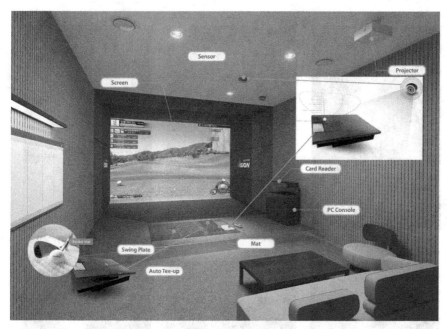

Fig. 5.3 An interaction case that uses metaphors: virtual golf simulator (courtesy of GolfZon, used with permission)

5.5.1.3   Narrative-Based Information Architecture

A narrative requires temporal causal relationships as a prerequisite. Therefore, narrative information architecture should be based on temporally sequential information (Carrozzino et al. 2005). Information architecture that uses narratives is organized on the basis of a connected series of events. Sequential information architecture is suited for information that is naturally narrative or follows the flow of time or information that has a clear logical structure between components. Movement within sequential architecture generally follows two directions. The first is movement to a previous event, and the other is to the following event. The information architecture of the virtual golf simulator, as shown in Fig. 5.4, follows a narrative as the second hole comes after the first hole, and the 17th hole before the 18th. If this system did not support a narrative architecture, then people would play on the 18th hole first and not be able to appreciate the relationship between plays. Therefore, narrative-based information architecture enhances narrativity and, in turn, increases the level of vividness.

1H Par4   2H Par4   3H Par3

4H Par4   5H Par5   6H Par3

7H Par5   8H Par4   9H Par4

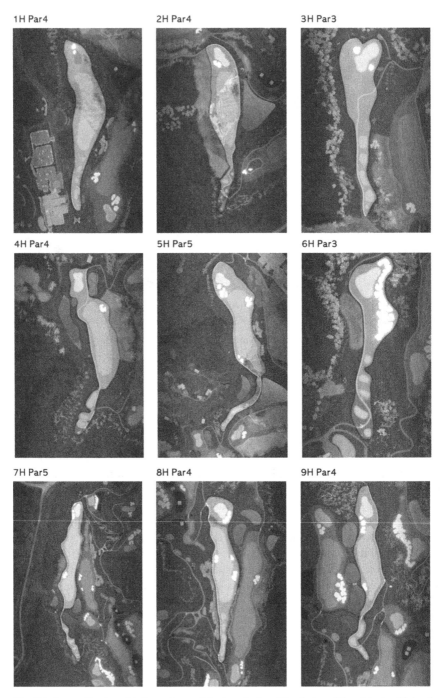

Fig. 5.4 A narrative-based information architecture design: Nine holes of the virtual golf simulator (courtesy of GolfZon, used with permission)

5.5.2   Concreteness

The wonderful part about my virtual golf simulator experience was that the product provided me with a very concrete experience compared to actual golf. When I first start a game, there are images of actual golf courses that I can select from. When I'm swinging on the field, the swing mats offer details regarding the surface I'm swinging on, and I can also control the precise angles for my putting.

In the perspective of judgmental experience, high concreteness refers to how clear an object is expressed; it should be perceived through seeing or touching and these stimuli should express in detail its real world counterpart. Therefore, a higher concreteness of a sensory stimulus enhances associative learning and image association (Paivio et al. 1968).

So, how does the UX factor of concreteness influence vividness? Generally, sensory experiences that resemble or utilize reality feel more vivid than basic sensory stimuli (Nisbett and Ross 1980). For example, the sounds of birds chirping are not directly associated with golf. However, it helps express the simulator closer to a real course and provides users with a more vivid experience.

Another good example that shows how high concreteness leads to high vividness is the musical "Cats." "Cats" expresses a world seen through the eyes of cats. In order to do this, their stage props such as tires, shoes, and typewriters are three to ten times larger than their actual sizes in real life. The musical also provides diverse noises from humans, and detailed props expand all the way to the back seats of the audience to provide a vivid story.

There are two types of design features that enhance concreteness: force feedback and micro feedback interface.

5.5.2.1   Force Feedback

The force feedback provides direct vibration based feedback on game context to a user's action. Feedback is usually a reaction that the system provides to the user as a result of the user's action towards the system (Shneiderman 1987). If feedback is too indirect or abstract, then users will have a hard time catching what it means, and vividness cannot properly be emphasized.

One design feature that provides direct feedback, known as force feedback, uses a mechanical interface that provides tactile physical force. In video games, force feedback provides vibrations on a joystick controller in situations that require impact such as a car crash or getting hit during a boxing match. The direct vibrations are felt by the user holding the joystick and increases the concreteness of the visual stimuli because vibrations provide a more natural means of providing feedback on changes in movement than does visual feedback (Everett and Nieusma 1994). When playing tennis on the Nintendo Wii, the controller vibrates when you hit the ball accurately. This vibration stimulus helps the user to directly feel the impact as if hitting an actual tennis ball with a tennis racquet. Through this, users can receive more concrete sensory stimuli and thereby experience enhanced vividness.

5.5.2.2 Micro Feedback Interface

Micro feedback interface is a detailed feedback interface design that helps people think, "wow, the feedback is so intricate, it doesn't miss the details." User and system, under the context of a product or a service, act as conversation partners (Clark and Wilkes-Gibbs 1986; Clark and Schaefer 1987, Clark and Brennan 1991). Detailed feedback carefully takes consideration of the user (Foley and Dam 1982). For example, the virtual golf simulator provides three different types of mats for fairway, rough, and bunker shots. When the ball comes up, I can manually select which mat to hit from, and micro feedback is provided accordingly. If I try to hit a bunker ball on a rough mat, then I receive a message that says "please place the ball on another location" and the game halts as shown in Fig. 5.5. On the other hand, I can use a fairway mat to hit a bunker ball, but since a fairway shot is easier than a bunker shot, the system provides appropriate feedback so as to reduce the effects of the fairway shot and make it feel more like a bunker shot. Such micro feedback from the system provides the experience of an actual shot rather than a simulated shot, and this is one of the features that heightens the experience of vividness.

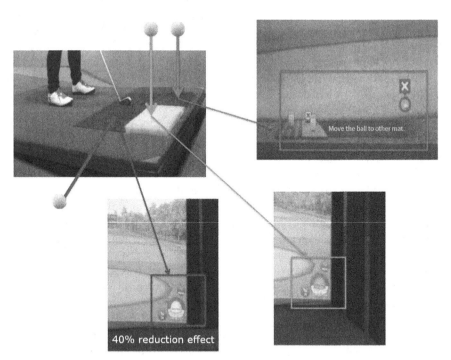

Fig. 5.5 A case of micro feedback interface: three types of mats of the virtual golf simulator (courtesy of GolfZon, used with permission)

5.5.3 Media Richness

The virtual golf simulator contains diverse sensory stimuli regardless of it being based indoors on a visual screen. Fairway, rough, green, and bunker mats offer situation-specific plays that reduce artificiality and allow more feel for the field. Also, my viewing angle of the course can be changed, and detailed slopes are offered based on the surface of the course. The degree of how well a stimulation medium provides messages that contain flourishing information is known as media richness (Carlson and Zamud 1999).

In the perspective of experience, higher media richness offers diverse methods to express information, thereby decreasing the uncertainty of users. Therefore, the influence of how we accept certain content is greater than how and at what time the information is provided. This is because there is a difference in the level of prior knowledge or information that every individual possesses (Schwitzgebel 2002).

Then how does the UX factor of media richness influence vividness? Vividness is also related to the quantity of detailed information, brightness, saliency, and degree of contour (Cornoldi et al. 1992; McKelvie 1995). If websites utilize diverse media tools such as videos, music, or animations, then the vividness perceived on the website increases. Therefore, sensually flourishing content that utilize many different senses that are a result of high media richness will enhance vividness (Coyle 2001).

A good example that supports enhanced vividness through the UX factor of media richness is 4D movies. In 4D, 3D visuals are provided along with moving chairs, wind, scents, and water. The moving chair doesn't just move in one dimension; they move in two dimensions and even tilt forwards and backwards to give the feeling of actually driving a car or flying. Due to the stimulation of senses, other than auditory and visual, such as olfactory and tactile, the richness of stimulations provides a vivid movie experience to audiences.

There are mainly three design features that enhance media richness: mapping modalities to tasks, augmented information, and multimodal combination of touch and motion.

5.5.3.1 Mapping of Modalities to Tasks

When designing products or services that utilize diverse sensory information, each piece of sensory information should be naturally mapped to the intended task (Sarter 2006). Therefore, a specific goal of what experience to provide to the user must be clear, and sensory information should be provided based on that goal.

For instance, the goal of Klive is to allow users to think that the holographic singer on the stage feels real. As shown in Fig. 5.6, the singer and the content are made more real by an actual performance team that performs with the holograms. It is quite hard to distinguish between the actual performance team and the hologram, and this provides concrete visual representations to the audience. Along with this,

Fig. 5.6 A case of mapping between sensory stimuli and content: Klive holograms and stage effects (courtesy of KLIVE, used with permission)

a 14.2 channel surround system helps the audience feel like they are in an actual concert hall. Furthermore, special effects such as smoke are used to provide new experiences to the audience. When diverse stimuli are provided as specific information with a clear goal, users feel high media richness, and this allows them to have a vivid concert experience.

5.5.3.2   Augmented Information

Augmented information refers to a combination of real world and virtual information that delivers augmented reality to users in a media environment (Azuma 1997). An example of augmented information is a detailed pop up window that is shown when putting your mouse cursor on top of a hyperlinked text (Kesim and Ozarslan 2012).

    As an example in the media, I can think of a Korean variety show called Infinite Challenge. Six celebrities are given a challenge in each episode such as being radio DJs, chefs, or Formula 1 racers. Based on this challenge, the celebrities fill out the episode without a script. Many improvised and unintentional scenes are shown. Many people evaluate the show as excellent because there are subtitles, animations, and computer graphics that complement the situations and add to the enjoyment of watching the show. These visual effects provide complementary augmented information to add to the fun and enhance content immersion. Diverse icons and phrases such as onomatopoeia, mimetic, and exclamations capture the situational context or essence of the characters involved to provide understanding and enjoyment of each scene. Such a show provides situations that are more dynamic and vivid.

Fig. 5.7 A case of augmented information: Virtual golf simulator (courtesy of GolfZon, used with permission)

Augmented information can also be found in the virtual golf simulator example. As shown in the left part of Fig. 5.7, in the practice mode the system takes a picture of my swing that I can then view. This is something that can be difficult to do in real golf, but the detailed information enhances my experience. In real golf, I have to follow the direction of my shots and walk all the way to my ball, but the simulator provides me with all that information as shown on the right part of Fig. 5.7.

In this way, augmented information provided through diverse sources enables users of products or services to help understand the context better, thereby enhancing their perceived vividness of experience.

5.5.3.3   Multimodal Combination of Touch and Motion

Touch interaction can be seen widely in mobile devices nowadays. Accelerometers and gyroscopes help detect movement to provide users with more sensual experiences. Touch and motion sensing are complementary, providing a synergy effect for new interaction technology (Hinckley and Song 2011). A multi-channel system that stimulates and utilizes diverse sensory channels such as touch and movement provide continually appropriate stimulation, thereby enhancing the media richness of users (Benoit and Le Goff 1998; Cohen et al. 1997; Pentland et al. 1996; Stork and Hennecke 1995; Turk and Robertson 2006; Vo and Wood 1996; Wang 1995; Zhai et al. 1999). Among the many types of stimuli, touch and movement can effectively help enhance the richness of stimuli and information.

While the virtual golf simulator works hard to accurately reproduce the experience of real golf through meticulous sensors, I was impressed with the slope that moves according to the situation as shown in Fig. 5.8. The slope causes changes in the way I need to hit the ball, and this provides a more realistic experience of golf.

Fig. 5.8 A case of complex touch and movement stimuli interface: Virtual golf simulator (courtesy of GolfZon, used with permission)

By controlling both my movement and the touch of the ball, the simulator can be seen as a rich media.

5.6   UX Factors and Design Features for Interactivity

The UX factors that enhance interactivity are controllability, exchange of meaning, and synchronicity. The next section explains each concept along with design features that can enhance these concepts.

5.6.1   Controllability

Let's go back to the Nintendo Wii. Before I start a game, I need to choose a title and choose a game character. The system reacts based on my choices and asks for more decisions on my part. There is a continuous action and reaction between the user and the system. Controllability, under this context, refers to how much influence a user can exert on a product or system during the process of action and the system's reaction (Quiring and Schweiger 2008; Liu and Shrum 2002). Controllability differs based on the degree of possible controls that the system offers through stimuli. For example, the controllability of a website is evaluated by whether I can control aspects such as the background or template.

Controllability can be explained through three features. The first feature is the selection option, which refers to input methods of the medium such as the keyboard, mouse, buttons, and touch (Goertz 1995; Ha and James 1998 Heeter 1989). The second feature is the modification option, which refers to system information that can be added, edited, and deleted after initial input (Coyle and Thorson 2001; Goertz 1995; Heeter 1989, 2000; Jensen and Lockwood 1998; Lombard and Snyder-Dutch 2001). This is the extent of a person's control. After this, a person chooses behavior based on what kind of information the system provides. This process is also called the 'Transfer Rule' and is how the actions and reactions of people and system control the entire process. Therefore, more selection and modification options mean there are more variables to consider. Ultimately, a higher controllability creates complex and diverse interactions (Durlak 1987; Kiousis 2002; Lombard and Ditton 1997; Steuer 1992).

Allow me to explain the relationship between controllability and interactivity through the case of Wikipedia. If I want to search for "Jinwoo Kim" on Wikipedia, then I will provide a modification option to the system by commanding it to search for that specific information in the search input box. Then, the site reveals information by comparing the search input with system entries through the transfer rule. Many Jinwoo Kims appear, such as a baseball player, a celebrity, a linguist, and more. This flow of interaction includes the three control processes. Inputting one type of information on an input system and comparing it with other search results is a very simple interaction process. Therefore, it may be difficult to find the desired information.

Let's try to control the three features of controllability to enhance interactivity. I can add photos to the search field, and I can also input additional information regarding the Jinwoo Kim that I want to find including his birth date and his occupation. The system becomes busier with this increased amount of input information. First, each input is checked and compared with system information. To enhance search results, Wikipedia provides the first results to users, and if this is not the right information for the user, then it asks for new information. This process continues until Wikipedia is able to find the correct Jinwoo Kim. The controllability of this process increases, and the interaction between product and user becomes more intensified. Therefore, more complex and diverse actions and reactions between a user and a system enlarge the range of users' choices and bring about more changes to experience.

There are two design features that enhance controllability: selective interface and interface for sensory activation.

5.6.1.1   Selective Interface Based on Diversity of Input Devices

A selective interface sets the range of selection and modification options (Kiousis 2002). This includes simple selections such as the number of links within a website to diverse input methods (i.e. mouse, keyboard). Modification also includes the number of words input to diverse input types such as images, voice, and motion. The greater the diversity, the controllability of the system experience is enhanced.

Ultimately, information with high controllability enables high interactivity through the appropriate extraction of results (Quiring and Schweiger 2008).

With the Nintendo Wii, users can utilize the standard bar-shape controller (http://en.wikipedia.org/wiki/Wii_MotionPlus) or a steering wheel device that looks similar to the real steering wheel in car (http://www.engadget.com/products/nintendo/wii/wheel/specs/) to play a game such as Mario Cart. The two devices provide different driving experiences to users. You can use the direction buttons on the bar-shape controller to drive, but this is much different than our real life driving experiences. Therefore, system reaction does not appear natural. However, when using the steering wheel to play the system shows that the direction of the wheel and the character's cart on the screen match each other naturally, and this enables direct feedback. Of course, there are cases opposite to this as well. People who are not accustomed to driving in real life may find that using the bar-shape standard controller to control a car may seem more natural. Ultimately, diverse user interfaces needs to be guaranteed rather than the mere strengthening of selective interfaces.

5.6.1.2   Interface for User's Sensory Activation

The second type of interface that enhances controllability is an interface that utilizes human senses in a product or service that users can feel directly (Chu et al. 1997). This interface is connected to the activation of human senses through direct or similar experiences. Examples of an interface for the user's sensory activation include game controllers that provide the perception of weight or vibration, basically the awareness of the use of the five human senses. This interface is closely related to the reaction of the system as we talked about earlier because a system's reaction that activates visual, auditory, tactile, and olfactory senses influence the controllability of the user (Durlak 1987, p. 746; Kiousis 2002, p. 378; Lombard and Ditton 1997; Quiring and Schweiger 2008). A good example that illustrates this type of interface is the golf simulator, Golfzon. As shown in Fig. 5.9, the simulator not only utilizes

Fig. 5.9 A case of an interface that induces sensory activation: real golf club (*left*) and motion remote control (*right*) (courtesy of GolfZon, used with permission)

auditory and visual stimuli through a computer device, it provides the experience that resembles an actual experience such as swinging an actual golf club and hitting an actual ball on the field. The fact that, in the simulator, I can swing with a real club and hit a real ball helps me perceive detailed sensory information. Activating senses, which I use in real life, allows me to know how to react and helps me get ready for the next play. On the other hand, the picture on the right in Fig. 5.9 shows how you can only use the motion remote controller to hit a shot. Since only the swinging motion is taken into factor, meticulous control is difficult and the stimuli that you receive from the system's reactions activate your senses relatively less. Compared to swinging a real golf club and hitting a real ball, sensory activation is much lower in the case of using the motion remote controller.

5.6.2   Exchange of Meaning

Let's go back to the example of internet radio I previously discussed in this chapter. The radio is considered an emotional medium because people send in stories about their lives for the DJs to read and share to those tuning in. These stories don't just end as "yeah, so this happened." They carry messages of inspiration, sadness, and joy that other people listening can relate to. These actions create meaning for the person sending in the story, the DJ reading it on air, as well as the listeners. A long time ago, a person sent in a message to suggest changing the show's title abbreviation. The new abbreviation carried a lot of meaning, and the DJ thanked the listener and started calling the show with that name. Now, more than a decade has passed and the show's name is still called by that name. Such an exchange between persons and a person to a medium (system) provides new meaning through organic communication, which is called exchange of meaning (Quiring and Schweiger 2008).

In the perspective of experience, exchange of meaning can be thought of as a good understanding and interpretation of the property of the information. Users are exposed to many types of information during product or service use. Users comprehend meaning through symbols that are transferred through the system. Based on the property of the system and personal interpretation, the meaning of the symbol may differ (Quiring and Schweiger 2008). For instance, let's say you were surfing the web and saw a HTTP 404 error code which means that the page could not be found. If you are someone with basic knowledge of internet codes, then you would choose an appropriate means of action such as letting the webmaster of the site know of this error. But if you are not familiar with the internet or the error code, then you will not be able to take additional steps other than to halt use of the website. Ultimately, understanding of the symbol behind a single error code can cause a breach in communication between a user and a system or a user and another user. Therefore, exchange of meaning can be interpreted as whether there is a mutual understanding of meaning between a user and a system or a user and another user.

Such exchange of meaning can be broken down into three processes. The first process is a technological method built within the product or service that delivers meaning to the user based on system specifications. The second is the transfer of meaning. The third is the decoding of that transferred meaning. This includes the process of restructuring the meaning of the received information. How actively the exchange of meaning is happening can be measured through the quality and quantity of a two-way communication. In other words, it refers to whether the user has a method to deliver his/her thoughts to the system, how well the user can express his/her thoughts to the system, and how well the system can accurately understand the user's intentions and provide appropriate feedback.

So then, how does the exchange of meaning influence interactivity? There is a close relationship between the directionality and composition of power of communication (McMillan and Downes 1998; Downes and McMillan 2000). The exchange of meaning is a basic condition for two-way communication and a necessary prerequisite for building a mutual communication relationship (Hoffman and Novak 1996). The better the exchange of meaning, a user can maintain continuous interaction with the system. A successful exchange of meaning is said to be established when the power between a user and a system or a user and another user is distributed proportionately so that the message to be delivered has been delivered clearly. The transfer of a clear message creates secondary interactions, and this circular structure induces the potential for more change in the system. This cycle ultimately enhances interactivity.

A good example of how the exchange of meaning enhances interactivity is Line Messenger. Prior messengers generally supported interaction through text, images, and videos. However, Line stickers express users' intentions through creative emoticons that help deliver more meaning.

Two design features, participatory interfaces and auxiliary information, support the exchange of meaning as design features of a system.

5.6.2.1 Participatory Interface

A participatory interface focuses on active participation and information exchange by users. There are three different types of users in interactive media in which many people participate. First, there are spectators that merely adhere to the media. Spectators are potential participants that can actively take part in a medium based on changes in their physical and psychological environments. The second type of users perform simple tasks through the medium. The third and last type, are performers who are active users that exceed actions provided by the system. Spectators, who lack action, change into active users who create relationships with other users and content, and further along the way, active users become performers (Dalsgard 2009).

A participatory interface that supports performers needs to show the relationship between the content and a user and be able to connect them together. It provides a basis for transferring and accepting messages that support profiles and content, real-time comments, and other information related to users and the system or network. This not only includes information that the service provider offers but also includes other people's opinions. In this way, the design should provide an equivalent level of interaction between service provider and users. For example, Fig. 5.10 shows an internet radio application that provides a comment section where users can voice

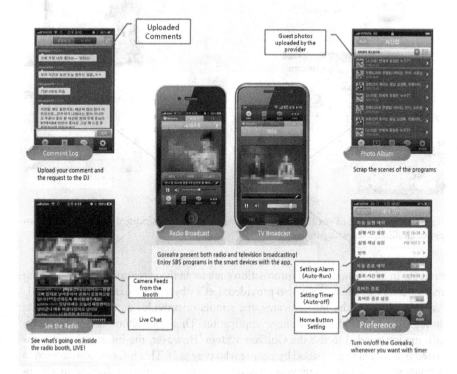

Fig. 5.10 Internet radio application that supports a chatting system (courtesy of SBS, used with permission)

their opinions in real-time. These service functions provide an opportunity for users and DJs to interact continuously by exchanging diverse meanings and content.

5.6.2.2   Auxiliary Information

Auxiliary information is a supporting dependent data for a main data and has been widely utilized as a means to enhance the accuracy of system data (Wang and Zhu 1998; Rytsar et al. 2003). Auxiliary data is a form of metadata that is also shown in the system. Metadata refers to structured data about a certain type of data (Caplan 2004). The combination of metadata and usage rules is called a schema or a scheme, which includes the meaning structure and content rules of data. Auxiliary data plays an important role in understanding the meaning of a particular content by structuring content based on a certain schema.

For example, the virtual golf simulator exchanges information through auxiliary data such as the length of a course, difficulty, the characteristics of each hole, and

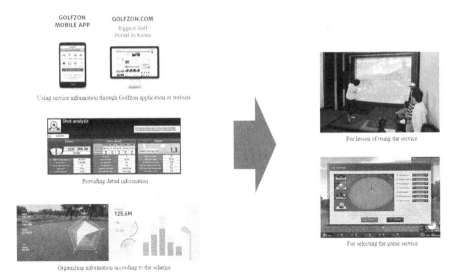

Fig. 5.11 An example of auxiliary data and utilization of data in the virtual golf simulator (courtesy of GolfZon, used with permission)

strategy. In addition, detailed information such as analysis reports of a user's swing and trajectory of the ball are also provided. Let's observe the example in Fig. 5.11. As the picture on the left indicates, the simulator provides auxiliary information through the web and a smartphone application. This information is not necessary information needed to use the Golfzon system. However, the information is comprised in a schema understood by people who play golf. This information, as seen in the picture on the right, is recycled based on the meaning of the information and intentions of the user. The auxiliary information, when reused, is useful in enhancing understanding regarding how to strategize for a certain hole in the simulator. While playing the evaluation of my swing or information on the direction of the shots lead to diverse actions of the player. Therefore, the provision of auxiliary information provides a basis for continuous interaction between the user and the system through the exchange of indirect meaning.

5.6.3   Synchronicity

Let's think back on the previous Nintendo Wii example. In Mario Cart, a popular driving game for the Wii, tilting the controller one way tilts the cart inside the game in the same direction, thereby providing the experience of driving. In Wii Sports, the game functions under the same principle. The user uses the controller to move it at a certain time, and the game character directly reacts in the same way. This direct reaction is crucial for victory in the game. In this way, synchronicity refers to feedback directly coordinated to the user's control (Liu and Shrum 2002).

In terms of experience, synchronicity is a UX factor that determines how fast a system reacts to a person's manipulation of the product or service. A user's manipulation can take place through many methods. In the Wii, a game consists of much tilting and shaking. If there was a lag in time between action and reaction during a game, the game would be severely interrupted. A time gap is an important factor that may disrupt game play.

Synchronicity is an important UX factor that helps users become aware of the task at hand. It is a factor that makes people to believe that they are actually doing something just like in the real world. as the user manipulates and the system reacts. For example, let's think about a multiplayer tennis match between two people on the Wii. As the users volley the ball between each other by manipulating their controllers, the avatars of the users react right away. This adds to the actual experience of competing against one another even though the users are not bouncing an actual ball between each other. The manipulation of the system and the system's reaction provides a synchronous experience that enables the users to think that they are hitting the ball between themselves.

So how does synchronicity affect interactivity? Because interactivity is a scale that indicates how much a user can change a system, more diverse manipulations through the system lead to increased interactivity. When the user manipulates the system, a more instant feedback results in enhanced interactivity because synchronicity is a factor that can maximize the influence of speed, which is one of the three levers of interactivity. If there is a lag in feedback no matter how much a user tries to manipulate the system, then not only will the user feel discomfort in using the product or service but also feel decreased interactivity. On the other hand, the perception of a more instant feedback by increased synchronicity helps the user understand and evaluate the feedback faster in order to proceed with more manipulations. Therefore, synchronicity also has the effect of increasing the range of interactivity.

Design features that enhance synchronicity include timing notification information and the progress indicator.

5.6.3.1   Timing Notification Information

Timing notification is a design feature widely used in products and services that alerts the user of the precise timing of a certain manipulation (Tam et al. 2013). Examples in real life include letting the user know when to change a car's gear and when to perform a certain action in a video game. Timing notification can be seen in Nintendo Wii games as well. It is often frequently displayed in sports games, such as baseball where swinging the bat at the right time shows a green highlight effect through the screen and the built-in speakers of the controller (http://www.pixlbit.com/feature/2374/marketing_101_nintendo/page5).

The timing notification helps users understand the right timing, thus enhancing synchronicity and inducing high interactivity.

5.6.3.2   Progress Indicator

The progress indicator is a basic design feature that shows the status of a file transfer (Brewster and King 2005). This feature provides synchronicity by helping the user

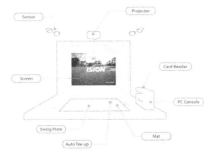

Based on sensing data showing the
scene and trajectory of a flying ball.

Fig. 5.12 An example of a progress indicator: An interface for real-time trajectory information in the virtual golf simulator (courtesy of GolfZon, used with permission)

directly see the changes to a system in the perspective of a UX rather than directly increase the reaction speed. After a user has induced a manipulation to the system, the progress indicator shows the reaction speed and status of change continually and instantly to maintain communication and enhance synchronicity between the user and the system. For example, Fig. 5.12 illustrates a progress indicator that shows the trajectory of the golf ball along with its speed and direction. Utilizing the progress indicator enables users to wait patiently while the ball flies in the air. Therefore, using the progress indicator, which continually updates the user with changes in the system, in appropriate ways, enhances synchronicity and ultimately raises the level of interactivity.

5.7   Summary

- Presence is a dimension that effectively deals with changes to the external environment and controls the sensual thread of experience.
- Presence is influenced by perceptual and behavioral levers. Vividness is a key perceptual lever, while interactivity is a key behavioral lever.
- Vividness is determined by the breadth and depth of a perceived stimulus.
- The depth of stimulation refers to the level of stimulation that a single channel offers.
- The breadth of stimulation refers to how many channels of stimuli are provided simultaneously.
- Interactivity refers to the level of change that the user can impact on the object of interaction.
- Interactivity is determined by speed, range, and mapping.
- In order to provide the desired level of vividness, it is important to provide the UX factors of narrativity, concreteness, and media richness.

- In order to provide an experience with high narrativity, design features such as a metaphor-based interface, actions for using the metaphor, and an information architecture that is based on sequential causal relationships must be effectively designed.
- An experience with high concreteness can be effectively provided through the design features of force feedback and micro feedback.
- Media richness can be enhanced through the design features of augmented information, the combination of touch and movement, and mapping between sensory information and user tasks.
- In order to provide the desired level of interactivity, it is important to provide the UX factors of controllability, active exchange of meaning, and high synchronicity.
- Controllability can be effectively enhanced through the design features of utilizing selective interfaces and interfaces that induce sensory activation based on input method diversity.
- For an active exchange of meaning, it is important to provide the design feature of a participatory interface that induces active user participation and diverse auxiliary information.
- In order to provide high synchronicity, the design features of timing notification information and progress indicators need to be effectively designed.

5.8 Discussion Topics

- Think of a product or service you recently experienced that offers high vividness. Why do you think the experience provided high vividness? What were the design features that induced this kind of experience?
- Think of a recent experience of a product or service that offered low vividness. Why do you think the experience provided low vividness? What were the design features that induced this kind of experience?
- Let's think of a recent digital product or a service that supports high interactivity. Why do you think interactivity was high? What were the design features that induced high interactivity?
- Let's think of a recent digital product or a service that supports low interactivity. Why do you think interactivity was low? What were the design features that induced low interactivity?

References

Azuma RT (1997) A survey of augmented reality. Presence 6(4):355–385

Benoit C, Le Goff B (1998) Audio-visual speech synthesis from French text: eight years of models, designs and evaluation at the ICP. Speech Commun 26(1):117–129

Biocca F (1992) Communication within virtual reality: creating a space for research. J Commun 42(4):5–22

Biocca F (1997) The Cyborg's dilemma: progressive embodiment in virtual environments [1]. J Comput Med Commun 3(2):1–18

Brewster SA, King A (March 2005) The design and evaluation of a vibrotactile progress bar. In: Eurohaptics conference, 2005 and Symposium on haptic interfaces for virtual environment and teleoperator systems, 2005. World haptics 2005. First joint, IEEE, pp 499–500

Caplan P (2004) Building a digital preservation archive: tales from the front. Vine 34(1):38–42

Carlson JR, Zmud RW (1999) Channel expansion theory and the experiential nature of media richness perceptions. Acad Manage J 42(2):153–170

Carrozzino M, Brogi A, Tecchia F, Bergamasco M (June 2005) The 3D interactive visit to Piazza dei Miracoli, Italy. In: Proceedings of the 2005 ACM SIGCHI International Conference on Advances in computer entertainment technology, ACM, pp 192–195

Chu CCP, Dani TH, Gadh R (1997) Multi-sensory user interface for a virtual-reality-based computeraided design system. Comput Aided Des 29(10):709–725

Clark HH, Brennan SE (1991) Grounding in communication. Perspect Soc Shar Cognit 13(1991):127–149

Clark HH, Schaefer EF (1987) Collaborating on contributions to conversations. Lang Cognit Process 2(1):19–41

Clark HH, Wilkes-Gibbs D (1986) Referring as a collaborative process. Cognition 22(1):1–39

Cohen PR, Johnston M, McGee D, Oviatt S, Pittman J, Smith I, Chen I, Clow J (November 1997) Quickset: multimodal interaction for distributed applications. In: Proceedings of the fifth ACM international conference on Multimedia, ACM, pp 31–40

Cornoldi C, de Beni R, Cavedon A, Mazzoni G (1992) How can a vivid image be described? Characteristics influencing vividness judgments and the relationship between vividness and memory. J Ment Imag 16(3–4):89–107

Coyle JR, Thorson E (2001) The effects of progressive levels of interactivity and vividness in web marketing sites. J Advert 30(3):65–77

Dalsgard (2009) Designing engaging interactive environments: a pragmatist perspective. PhD Thesis. Department of Information and Media Studies, Aarhus University

Downes EJ, McMillan SJ (2000) Defining interactivity a qualitative identification of key dimensions. New Med Soc 2(2):157–179

Durlak J T (1987) A typology for interactive media. Commun Yearb 10:743–757

Escalas JE (2004) Imagine yourself in the product: mental simulation, narrative transportation, and persuasion. J Advert 33(2):37–48

Everett Jr HR, Nieusma JM (1994) U.S. Patent No. 5,309,140. U.S. Patent and Trademark Office, Washington, DC

Foley JD (1982) Fundamentals of interactive computer graphics (Systems Programming Series) Addison-Wesley Longman Publishing Co., Inc., Boston

Gibson BS (1996) The masking account of attentional capture: a reply to Yantis and Jonides (1996). J Exp Psychol: Hum Percept Perform 22(6):1514–1520

Goertz L (1995) Wie interaktiv sind Medien?. na. Rundfunk Fernsehen 4:477–493

Graesser AC, Hauft-Smith K, Cohen AD, Pyles LD (1980) Advanced outlines, familiarity, and text genre on retention of prose. J Exp Educ 48:281–290

Ha L, James EL (1998) Interactivity reexamined: a baseline analysis of early business web sites. J Broadcast Electron Med 42(4):457–474

Heeter C (1989) Implications of new interactive technologies for conceptualizing communication. Media use in the information age: emerging patterns of adoption and consumer use, pp 217–235

Heeter C (1992) Being there: the subjective experience of presence. Presence: Teleoperators Virtual Environ 1(2):262–271

Hinckley K, Song H (May 2011) Sensor synaesthesia: touch in motion, and motion in touch. In: Proceedings of the SIGCHI Conference on Human Factors in Computing Systems, ACM, pp 801–810

Hoffman DL, Novak TP (1996) Marketing in hypermedia computer-mediated environments: conceptual foundations. J Mark 60(3):50–68. (ISO 690)

Jensen H, Lockwood B (1998) A note on discontinuous value functions and strategies in affine-quadratic differential games. Econ Lett 61(3):301–306

Kesim M, Ozarslan Y (2012) Augmented reality in education: current technologies and the potential for education. Proc Soc Behav Sci 47:297–302

Kiousis S (2002) Interactivity: a concept explication. New Med Soc 4(3):355–383

Lakoff G, Johnson M (1980) The metaphorical structure of the human conceptual system. Cognit Sci 4(2):195–208

Laurel, B. (1993) Computers as theatre. Addison-Wesley, New York (1991)

Laurel B (1997) Interface agents: metaphors with character. Hum Val Des Comput Technol 207–219

Liu Y, Shrum LJ (2002) What is interactivity and is it always such a good thing? Implications of definition, person, and situation for the influence of interactivity on advertising effectiveness. J Advert 31(4):53–64

Lombard M, Ditton T (1997) At the heart of it all: the concept of presence. J Comput Med Commun 3(2). doi:10.1111/j.1083-6101.1997.tb00072.x

Lombard M, Snyder-Duch J (2001) Interactive advertising and presence: a framework. J Interact Advert 1(2):56–65

Mar RA, Oatley K (2008) The function of fiction is the abstraction and simulation of social experience. Perspect Psychol Sci 3(3):173–192

McKelvie SJ (1995) The VVIQ and beyond: vividness and its measurement. J Ment Imag 19(3–4):197-252

McMillan S, Downes E (1998) Interactivity. Handbook of new media: social shaping and social consequences. Sage, London

Nisbett R, Ross L (1980) Human inference: strategies and shortcomings of social judgment. Prentice-Hall, Englewood Cliffs, p 334

Paivio A, Yuille JC, Madigan SA (1968) Concreteness, imagery, and meaningfulness values for 925 nouns. J Exp Psychol 76(1p2):1–25

Pentland A, Picard RW, Sclaroff S (1996) Photobook: content-based manipulation of image databases. Int J Comput Vision 18(3):233–254

Quiring O, Schweiger W (2008) Interactivity: a review of the concept and a framework for analysis. Communications 33(2):147–167

Rheingold H (1991) Virtual reality: exploring the brave new technologies. Simon & Schuster Adult Publishing Group, New York

Ryan ML (2002) Beyond myth and metaphor: narrative in digital media. Poet Today 23(4):581–609

Rytsar Y, Voloshynovskiy S, Ehrler F, Pun T (December 2003) Interactive segmentation with hidden object-based annotations: toward Smart Media. In: Electronic imaging 2004. International Society for Optics and Photonics, pp 29–37

Sarter NB (2006) Multimodal information presentation: design guidance and research challenges. Int J Ind Ergon 36(5):439–445

Schwitzgebel E (2002) Why did we think we dreamed in black and white? Stud Hist Philosophy Sci Part A 33(4):649–660

Shneiderman B (1987) Designing the user interface: strategies for effective human-computer interaction. Addison-Wesley Publishing Co., Reading, Masachusetts

Short J, Williams E, Christie B (1976) The social psychology of telecommunications. Technology and Engineering

Steuer J (1992) Defining virtual reality: dimensions determining telepresence. J Commun 42(4):73–93

Stork DG, Hennecke ME (eds) (1995) Speechreading by humans and machines. Springer, New York

Tam D, MacLean KE, McGrenere J, Kuchenbecker KJ (April 2013) The design and field observation of a haptic notification system for timing awareness during oral presentations. In: Proceedings of the SIGCHI Conference on Human Factors in Computing Systems, ACM, pp 1689–1698

Taylor SE, Thompson SC (1982) Stalking the elusive "vividness" effect. Psychol Rev 89(2):155–181 (Cited: 603)

Turk M, Robertson G (2000) Perceptual user interfaces (introduction). Commun ACM 43(3):32–34

Vo MT, Wood C (May 1996) Building an application framework for speech and pen input integration in multimodal learning interfaces. In: Acoustics, Speech, and Signal Processing, 1996. ICASSP-96. Conference Proceedings, 1996 IEEE International Conference on (vol 6, pp 3545–3548), IEEE

Wang J (October 1995) Integration of eye-gaze, voice and manual response in multimodal user interface. In Systems, Man and Cybernetics, 1995. Intelligent systems for the 21st century, IEEE International Conference on (vol 5, pp 3938–3942), IEEE

Wang Y, Zhu QF (1998) Error control and concealment for video communication: a review. Proc IEEE 86(5):974–997

Weghorst S, Billinghurst M (1993) Spatial perception of immersive virtual environments. HIT Lab Technical Report, University of Washington

Welch RB, Blackmon TT, Liu A, Mellers BA, Stark LW (1996) The effects of pictorial realism, delay of visual feedback, and observer interactivity on the subjective sense of presence. Presence: Teleoperators Virtual Environ 5(3):263–273

Zeltzer D (1992) Autonomy, interaction, and presence. Presence: Teleoperators Virtual Environ 1(1):127–132

Zhai S, Morimoto C, Ihde S (May 1999) Manual and gaze input cascaded (MAGIC) pointing. In: Proceedings of the SIGCHI conference on Human Factors in Computing Systems. ACM, pp 246–253

Chapter 6
Design for Valuable Experience

6.1 Introduction

In the perspective of judgmental experience, we seek valuable experiences while using a product or service to help us achieve our intended goals. In order to achieve a valuable experience, it is important to consider what values can be achieved through what means. The key dimension of the judgmental thread of experience that sheds light on these questions is the locus of causality. This is because the locus of causality can effectively control a person's judgmental experience according to changes in the external environment. So what levers control the locus of causality? And which UX factors make up these levers? Lastly, what are the design features that provide these UX factors effectively?

6.2 Korean e-Government Service

Recently, I had to print out a copy of my certified resident registration in a hurry. The time and hassle of going to the district office to request a document was not what I was excited to do with the long que, problem with finding a parking spot, taking time from teaching, etc., and then hoping that there would be no problems with the application and that I brought all the correct supporting documents.

As I worried about the dreadful experience, my wife told me some good news. She told me that an online government service called "Minwon 24" had opened where I would be able to print out my copy of the resident registration without having to visit the district office. I was pleasantly surprised to hear about this and gave it a go.

Minwon 24 is a 24 hour service, as the name suggests, which is very convenient for a person like me that works during business hours. I logged in through my online certificate of authentication (a prerequisite for government and banking services in

The online version of this chapter (doi: 10.1007/978-3-319-14304-0_6) contains supplementary material

J. Kim, *Design for Experience*, Human-Computer Interaction Series,
DOI 10.1007/978-3-319-14304-0_6

Korea). The process was divided into a few steps, and each step required user consent to proceed. The steps were not too inconvenient because they were automated, and I reached the last step in no time. The system had already filled in most of my personal information so filling out the forms was very convinient. Despite the security precautions I had a feeling of unrest that my private information could be leaked. But a pop-up window ensured me that a security program was protecting my information, so I felt a relief. In the last step, I requested to print my document and after the service automatically detected printers nearby, I was able to select my printer of choise.

A more dramatic indicent happened a few weeks ago. My mother called me while I was at the airport waiting for a plane to go on a business trip overseas. She needed a family relation certificate for insurance purposes. I only had a limited amount of time before I had to board, and I didn't have any time to visit a district office nearby. I therefore went to the Minwon 24 and selected the "request for other persons" service. I selected the corresponding officer at my mother's district office as the issuer of the document. Few minutes later I received a text message confirming that the request had been received. I was very thankful for being able to take care of this issue so conveniently.

Many useful services are being provided and even exported under the name of the e-government and the UN has even recognized this by naming it as one of the best in the world on consequtive occations.

6.3   Locus of Causality

As I mentioned in Chapter 2, the judgmental thread of experience evaluates the value of my experience. It evaluates whether and how I achieved my goals through my experience. For example, in terms of the Minwon 24 service, the judgmental thread of experience evaluates what kind of value I received when printing the document out based on the online process I had to go through to achieve my goal. An important standard of evaluation is known as the locus of causality that mainly has two aspects. The first is the objective or result of the use of a product or a service. This aspect helps judge whether the objective or motivation for the experience stems from the experience itself or other external elements. If I have the objective to enjoy the experience itself, then the usefulness of that experience is determined through the experience itself; therefore, the locus of causality is internal. For example, if I think that the act of printing out a document through Minwon 24 made my experience valuable, then the basis for judgment is from an internal locus of causality. On the other hand, if it was something other than the experience itself, then the locus of causality is external. For example, if I considered Minwon 24 valuable because it helped me request a certificate that my mother needed for insurance purposes that saved me both time and money, then the origin of my motivation comes from an external locus of causality.

Another perspective of locus of causality is related to the process of experience. It refers to the user's direct control of a process of experience. For instance, Minwon 24 issues the documents that I need without me having to do much. It doesn't require me to input a lot of information, it detects my printer automatically, and protects my information through a security program. When I think of these things, then the locus of causality is external. On the other hand, if I am able to select the document I need and choose the method in which to receive it, then there are more aspects I can control; then, I can say that my experience stems from an internal locus of causality. Therefore, locus of causality refers to how much of what I perceive is under my control during product or service usage.

Because judgmental locus of causality possesses both result-oriented and process-oriented characteristics, it is important to investigate both characteristics. This book presents "a hedonistic-utilitarian value" as a result-oriented lever and "an autonomy and automation" as a process-oriented lever of locus of causality. Let's take an in-depth look into these levers that determine locus of causality.

6.3.1 Hedonistic vs Utilitarian: Key Result-Oriented Levers for Judgmental Experience

There is currently a very popular video game called League of Legends. League of Legends is a real-time strategy game that consists of three to five people per team whose goal is to destroy the other team's buildings. The most popular method of gameplay is five against five. Users can choose from over 100 heroes and participate with four other players to destroy the other team's nexus. Continuous cooperation with teammates and the competition with other teams makes this game fun and easy to immerse in. The game also provides elements of luck such as selecting random teammates or choosing 10 random heroes for a week to provide a serendipitous enjoyment.

On the other hand, PayPal is a service that helps people transfer money and make payments online. Because PayPal enables payments without requiring users to share detailed personal information, it is a useful service at a time where online privacy is a videly discussed topic. PayPal is also convenient because it uses bank accounts or credit cards to make payments, thus providing familiar methods for the users. The primary goal of using PayPal is to conduct financial transactions with other people. People use PayPal not because the experience is enjoyable or hedonistic; it is used to purchase products online. Therefore, the value of PayPal stems from effectively being able to achieve other purposes that exist outside the realms of PayPal rather than the experience of using PayPal itself.

People have many different goals for using a product or a service (Hidi and Harackiewich 2000). When this goal has been achieved, the experience is deemed to be useful and valuable (Ho et al. 2010; Li 2006). While people may have many different goals for using a product or service, the goals can be primarily divided into utilitarian and hedonistic goals (Batra and Ahtola 1991).

A utilitarian goal is used as a means to achieve other goals. Therefore, products or services that seek to provide utilitarian goals focus on efficiency or effectiveness and attempt to approach them logically and rationally. For instance, PayPal places importance on how quickly and safely a financial transaction can be performed because it seeks to provide a utilitarian goal.

On the other hand, hedonistic goals refer to the enjoyment that arises out of the experience of using a product or service (Boo and Mattila 2003). Therefore, subjective experience is important for hedonistic goals. For instance, the goal of playing League of Legends is achieved based on how enjoyable the experience of playing the game is.

But people don't always seek to fulfill goals that have been laid out for them. People can possess special values based on which desires they seek to fulfill (Pintrich 2000; Arias 2004). For example, ordinary users would probably possess the goal of enjoying the game itself. However, employees of rival game companies may play it to understand its dynamics and popularity. Since this is a utilitarian goal, these users will feel like the experience is more valuable when they are able to apply their findings to their own games rather than when enjoying the game itself.

The locus of causality of judgmental experience is influenced by whether the experience possesses hedonistic or utilitarian value. Once the value is determined to be hedonistic or utilitarian, it is a crucial factor that decides the type of locus of causality in a judgmental experience.

6.3.2 Autonomy vs. Automation: Key Process-Oriented Levers for Judgmental Experience

I no longer use paper to write notes. Instead, I use my tablet device to freely write down my thoughts and experiences. Until recently a tablet touch pen felt dull, and it was difficult to efficiently write down the things I wanted to express. However, a recently released graphic tablet for professionals provides a completely different experience. First, it senses pressure as little as 1 g and supports over 2000 levels of pressure sensing, and it senses the detailed slants of my pen to provide more meticulous control than a conventional brush or pen. I press hard when I want thick lines, and I press lightly to make thinner lines. In addition, free control of the tablet's orientation and angles allows more detailed tasks to be completed. Due to the minute sensing capabilities, I can express more details than with a brush and canvas.

On the other hand, let's think of an automated parking system in a metropolis like Seoul. There is an automated parking system at a movie theater I visit frequently in the center of Seoul. When I attempt to park, there is very little that I can control. I park my car on a round metal floor in front of the parking tower and get off. This is the extent of what I do. After this, the system first recognizes the plate number of my car, and then the metal floor rotates automatically to take my car inside the parking tower. I have no idea on which floor my car will be parked. Once the movie ends and I insert my plate number into the automated system, it locates my car and delivers it to the spot at which I dropped it off. During this process, there is nothing I can control.

The concept of automation refers to a machine or a system performing a function that was normally reserved for humans (Parasuraman et al. 2000). The level of automation refers to how long human attention does not have to be on a robot when it performs its intended tasks (Goodrich and Schultz 2007). The higher the level of automation the less interference into its tasks is needed.

Humans typically process information in four stages. The level of automation can be determined based on these four stages of automation. The first stage is the stage of collecting information by recognizing and recording input information. During this stage, the task of scanning the environment, observing, and recording can be automated. In the automated parking example, the system scans the car's plate number and records it. The second stage cognitively processes the recorded information and analyzes it appropriately. For example, this stage refers to if the automated car parking system can analyze which movie the car owner will watch and at what time the movie ends. In the third stage, a decision making process is conducted based on the results of the analysis in the prior stage. For instance, the automated parking system can determine which parking space would be most appropriate for a certain car. Lastly, the fourth stage performs the actions necessary for executing the decision. For example, the automated parking system, not the owner, can move the car to a specific parking spot.

The level of automation refers to how much of the stages a machine or a system can fulfill. For example, the lowest level of automation would not help a person in any way; the person would conduct all four stages him/herself. The tablet I mentioned earlier provides the lowest level of automation since users are offered various options on how to use the pen and must manually place pressure on the screen to write in thick ink. On the other hand, a system that automatically gathers data, analyzes it, and provides action offers the highest level of automation. For example, a high level of automation would be if the automated parking system would predict at what time I'd be back and placed my car in front of the movie theater accordingly.

Automation is closely related to the concept of controllability, which is the process aspect of the locus of causality. People perceive that the greater number of automated systems in of their environment, such as the automated parking system, reduces the range of their controlability, and this leads their judgmental experience to shift towards an external locus of causality. On the other hand, low-level automated devices such as the graphic tablet helps people perceive themselves as more in control, thus shifting their experience to an internal locus of causality.

Automation is the opposite of user autonomy (Ryan and Deci 2000). While automation refers to the amount of control that a product or service has on a person, autonomy refers to the amount of control that a person has on a product or service. Therefore, a system with high automation is system-driven, while a system with low automation provides a human-driven experience.

6.3.3 Result-Oriented and Process-Oriented Levers

What is the relationship between result-oriented and process-oriented loci in the perspective of the judgmental thread of experience? While these two levers are closely related to each other, they are not the same lever. Just because I judge that internal goals influenced my experience, doesn't necessarily mean I must be able to control every single aspect of the system. Similarly, just because a utilitarian goal influences my experience doesn't mean the system must be fully automated and I shouldn't be able to control anything at all. For example, I can evaluate that the direct controls I have in the Minwon 24 service may deem my procedural locus of causality to be internal, while my objective of using the service for an external goal such as taking care of my medical insurance reveals that my result-oriented locus of causality is external.

However, since both process-oriented and goal-oriented loci are about judgmental aspects of experience, an interaction effect will exist between them. For example, a person who uses the graphic tablet for leisure purposes will possess a more internal locus of causality than a person who uses it for professional design because both the result-oriented and process-oriented locus of causality of the person who uses it for leisure will be internal. On the other hand, an automated parking system for a movie theater in the middle of the city is highly automated and the locus of causality of the experience of using it is external. The high automation already makes the process-oriented locus of causality externalized, while the result-oriented locus of causality is also externalized. In this sense, the locus of causality of the parking system for a movie theater is external in both process-oriented and result-oriented levers as shown in the three-dimensional model of experience in Fig. 6.1.

As the above examples demonstrate, process-oriented and result-oriented loci of causality are closely related while also mutually exclusive. Therefore, each lever possesses different UX factors and design features. The next section explains multiple cases of each lever and identifies key UX factors and design features.

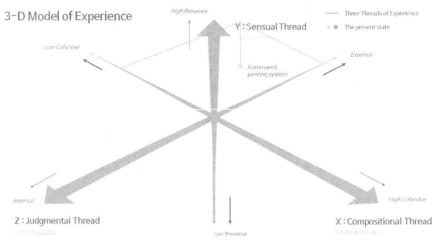

Fig. 6.1 A three-dimensional experience model of an automated parking system for a District Office

Table 6.1 Eight cases used in the case study

Product/service	Hedonistic (internal)	Utilitarian (external)
Automation (external)	Product: Philips Hue Service: Beat	Product: LG Robotking Service: Minwon 24
Autonomy (internal)	Product: Tamiya RC Car Porsche 934 Turbo RSR Service: I Love Coffee	Product: Aimsak AD 418R, 18V Rechargeable Driver Drill Service: Easy Taxi

6.4   Eight Case Studies on Result-Oriented and Process-Oriented Levers

In the prior section, I selected result-oriented and process-oriented loci of causality as key levers that influence the judgmental locus of causality. I then divided each lever into internal and external cases. I created a 2×2 table that illustrates this division as shown in Table 6.1. I also provided examples of a product and a service that corresponds to each cell. These products and services are either in the position of a dominant design or are predicted to be in such a position. A total of eight cases are summarized in Table 6.1.

I conducted a case study on these eight cases. The purpose of this study was to investigate the UX factors that led to the success of each product or service and the specific design features that made the UX factors effective. Further and more specific explanations on each case are shown in (http://extras.springer.com) . In this chapter, I want to summarize each case and emphasize the UX factors that were deduced and the design features that were utilized.

6.4.1   I Love Coffee

A service case with internal results and internal process. (http://www.pati-games.com/)

"I Love Coffee" is a mobile game, released in 2012, that allows users to set up and manage a coffee shop. The process of managing itself provides fun and enjoyment. It is fun because the user can decorate its coffee shop in any way he wants, and it is enjoyable to play socially with friends or other users. People feel hedonistic values through this process, and this places the result-oriented locus of causality on the internal. "I Love Coffee" also possesses a high internal process-oriented locus of causality. The user is able to control finite details of the management such as creating the coffee menu and choosing what to display in the shop. This high user autonomy determines the image of the coffee shop and its revenue; therefore, process-oriented locus of causality is internal as well.

6.4.2   Tamiya RC Car Porsche 934 Turbo RSR

A product case with internal results and internal process. (modelkits123.com. au/)

The Tamiya RC Car Porsche 934 Turbo RSR is a remote control (RC) car. The process of assembling the car manually is enjoyable to many people. In the process of controlling the RC car, users are able to feel enjoyment. People feel hedonistic values through this process, and this places the result-oriented locus of causality as internal. The Tamiya RC car also possesses a high internal process-oriented locus of causality. The user is able to meticulously control both assembly and driving. Users are able to choose the interior and exterior parts to install in their car. They can choose customized engines and frames. This high user autonomy to be able to control all aspects of the building and driving process places both the result-oriented and process-oriented loci of causality as internal.

6.4.3   Beatpacking Company—BEAT

A service case of internal results and external process. (https://itunes.apple. com/kr/app/beat-music-player)

BEAT is a music player released in 2014 that recommends music based on context awareness. BEAT provides mix playlists, and users can select the type of music they would like to listen to. Once a mix playlist is selected, BEAT starts playing music randomly. When a user is listening to a mix that is popular in terms of the time of day or genre, BEAT enables the user to find other music and playlists serendipitously. Selecting a mix and listening to music on BEAT itself can bring fun and enjoyment to users. There are also many users who feel enjoyment in selecting a mix. During this process, people feel hedonistic values, and this places the result-oriented locus of causality on the internal. On the other hand, BEAT possesses a high external process-oriented locus of causality. BEAT automatically offers music to users based on different preferences of the user; therefore, users entrust BEAT with music recommendation during usage of its service.

6.4.4   Philips Hue

A product case with internal results and external process. (www.newscenter. philips.com)

I refer to previous discussion on the Philips Hue in Chapter 4. Hue is a smart light bulb that can be turned on and off automatically, and it can produce diverse colors as well. The Hue application for mobile and tablet allows users to automatically search for a dedicated bridge that can control lighting and brightness. For example, Hue offers colors for a certain theme such as a game or movie, and multiple Hue lamps can be used to express diverse colors such as a rainbow or a macaroon. During this process, people feel hedonistic values, and this places the result-oriented locus of causality on the internal. On the other hand, the Hue possesses a high external process-oriented locus of causality. No extra effort is needed after setting up a dedicated bridge. Conventional light bulbs require the user to control the device for each use, but the Hue analyzes user movement and lifestyle patterns to automatically control the lighting.

6.4.5 Easy Taxi

A service case with external results and internal process. (http://www.easytaxi. com)

Easy Taxi is a taxi reservation application that is available worldwide. When a user reserves a taxi through the application, then a GPS location is utilized to request a pickup by the nearest taxi driver who is also using the application. Easy Taxi emphasizes safety as one of its most important values. Taxi information such as the name of the driver, contact number, license plate, and car type are registered in the application. Therefore, it is easy to deal with safety and security problems that may arise. In this sense, users can feel a high utilitarian value for this service; therefore, the result-oriented locus of causality is placed on the external. On the other hand, Easy Taxi possesses a highly internal process-oriented locus of causality. For instance, taxi drivers and users can be connected one-on-one, so users can feel that they can deliver their intentions more strongly. Also the GPS location on a map is an effective way to help the user pinpoint the exact pick up location. Since users feel a greater sense of control during the pick up process, Easy Taxi possesses a highly internal process-oriented locus of causality.

6.4.6 AD 418R, 18V Rechargeable Driver Drill

A product case with external results and internal process. (http://www.aimsak. com/)

The rechargeable driver drill is often used in homes or offices for repair works, and it is also frequently used by amateur users who make their own furniture or conduct their own repairs. The advantage of the rechargeable driver drill is that it is simple enough for amateurs to use, and it also doesn't require much strength. Tasks can be completed using the driver drill with little effort. Users consider the ease of use as an important value in using the driver drill. Therefore, users feel more utilitarian value through the rechargeable driver drill, and the result-oriented locus of causality is placed on the external. On the other hand, the Aimsak 418 series possesses a highly internal process-oriented locus of causality. Users can set the performance of the device according to their needs. The rotation direction and work/safety mode can be set through a single button, and the strength of the drill can be minutely set with over 20 levels. Since the process offers users many different aspects of control, the process-oriented locus of causality is positioned on the internal.

6.4.7   E-Government Portal, Minwon 24

A service case with external results and external process. (http://www.minwon. go.kr/)

As I mentioned in the introduction to this chapter, Minwon 24 is an e-government portal service. Minwon 24 provides diverse administrative services such as issuing certificates and searching for official documents. Users feel utilitarian value with the service because they can choose the service they want to receive for practical purposes. Therefore, Minwon 24 provides a highly external result-oriented locus of causality. Minwon 24 also possesses a highly external process-oriented locus of causality. It completes forms with my personal information automatically from government databases. There are not many steps the user has to take to issue a certificate from start to finish. The user entrusts the autonomy of the system, and the system automation level is very high. Therefore, the process-oriented locus of causality is positioned on the external.

6.4.8   LG Robot Vacuum Cleaner—Roboking

A product case with external results and external process. (cyking.lge.co.kr)

The LG Roboking reduces the uncomfortable hassle of cleaning. The Roboking provides both vacuuming and mopping functions. It offers cleaning mode, auto-cleaning mode, and it has a rectangular design that raises the efficiency of cleaning corners. People get practical and useful values through the robot vacuum cleaner, and this leads to a high external result-oriented locus of causality. The Roboking also possesses a highly external process-oriented locus of causality. Users do not need to control any aspects of its tasks except turning it on and off. The robot vacuum cleaner is highly automated as it analyzes its context and cleans different parts of the house. The high system automation places the process-oriented locus of causality on the external.

These eight cases are currently or have been dominant designs in their respective markets. As the eight cases reveal, some dominant products and services are extremely internal and others are extremely external, which means that being internal or external by itself does not gurantee a product or a service to become a dominant design. The important point is to provide a good experience with each product, and how to provide a good experience is different with each product according to the locus of causality. Based on these eight cases, I was able to deduce the UX factors for high hedonistic value, high utilitarian value, high user autonomy, and high system automation. I also identified specific design features that can effectively facilitate these UX factors.

6.5 UX Factor and Design Features for Hedonistic Value

6.5.1 Serendipity

I received the impression while using the BEAT service that I was able to experience unexpected enjoyment. The more I use BEAT, the better music recommendations it provides based on time and place. I didn't have much expectation from a streaming service like that, but I was able to have this sort of unexpected enjoyment due to its appropriate music recommendations.

Such unexpected enjoyment in a UX is known as 'serendipity.' Serendipity refers to an unexpected but positive experience while using a system (Hart et al. 2008). There are mainly two ways that people perceive serendipity (Erdelez 1999). First, serendipity is determined based on past experiences. This is when a user is exposed to non-encountered information, or information that he/she has not been exposed to in prior experiences. The second way that people perceive serendipity is when they judge that an experience provides a completely new contextual situation. This refers to when a user feels enjoyment when he/she comes upon information that is highly relevant in a new context.

So why is the UX factor of serendipity effective in enhancing hedonistic value? It is because of the effects of unexpected value-facilitation or creativity (André et al. 2009; Lieberman 1995). Users who discover serendipity through unexpected experiences tend to use the system in their daily lives. For example, the recommended mixes in BEAT makes people look forward to further recommendations. Then users select a new mix, and they expect to enjoy an experience with new recommendations. Since users naturally seek a hedonistic value through enjoyment, serendipity has a direct influence on the hedonistic value.

Furthermore, serendipity enhances users' creativity through the product or service (André et al. 2009). In order for me to receive a hedonistic value through a certain system, then it is helpful for the system to provide me with opportunities to discover new things and stimulate creativity. A creative experience through a system affects the enjoyment of a new product or service, and this helps users achieve their goal of receiving a hedonistic value.

An example of how serendipity helps enhance hedonistic value is social dating services. Think about it. How would a user feel if a mobile dating application recommends a potential date's profile every morning? The user would then anticipate a recommendation every day at that specific time. Social dating applications have already seen explosive growth as users make in-app purchases to increase their chances of serendipity.

There are two types of design features that enhance serendipity: context-based contingent information and serendipitous pop-up interface.

6.5.1.1 Context-Based Contingent Information

Recent trends reveal that services that provide interaction based on usage context are popular. Analyses of usage contexts can help provide unexpected con-

Fig. 6.2 An example of context-based contingent information: BEAT. (Courtesy of BEAT, used with permission)

tent. A wide variety of content can be tailored to users based on algorithms that understand the connections between user preference and usage context information. For example, BEAT doesn't simply recommend similar genres or popular songs in a mix. It induces a serendipitous experience by recommending music based on how many users listened to a certain song under similar contexts. Figure 6.2 expresses unexpected song recommendations that made a user in our case study feel serendipity. The user said, "These three songs don't seem related in terms of genre or popularity, but they really helped relieve my stress after work. Two of them, 'I Don't Feel' and 'Living Like I Do' were hidden songs that I heard for the first time."

6.5.1.2 Serendipitous Pop-Up Interface

Pop-ups can provide serendipity to users without the user having to interact with the system first. For example, I Love Coffee induces users to experience serendipity in its world, even those who do not participate on a frequent basis, through continual pop-ups. When a regular guest comes near my coffee shop, the system launches a pop-up to persuade me to sell coffee to the guest. At times, the system also provides appropriate compensation to provide serendipity. Figure 6.3 shows that as my experience level increases, my employees' levels also increase, and a pop-up reveals an unexpected compensation for what I was able to achieve.

6.5.2 Playability

The Philips Hue light bulb transforms a practical product into a hedonistic one. For example, people turn on music and have a party at home with friends while the Hue changes its lights based on the beat of the music.

Fig. 6.3 An example of serendipitous pop-up interface: I Love Coffee. (Courtesy of I Love Coffee, used with permission)

Such UX is known as playability, which is an important UX factor that affects game experience. Playability refers to the degree of how much a user enjoyed a certain object under a given context (Sánchez et al. 2011; Sánchez et al. 2012). For example, a user can watch a movie while the Hue changes colors based on the scenes of the movie to provide a more vivid and enjoyable experience. This type of experience possesses high playability.

So why is the UX factor of playability effective in enhancing hedonistic values? It is because playability is related to the experience of gamers. A high playability makes people feel positive feelings towards the corresponding product or service (Norman 2004; Lazzaro 2008). For example, the Hue Christmas for Philips Hue application can be installed so that the lights and sound effects can change based on Christmas carols. This helps users to have a more enjoyable experience with the Hue. Hedonistic experience is related to the intrinsic value of how subjectively positive an experience is. Therefore, playability directly influences the creation of such intrinsic values.

A good example of how playability enhances hedonistic value is Candy Crush Saga, which is a mobile game that comprises of diverse colors of candy. The basic background of Candy Crush Saga is a candy factory. As gamers level up, the game background changes from bubble gum bridges, candy clouds, and other elements that portray fantasy worlds in fairy tales. There are also different types of candies such as striped candies, wrapper candies, and fish-shaped jelly that make users savor the candies while playing the game. Imagine if the game used blocks instead of candies while maintaining the same principles. It would be hard to imagine that it would have attracted the current 50 million daily users or even any interest whatsoever in the beginning of its launch. Without the candies, Candy Crush Saga would not be able to provide playability.

Two design features that enhance playability are tangible game interaction and share-based interaction.

6.5.2.1 Tangible Game Interaction

Tangible interaction utilizes physical objects to interact with digital information (Ishii and Ullmer 1997; Hornecker 2005). For example, in I Love Coffee, users must physically tilt the smartphone in order to pour milk in coffee during a barista test. As users tilt the angle of their smartphones and their bodies alike, milk gets poured in faster. As this type of interaction reflects that of physical properties, it is more enjoyable than interacting through taping or swiping on the screen (Fig. 6.4).

6.5.2.2 Share-Based Interaction

Interaction methods of sharing information with other users, such as the "share" button or a button that moves a user to another person's profile, help enhance playability. For example, the Philips Hue is merely a lightbulb but people have different ways of utilizing it so they are able to share themes and usage methods through meethue.com and discover new ways provided by other users and in that way feel enhanced playability.

Fig. 6.4 An example of tangible game interaction that enhances playability: I Love Coffee. (Courtesy of I Love Coffee, used with permission)

6.6   UX Factor and Design Features for Utilitarian Value

6.6.1   Compatibility

I was impressed by the Aimsak rechargeable driver drill 418 series because I could use it easily in many different circumstances. With a single driver drill, I can switch the tip and use for different purposes. Even if the same manufacturer does not make the tips, I can use the tips that fit the industrial standard. The method of use is the same for any tip, so I do not need to learn anything new to use it. Moreover, regardless of manufacturer or model, I can use the same voltage for the recharger and do not need to carry multiple rechargers.

This type of experience is known as compatibility, which refers to how well a person's value and the experience match with each other during the use of a product or service (Carter and Bélanger 2005; Rogers 1995). Compatibility is related to the attitude of how a person accepts an innovative service or product and their intention to use continually (Agarwal and Karahanna 1998; Wu and Wang 2005). For instance, if a person can use the same beats for a new drill product, then the person will perceive that the experience of using the new drill is compatible with the experience of using a prior drill and will then show a positive attitude towards it.

So why is the UX factor of compatibility effective in enhancing utilitarian value? It is because compatibility reduces the user's perceived risk and enhances the effectiveness of use. Compatibility refers to how well a prior experience, value, and need is reflected in the new experience. As such, it is easy to meet the user expectations of a product or service if compatibility is high (Wu and Wang 2005). For example, a drill recharger with high compatibility reflects well the experience and requirements of users who complain about how heavy it is to carry around multiple rechargers. A new experience with high compatibility enhances the utilitarian value of a product or a service by reducing risk and raising the efficiency of a task for the same purpose as that of a prior experience (Agarwal and Karahanna 1998).

Dropbox is a good example that illustrates how compatibility enhances utilitarian value. Dropbox supports Windows, Mac, Linux, and even other operating systems such as Blackberry's. Irrelevant of the device or operating system, I do not need to log in each time. I can open the Dropbox folder like I open any other folder to save and open files. It is also highly compatible with other applications when using Dropbox through mobile or tablet. The "export" function in Dropbox makes it easy to save and move files on a mobile device where it can ordinarily get quite tricky to do the same without Dropbox. It maintains the same experience as the desktop version in being able to open and save files. If Dropbox did not offer the range of compatibility that it does, it would not have been able to meet the utilitarian need of users to use the service quickly, easily, and efficiently.

Design features that enhance compatibility include standardization and human-like interaction.

Battery   Compatible Models

Fig. 6.5 An example of standardized interface that enhances compatibility: Rechargeable driver drill battery. (Courtesy of Aimsak Drill, used with permission)

6.6.1.1   Standardized Interface

A design has a greater compatibility when it follows a common standard (Collins 2013). It is important to design a product or service so that its functions are not just specialized for itself but shareable with other products and services. As Fig. 6.5 shows, a good example of standardization is a rechargeable driver drill battery compatible between 10.8V and 18V as long as the size fits, or an Android smartphone charger that can charge any Android phone regardless of manufacturer.

6.6.1.2   Human-Like Interaction

Human-like interaction refers to the application of interaction between human and system to be similar to that of human to human interaction such as a conversation

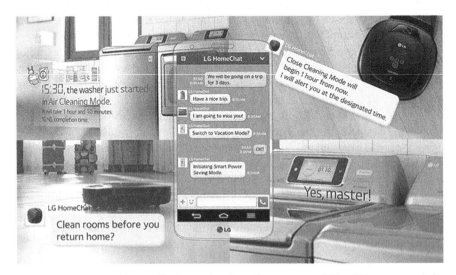

Fig. 6.6 An example of human-like interaction that enhances compatibility: Voice commands for LG Roboking. (Courtesy of LG, used with permission)

or gestures (SIRI 2014). For instance, the LG Roboking in Fig. 6.6 understands and follows the commands "come here," "start cleaning," "stop now," and "recharge." When the user says, "come here the robot finds the direction of where the voice is coming from and moves towards the user. The interaction of the product was designed to use natural commands rather than unnatural ones like "activate," "stop," and "clean" in order for the robot to perform its tasks. This is the same as Siri in Apple's iOS, which utilizes human-like interaction to listen to users and tell them interesting stories.

6.6.2 Consistency

When I used the Korean e-government's Minwon 24 the second time for another kind of certificate I needed, I saw how consistently it was assembled. Most of the screens in Minwon 24 are designed similarly. For example, the "issue certificate" button is always on the lower end of the screen in the form of a rectangular button.

This type of experience is known as consistency, which refers to the uniformity of the experience of using a system (Alonso-Ríos et al. 2009). There are two aspects of consistency, the first of which is the internal consistency while using a single system (Lin et al. 1997). For example, if the introduction page and the log out page of a system appear uniform during use, then the system possesses high internal consistency. The second type of consistency is called external consistency between systems. If I feel that the experience of using Minwon 24 is similar to another government website, then it possesses high external consistency.

So why is the UX factor of consistency effective in enhancing utilitarian value? It is because of the effects of transfer of skill and credibility that consistency provides (Monk 2000b). A highly consistent experience enables users to learn from the experience and apply it in another situation. For example, since I used Minwon 24 to issue my resident certificate, I was able to predict that issuing a land register would be a similar experience. I was correct and was able to issue the document with ease. Through such consistency, it will be easier to design utilitarian value since new tasks and situations will not prevent the user from performing a given task quickly and efficiently (Neilsen 1988). Furthermore, consistency creates more trust for the user towards the corresponding product or service (Clark and Montgomery 1998). Trust is a very important concept in designing utilitarian value because I need to first trust that the system will bring me my desired results before I place a utilitarian value on that system (Lee et al. 2013).

A good example that supports the notion that consistency enhances utilitarian value is the rental car service. No matter where we travel, we can start driving a rental car without too much difficulty. We get into the car, adjust the back and side mirrors, and drive away. Usually, we have never driven that specific type of car before, but there is no difficulty because most cars offer consistent UXs. I use my left hand to turn on the headlights, and I use my right hand to turn on the windshield wiper. Most buttons are also quite consistent throughout cars, thus enabling me to drive with ease. If I needed to learn and practice driving a rental car for a few hours before heading off, this service would have failed ages ago because it would not have been able to fulfill the utilitarian value of reaching a destination quickly and efficiently.

There are three design features that enhance consistency: consistent graphic interface, consistent interaction, and friendly information.

6.6.2.1 Consistent Graphic Interface

Screens of a single system should be designed with consistent themes and colors. Icons must also possess a consistent look, feel, and concept. In terms of a service, one way to provide consistency is to provide buttons at the same location on every page. For example, Easy Taxi uses the star icon to indicate "Favorites," which is an indirect way of letting the user know that this space is where the user's favorite content is stored, as shown in Fig. 6.7. Such consistent graphic user interface helps users navigate through a product or service more efficiently.

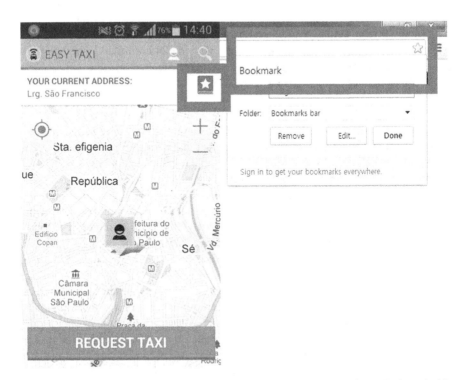

Fig. 6.7 An example of consistent graphic interface: Easy Taxi. (Courtesy of Easy Taxi, used with permission)

6.6.2.2   Consistent "Action-Results" Interaction

When a user performs a certain action, a system should provide consistent results relevant to the action. The LG Roboking robot vacuum cleaner can be controlled through a remote control or the smartphone application. As Fig. 6.8 reveals, each method of control provides consistent actions that lead to consistent results. For instance, using the arrows of the remote control moves the Roboking in the same way as using the arrow icons in the smartphone application. This type of design feature is known as consistent action-results interaction design. This design feature is similar to what design style guidelines require in general. For instance, the Microsoft style guide emphasizes consistent action-results, which is why pressing CTRL+C in Microsoft Word provides the same results of copying as pressing CTRL+C in Microsoft Excel.

6.6.2.3   Friendly Information Design

This type of design feature provides system information based on everyday life experience. This could be the choice of everyday life words or words from familiar tools or devices. For instance, Easy Taxi uses familiar words from everyday life in

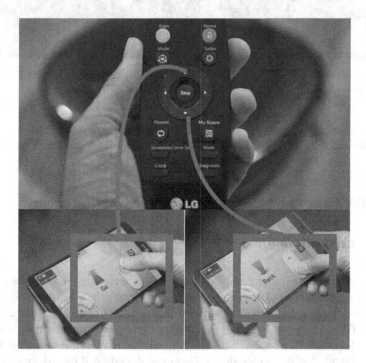

Fig. 6.8 An example of consistent "action-results" interaction that enhances consistency: LG Roboking. (Source: social.lge.co.kr/view/the_bloger/roboking-single, courtesy of LG, used with permission)

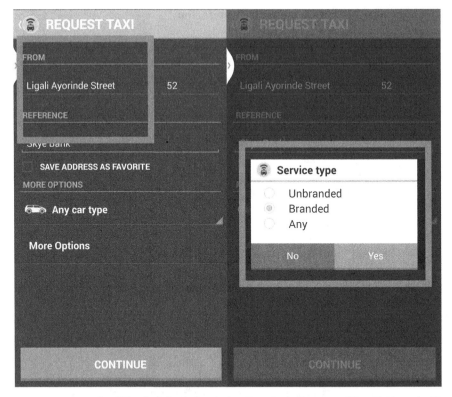

Fig. 6.9 An example of friendly information design: Easy Taxi. (Courtesy of Easy Taxi, used with permission)

the taxi reservation screen as shown in Fig. 6.9. Familiar words are also used for examples and other additional information that is provided when reserving a taxi.

6.7   UX Factor and Design Features for User Autonomy

6.7.1   Customizability

As I mentioned previously, Easy Taxi has many aspects that the user can control while using the service. For example, users can input detailed information about nearby buildings or landmarks in addition to automatically registering their addresses using GPS. This enables users to accurately express their intentions of where to be picked up, and the location of the taxi is illustrated in real-time on a map, where users can send feedback to the driver. Users can directly call the driver to request something, and they can easily cancel a pick up if they no longer need the taxi.

This type of experience has high customizability, which refers to the perception of how the user can change the system based on preference and circumstance (Nidumolu and Knotts 1998; Teng 2010; Orehovacki 2010). In the sense that the system changes based on circumstance, customizability is often compared to personalization. However, while personalization enables changes to the system without the user knowing, customization provides users with direct autonomy and options to create the circumstances they want. For example, showing the option to select a frequently selected address at the top of the screen in Easy Taxi is personalization, while being able to change the order of the addresses provides high customizability (Teng 2010; Nurkka 2013).

So why is the UX factor of consistency effective in enhancing user autonomy? It is because of process flexibility and a process that is user initiated (Nidumolu and Knotts 1998; Nurkka 2013). An experience with high customizability provides users with the authority to control or change a product or service according to specific circumstances. For example, if I want to change my pickup location in Easy Taxi, I can press the call button and discuss it directly with the driver. This speedy change after a user's control provides the perception that the user is in control. Also, the user who controls the system also knows the result of his/her required resource, time, and actions and is able to autonomously input control to the system. Therefore, the user customizes the system to suit his/her need. For example, detailed location settings in Easy Taxi enable users to perceive autonomy over the system, and they feel as if Easy Taxi is their personal driver.

A good example of customizability is the Android smartphone launcher. The preloaded launcher does not cause any problems while using a mobile phone's functions, but many people download third-party launchers. This is because launchers can help customize users' phones to make them "theirs." By downloading an Android launcher, many elements such as the dock bar, icons, and background can be customized. Users can reorganize their screens to fit their use patterns. If launchers were pre-designed and users were not able to change the icons, background color, themes, etc., then not as many people would be using launchers nowadays because it would not be able to fulfill their desires and to reveal their personalities.

There are two design features that can enhance customizability: preview and task manager.

6.7.1.1 Preview

A preview shows the results of an action before it actually takes place so that the user can check and revise it (Create a Sim 2014). For example, as shown in Fig. 6.10, I Love Coffee provides a preview of the coffee shop when I first buy and decorate it. I can check different areas to select, and I can rotate or delete items. An example of a preview in a product is the feature to check the performance of the device even when it is not processing something. For instance, a driver drill should indicate in which direction the drill will rotate and how fast the speed will be even when I am not using it. The process of preview, as well as revision based on the preview

Fig. 6.10 An example of graphic interface that provide preview: I Love Coffee. (Courtesy of I Love Coffee, used with permission)

results, enables users to conduct their tasks with precision and helps them perceive that they are directly in control of the system.

6.7.1.2 Task Manager

A task manager shows information to the users that helps them understand the mechanisms of the system (Windows Task Manager 2014). This can be explained through the process monitoring a system. As Fig. 6.11 shows, a user needs to know exactly how each part functions, whether the parts are replaceable, and whether they are

Battery (sold separately)

Steering Servo Front Bumper
(sold separately)

Friction Damper

Receiver
(sold separately)

Diff. Gear built-in
closed gear box

Front
Suspension

Bath Tub Frame

Electronic Speed
Controller

Wide Grooved Tire

540 Type Motor

Rear Suspension

Square Spike Tire

One-Piece Wheel

Fig. 6.11 An example of information design with high customizability: RC car. (Courtesy of Tamiya, used with permission)

compatible with other products in order to predict how to tune the RC car according to the user's needs. During this time, information about the mechanism of the RC car should be shown in an understandable level to users. As another example, if the real-time taxi indicator on the Easy Taxi map was shown as coordinates rather than an icon, users would feel unclear as to where the taxi is and when it will arrive. A task manager provides users with the option of controlling what they used to think of as areas of the system. Through this process, users can adjust how the system should be set up to enhance their efficiency, and this strengthens user autonomy.

6.7.2 Challenge

'I Love Coffee' continually provides an appropriate level of goals to users. When you first start the game, there is a series of easy level quests. Not all quests are required to be completed to play the game, but the quests help the user become familiar with the game and its functions. As the game progresses, harder quests arise. For example, a user needs to understand the preferences of regular customers and provide them with the appropriate drink. During this process, the user must figure out the correct milk temperature and the type of syrup the customer prefers, to get his or her attention. Once the user gets the customer's attention, then the customer provides the user with a gift to compensate the user for the effort.

This kind of experience is called an experience with an appropriate challenge. Challenge refers to the matching of a user's skills and experience to ignite positive motivation (Wang and Wang 2008; Chung and Tan 2004; Kiili 2005). Challenge can be explained through the degree of difficulty that a user perceives. Challenge is an important concept that is part of Mihaly Csikszentmihalyi's (Hungarian psychologist) optimal experience. If a challenge related to a task is in an optimal level that is neither too difficult nor easy, then a user can be fully immersed into the corresponding task (Csikszentmihalyi 1991).

So why is the UX factor of challenge effective in enhancing user autonomy? It is because of the intention and level of difficulty that a user perceives during a challenge (Wong et al. 2006). When a high challenge experience is provided to a user with the appropriate level of skill, the motivation to overcome perceived difficulty is created along with the intention to use. For example, it is difficult at first to perform graphic tasks through a professional tablet. But after using it multiple times and adjusting the sensitivity of the tablet to suit my skills, the tasks become as easy as performing them on paper, which encourages me to perform more graphic tasks on the tablet. As users desire to control more aspects of the system, they feel high autonomy.

The game Angry Birds provides a good example of how an experience with a high challenge helps enhance user autonomy. In Angry Birds, a user uses his/her finger to touch a bird character and throw it with a pellet gun towards a group of pigs. There are finite numbers of birds to throw in each stage. The objective of the game is to score high with the same finite number of birds. At the end of each stage, the user's score is displayed through stars. The highest score is three stars, and the lowest score is one star. Users generally set their aim to get the three stars before they start the game. The perceived difficulty is high, as users must consider obstacles, the angle of the throw, and the weight of the bird into consideration. Nevertheless, users continually attempt to achieve their objective of three stars. This is an example of a game with high challenge that provides users with active control of the game's elements.

There are two design features that enhance a challenge: personalized difficulty and goal-oriented information.

6.7.2.1   Personalized Difficulty

One way to design a high challenge is to provide interaction with personalized difficulty. In the field of system development, this interaction design pattern is known as dynamic difficulty adjustment (DDA), which allows users to select their own difficulty level (Yun et al. 2010). For example, 'I Love Coffee' provides quests that are different based on a user's level as shown in Fig. 6.12. Users receive quests fit for their level and also receive additional assistance to fulfill them so that they don't give up.

Fig. 6.12 An example of personalized difficulty that enhances challenge: I Love Coffee. (Courtesy of I Love Coffee, used with permission)

6.7.2.2 Goal-Oriented Information

Goal-oriented information shows how much the results of a user's actions contribute to the achievement of a goal. Let's take the customization example of 'I Love Coffee.' In I Love Coffee, decoration points are important in expanding a user's coffee shop. Regardless of the profit of a coffee shop, a user needs to achieve a certain number of decoration points in order to expand his/her coffee shop. As Fig. 6.13 shows, each item in the item shop shows how many decoration points it is worth through an image and a number. This type of information help users buy items to fill their decoration points. When users need a lot of decoration points, they can buy items that provide many points, while if they only require few points, they can buy an item worth the few points needed in order to reach the goal.

6.8 UX Factor and Design Features for System Autonomy

6.8.1 Agent-Awareness

Let's go back to the example of the robot vacuum cleaner. The more someone uses a robot vacuum cleaner, the less attention is required since the robot lets the user know of its progress. The robot vacuum cleaner does not merely function as a vacuum cleaner but it is also designed to let the user be aware that it aids his/her overall cleaning experience. For example, the robot vacuum cleaner lets the user know when the cleaning starts and ends with its voice and can do that as well via a smart-

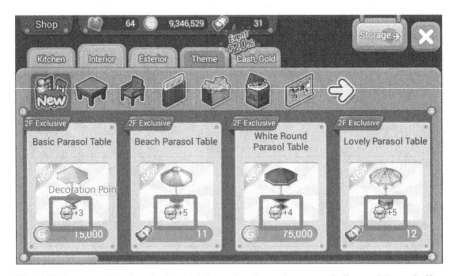

Fig. 6.13 An example of goal-oriented information that enhances a challenge: I Love Coffee. (Courtesy of I Love Coffee, used with permission)

phone application. Through this experience, users perceive the robot as an agent that helps them clean rather than a mere product that is being used.

This type of experience is known as agent-awareness. The agent here refers to a computer system that can take autonomous action within a certain environment for a specific purpose (Wooldridge and Jennings 1995).

The agent can be explained through the concept of situational awareness because the agent is aware of its surroundings until it arises to complete a specific objective. Situational awareness refers to the instant awareness of the surrounding environment (Neerincx et al. 2000). A more specific definition refers to it as the awareness of the components within a spatio-temporal environment. This type of awareness helps users instantly understand the elements of the near future that may influence them (Fore and Sculli 2013). Situational awareness helps provide an experience for a product or service without having to continually be aware. For example, the robot vacuum cleaner can come across many obstacles in its process, but it doesn't inform the user; it only provides the procedural situation to the users so that they perceive they are getting the experience of cleaning.

So why is the UX factor of agent-awareness effective in enhancing system autonomy? It is because the effects of the predictability and task-technology fit the agent-awareness of the product or service provides to users (Huang et al. 2012; Merikle et al. 2001; Fore and Sculli 2013). As it becomes easier to predict the pattern of a product or service, users seek to give their autonomy to an agent-aware product or service. For example, as users learn to predict how a robot vacuum cleaner cleans automatically without having to pay attention to it, users perceive the robot vacuum cleaner as an agent related to cleaning. Users can expect to have the experience of cleaning through the robot, and the fulfillment of this desire enhances the experience of system autonomy. Because system autonomy can be experienced without the user having to control or intervene, it is important to perceive the possibility of prediction that this experience will be fulfilled. Therefore, agent-awareness directly influences the development of such system autonomy. Furthermore, agent-awareness shows differences in the effect of how accurate the performance of the agent's task is (Dishaw and Strong 1999; Serenko 2008). In order for an experience of system autonomy to take place, the system must help the user perceive agent-awareness in terms of process by reducing the amount of intervention by the user while performing the desired task.

Smart keys for automobiles provide a good example of how agent awareness can enhance a system's autonomous experience. The automobile's antenna communicates with the smart key to provide a diverse UX such as automatic door unlock and ignition initiation to the car. It also provides situationally aware experiences such as unlocking a door when the automobile senses that a user is pulling the door handle. Based on these interactions the user perceives that the smart key possesses autonomy for the benefit of the user, and the automobile is considered as an agent. Such agent-awareness helps the user naturally provide control of the system without feeling the pressure of having to control the system.

There are two design features that enhance agent-awareness: situation-based system initiated interaction and responsive interface.

6.8.1.1   Situation-Based System Initiated Interaction

This interaction technology predicts the objective of a user and provides situational interaction fit to fulfill that objective. Such interaction does not need human intervention; it makes users give up their control to the experience of the system. Through the experience, the robot provides users the perception that it is not merely a cleaning device; it is a product that helps users feel the experience of cleaning. The development of interaction technology utilizing cameras and sensors has helped products such as the robot vacuum cleaner to become a smart product that understands its context and performs actions appropriate to its environment. As shown in Fig. 6.14, the LG Roboking uses cameras and sensors to avoid obstacles and sense the texture of the floor in order to select the appropriate method of cleaning.

6.8.1.2   Responsive Interface

Responsive interface refers to a type of interface that organically interacts with people based on situation and context rather than function in a mechanical, static manner. For example, the BEAT music service uses a responsive interface to provide users with mixes that are appropriate for the situation and context; this helps users become aware that a system agent is present. More specifically, BEAT uses data such as the day's weather, temperature, genre, and other basic information to help users select an appropriate mix name. This helps users experience the awareness of BEAT as an agent that helps recommend music. For example, Fig. 6.15 shows that BEAT recommended "twenty-first century Lullaby," "Coffee Shop Atmosphere," and "Time with You" (left) during the night when I couldn't fall asleep, while it recommend "Morning Stretching," "Mom, I Think I Like Somebody," and "Shall we Run Today" in the morning.

'Magic Eye' for
detecting environmental situation   Sensor can detect the floor material

Fig. 6.14 An example of situation-based system initiated interaction: The LG Roboking. (Courtesy of LG, used with permission)

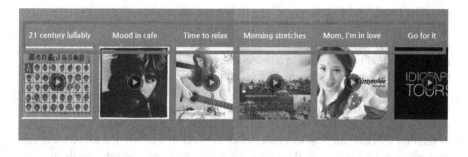

in the night   in the morning

Fig. 6.15 An example of responsive interface: BEAT. (Courtesy of BEAT, used with permission)

6.8.2 *Adaptivity*

The robot vacuum cleaner was impressive to me because it adapted to my house right away. When I use the Home Master function, I could tell how well my robot vacuum cleaner had adapted to my house as it remembered where furniture and other obstacles were and minimized crashes with them. Also, other functions of the robot vacuum cleaner adapted to the situation. For example, when a problem arises with the robot, it diagnoses itself and informs the user of the proper procedures on how to solve the problem.

This type of a UX factor is called adaptivity, which refers to how system adapts to what users desire (Heerink et al. 2010). Adaptivity is largely divided into eight elements:

- Input
- Selected user variables
- Identification Inference Mechanism
- Interaction Model
- Decision Inference
- Environmental Variables
- Selection Mechanism
- Evaluation Mechanism

The first element is input (Rothrock et al. 2002). For example, if a user is familiar with using the keyboard or mouse to input information on the computer, then adaptivity has taken place with the input element. The second element is selected user variables. For instance, if a system can change a user address throughout all of the user's registered accounts on websites at once, then the user does not need to go to every website changing the address. The third element is identification inference mechanism, which combines user's personal information and analyzes what the user thinks is important in terms of product value, and then this analysis is utilized in marketing or advertisement by the company that provides the service or system. The fourth and fifth elements are an interaction model and decision inference. These refer to adjusting the interaction method by understanding the age of the user or device usage capability. The sixth is environmental variables. An example of this is when air conditioning units in a home adapt to a hot summer day and accordingly maintain the indoor temperature. The seventh is known as the selection mechanism, which controls the range and level of automation. For example, during the purchasing process in an internet shopping mall, the system controls the length of an advertisement that reflects a user's needs. Finally, the eighth element is called the evaluation mechanism. For example, after evaluating whether the previous seven elements were adapted well through service usage patterns, or other tools to measure satisfaction, the evaluation mechanism takes these results to provide changes to the system for adaptation. These eight elements of adaptability help to identify specifically how adaptability must take place at which stage.

So what is the reason adaptability enhances system autonomy? It is because of the low cognitive workload that adaptability provides (Rothrock et al. 2002). A high adaptability experience does not need to consider many variables since the need for situational awareness is reduced, and then cognitive workload is lowered to enhance system autonomy. For example, the ultrasound sensor of the robot vacuum cleaner can analyze every space and, as a result, clean more efficiently.

A good example of how adaptivity enhances the value of automation is the "find road" function of a GPS navigation system. When driving our car using the GPS navigation system, the first thing we do is to look for traffic conditions. However, the further the destination, the harder it is to consider all the traffic conditions and the roads we must drive. Also, traffic conditions change by the hour, so it is almost impossible to drive while considering all of these variables. This is when the GPS navigation comes in handy as it calculates the optimal roads to take while calculating all sorts of variables. It does not require much cognitive effort by users. Furthermore, users do not have to rely on the GPS navigation during the entire trip. I can configure the system so that it recalculates my route if I deviate from the original proposal. If the GPS navigation system was to inform me only of the optimal path at the beginning of my drive, it would most likely not have become such a popular system for users because all cars would then take the same road and cause immense traffic as well it would be troublesome for the user to ask for new directions every time he or she deviates from the original path.

There are two design features that enhance adaptivity: adaptive interface and context-aware computing.

6.8.2.1   Adaptive interface

This interface changes its graphic interface by considering the user and situational variables (Rothrock et al. 2002). For example, a user can configure the main page of a frequently visited website. The main page is the first interaction point between the user and the website. How quickly a user can move from the main page to its destination affects the mobility of the user greatly. In this case, the main page can

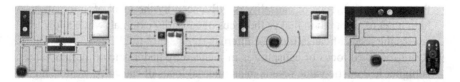

Fig. 6.16 An example of context-aware computing: LG Roboking. (Source: http://www.lge. co.kr/lgekr/product/detail/LgekrProductDetailCmd.laf?prdid=EPRD.278653, courtesy of I Love Coffee, used with permission)

provide links or menu icons that lead the user to his/her desired destination. This is the reason why many main pages have sections that show links to frequently visited pages. As another example, the Philips Hue analyzes when the user is asleep or awake to automatically provide different brightness. It also analyzes the weather so that when it rains, it alerts the user by displaying a different color. Through these actions, an adaptive interface can enhance adaptability (http://www.pcmag.com/article2/0,2817,2417107,00.asp).

6.8.2.2 Context-Aware Computing

This technology is utilized for dynamic and flexible interaction where the contextual change of the user is important (Schilit et al. 1994). Basically, context-aware computing adapts interaction elements by adjusting interaction based on the user's context without any effort required by the user. For example, playing a multiplayer role-playing video game well through the night can cause user's eyes to become tired. Context-aware computing analyzes that and increases the brightness of the screen so that the user's eyes feel more comfortable. In another example, Fig. 6.16 shows how the robot vacuum cleaner analyzes the structure of the house and optimizes its cleaning path. The ultrasound sensors attached to its front and the Home Master function that provides spatial recognition enable the robot vacuum cleaner to utilize the location information.

6.9 Summary

- Locus of causality is a strategically effective dimension that controls the judgmental thread of experience.
- Locus of causality is divided into two types of levers, process-oriented and result-oriented loci of causality.
- Process-oriented locus of causality refers to how much of the process of using a product or service a person can control.
- Result-oriented locus of causality refers to how a person evaluates the value of an experience after the use of a product or a service.

- Process-oriented locus of causality is influenced by the level of automation. A high level of automation makes the locus of causality external, while a low level causes the locus of causality to be internal.
- Result-oriented locus of causality is influenced by hedonistic/utilitarian values. A higher hedonistic value results in an internal locus of causality, while a higher utilitarian value results in an external locus of causality.
- The UX factors of serendipity and playability are important in providing a hedonistic value.
- The UX factors of compatibility and consistency are important in providing a utilitarian value.
- The UX factors of customizability and challenge are important in enhancing user autonomy.
- The UX factors of agent-awareness and adaptability are important in enhancing system autonomy.

6.10   Discussion Topics

- Think of a recent case when the process-oriented locus of causality was very internal while using a digital product or service. Why do you think the process provided an internal process-oriented locus of causality? What were the design features that induced this?
- Think of a recent case when the process-oriented locus of causality was very external while using a digital product or service. Why do you think the process provided an external process-oriented locus of causality? What were the design features that induced this?
- Think of a recent case when the result-oriented locus of causality was very internal after using a digital product or service. Why do you think the result provided an internal result-oriented locus of causality? What were the design features that induced this?
- Think of a recent case when the result-oriented locus of causality was very external after using a digital product or service. Why do you think the result provided an external result-oriented locus of causality? What were the design features that induced this?

References

Agarwal R, Karahanna E (1998) On the multi-dimensional nature of compatibility beliefs in technology acceptance. In Proceedings of the 19th Annual International Conference on Information Systems (pp 13–16). End Fragment

Alonso-Ríos D, Vázquez-García A, Mosqueira-Rey E, Moret-Bonillo V (2009) Usability: a critical analysis and a taxonomy. Int J Hum-Comput Interact 26(1):53–74

André P, Teevan J, Dumais ST (2009) Discovery is never by chance: designing for (un) serendipity. In Proceedings of the seventh ACM conference on Creativity and cognition (pp 305–314). ACM

Arias JDLF (2004). Recent perspectives in the study of motivation: goal orientation theory. Electron J Res Educ Psychol 2(1):35–62

Batra R, Ahtola OT (1991) Measuring the hedonistic and utilitarian sources of consumer attitudes. Mark lett 2(2):159–170

Boo HC, Mattila A (2003) Effect of hedonistic and utilitarian goals in similarity judgment of a hotel-restaurant brand alliance. In The 3 rd international conference on electronic business conference, National University of Singapore

Carter L, Bélanger F (2005) The utilization of e-government services: citizen trust, innovation and acceptance factors*. Inf Syst J 15(1):5–25

Chung J, Tan FB (2004) Antecedents of perceived playfulness: an exploratory study on user acceptance of general information-searching websites. Inf Manage 41(7):869–881

Clark BH, Montgomery DB (1998) Deterrence, reputations, and competitive cognition. Manage Sci 44(1):62–82

Collins, K (19 December 2013) Mobile phone chargers to be standardised under EU law. Wired. http://www.wired.co.uk/news/archive/2013-12/19/universal-phone-charger. Accessed 4 Aug 2014

Create a Sim (16 August 2014) The sims wiki. http://sims.wikia.com/wiki/Create_a_Sim. Accessed 4 Aug 2014

Csikszentmihalyi M (1991) Flow: the psychology of optimal experience, vol 41. HarperPerennial, New York

Dishaw MT, Strong DM (1999) Extending the technology acceptance model with task–technology fit constructs. Inf Manage 36(1):9–21

Erdelez S (1999) Information encountering: it's more than just bumping into information. Bull Am Soc Inf Sci Technol 25(3):26–29

Fore AM, Sculli GL (2013) A concept analysis of situational awareness in nursing. J Adv Nurs 69(12):2613–2621

Goodrich MA, Schultz AC (2007) Human-robot interaction: a survey. Found trends Hum-Comput Interact 1(3):203–275

Hart J, Ridley C, Taher F, Sas C, Dix A (2008) Exploring the facebook experience: a new approach to usability. In Proceedings of the 5th Nordic conference on Human-computer interaction: building bridges (pp 471–474). ACM. End Fragment

Heerink M, Kröse B, Evers V, Wielinga B (2010) Assessing acceptance of assistive social agent technology by older adults: the Almere model. Int J Soc Robot 2(4):361–375

Hidi S, Harackiewicz JM (2000) Motivating the academically unmotivated: a critical issue for the twenty-first century. Rev Educ Res 70(2):151–179

Ho LA, Kuo TH, Lin B (2010) Influence of online learning skills in cyberspace. Internet Res 20(1):55–71

Hornecker E (2005) A design theme for tangible interaction: embodied facilitation. In ECSCW 2005. Springer, Netherlands, pp 23–43

Huang YY, Moll J, Sallnäs EL, Sundblad Y (2012) Auditory feedback in haptic collaborative interfaces. Int J Hum-Comput Stud 70(4):257–270

Ishii H, Ullmer B (March 1997) Tangible bits: towards seamless interfaces between people, bits and atoms. In Proceedings of the ACM SIGCHI conference on human factors in computing systems (pp 234–241). ACM

Kiili K (2005) Digital game-based learning: towards an experiential gaming model. Internet High Educ 8(1):13–24

Lazzaro M (2008) Game usability: advice from the experts for advancing the player experience. In: Isbister K, Schaffer N (eds) Morgan Kaufmann. pp 315–345

Lee J, Lee D, Moon J, Park MC (2013) Factors affecting the perceived usability of the mobile web portal services: comparing simplicity with consistency. Inf Technol Manage 14(1):43–57

Li D, Ji S, Li W (2006) Information management environment, business strategy, and the effectiveness of information systems strategic planning. PACIS 2006 Proceedings, pp. 531–547

Lieberman H (1995) Letizia: an agent that assists web browsing. IJCAI 1:924–929

Lin HX, Choong YY, Salvendy G (1997) A proposed index of usability: a method for comparing the relative usability of different software systems. Behav Inf Technol 16(4–5):267–277

Merikle PM, Smilek D, Eastwood JD (2001) Cognition perception without awareness: perspectives from cognitive psychology. Cognition 79(1–2):115–134

Monk A (2000a) Noddy's guide to consistency. Interfaces 45:4–7

Monk A (2000b) User-centred design. In Home informatics and telematics. Springer, US, pp 181–190

Neerincx MA, Lindenberg J, Rypkema J, Van Besouw S (2000) A practical cognitive theory of web-navigation: explaining age-related performance differences. In Position Paper CHI 2000 Workshop Basic Research Symposium

Neilsen J (1988) Coordinating user interfaces for consistency. Technical report Department of computer science, Technical University of Denmark

Nidumolu SR, Knotts GW (1998) The effects of customizability and reusability on perceived process and competitive performance of software firms. MiS Q 22(2):105–137

Nurkka P (2013) "Nobody other than me knows what I want:" customizing a sports watch. In Human-Computer Interaction–INTERACT 2013. Springer, Berlin, pp 384–402

Orehovacki T (June 2010) Proposal for a set of quality attributes relevant for Web 2.0 application success. In Information Technology Interfaces (ITI), 2010 32nd International Conference on (pp 319–326). IEEE

Parasuraman R, Sheridan TB, Wickens CD (2000) A model for types and levels of human interaction with automation. IEEE Transact Syst Man Cybern Part A Syst Hum 30(3):286–297

Pintrich PR (2000) Multiple goals, multiple pathways: the role of goal orientation in learning and achievement. J Educ Psychol 92(3):544–555

Rothrock L, Koubek R, Fuchs F, Haas M, Salvendy G (2002) Review and reappraisal of adaptive interfaces: toward biologically inspired paradigms. Theor Issues Ergon Sci 3(1):47–84

Rogers E (1995) Diffusion of innovations. The Free Press, New York

Ryan RM, Deci EL (2000) Self-determination theory and the facilitation of intrinsic motivation, social development, and well-being. Am Psychol 55(1):68–78

Sánchez JLG, Iranzo RMG, Vela FLG (2011) Enriching evaluation in video games. In Human-Computer Interaction–INTERACT 2011. Springer, Berlin, pp 519–522

Sánchez JLG, Vela FLG, Simarro FM, Padilla-Zea N (2012) Playability: analysing user experience in video games. Behav Inform Technol 31(10):1033–1054

Schilit B, Adams N, Want R (December 1994) Context-aware computing applications. In Mobile computing systems and applications, 1994. WMCSA 1994. First Workshop on (pp 85–90). IEEE

Serenko A (2008) A model of user adoption of interface agents for email notification. Interact Comput 20(4):461–472

SIRI (15 April 2014) What is better? Mac Or Windows? Siri-ism. http://www.siri-isms.com/better-mac-windows-2054/. Accessed 4 Aug 2014

Teng CI (2010) Customization, immersion satisfaction, and online gamer loyalty. Comput Hum Behav 26(6):1547–1554

Wang HY, Wang YS (2008) Gender differences in the perception and acceptance of online games. Br J Educ Technol 39(5):787–806

Windows Task Manager (6 June 2014). Wikipedia, the free encyclopedia. http://en.wikipedia.org/wiki/Windows_Task_Manager. Accessed 28 Aug 2014

Wong KW, Fung CC, Depickere A, Rai S (2006) Static and dynamic difficulty level design for edutainment game using artificial neural networks. In Technologies for E-Learning and Digital Entertainment. Springer, Berlin, pp 463–472

Wooldridge M, Jennings NR (1995) Intelligent agents: theory and practice. The Knowl Eng Rev 10(02):115–152

Wu H, Wang SC (2005) What drives mobile commerce? An empirical evaluation of the revised technology acceptance model. Inf Manage 42(5):719–729

Yun C, Trevino P, Holtkamp W, Deng Z (July 2010). PADS: enhancing gaming experience using profile-based adaptive difficulty system. In Proceedings of the 5th ACM SIGGRAPH symposium on video games (pp 31–36). ACM

Chapter 7
Design for Harmonious Experience

7.1 Introduction

From the perspective of compositional experience, we want to achieve harmonious relationships between people, products, and services in our environment. In order to achieve a harmonious relationship between any one of those items and within each category, the right level of relational cohesiveness is necessary. Relational cohesiveness is an important dimension that affects the compositional thread of experience with respect to changes in the environment. If so, which levers control relational cohesiveness? Which UX factors are important for achieving a harmonious experience? What types of design features help us to have harmonious experiences with products and services?

7.2 Incheon Airport: A Highly-Cohesive International Travel Service

I had to go on a business trip to Munich recently. As usual, I had finish off some academic work before the trip, so I stayed up late the evenings running up to the trip. I then had to get up early to catch the early-morning flight. I tried to figure out what would be the most convenient and quickest way to get to the airport. A ride with a taxi from my doorstep to the terminal might be the best option but another very convenient option would be the express train from Seoul station to the airport.

I can easily take the metro from close to my house to Seoul station, where they offer an express train service to Incheon airport. I can even check my luggage in at the station and finish the passport control procedure before getting on the train. By choosing this option over a taxi saves me much time, not to mention that I can get rid of all the physical and psychological burden of riding in the traffic.

The online version of this chapter (doi: 10.1007/978-3-319-14304-0_7) contains supplementary material.

J. Kim, *Design for Experience*, Human-Computer Interaction Series,
DOI 10.1007/978-3-319-14304-0_7

Furthermore, I can use the free Wi-Fi available on the metro and on the express train. So I deemed the metro and the express train as the optimal choise. On the way I replied to several emails and wrapped up the unfinished work, before safely arriving at the airport.

I always try to arrive at the airport well before departure just to be sure and to have time to successfully finish the homework assigned by my wife at the duty-free shop or terminal. It takes quite some time to shop for gifts, but luckily I don't have to carry them around throughout the shop or terminal. The products I shopped for are directly sent to the pickup desk nearby my departure gate. After I finish my shopping, I can just walk towards my gate and present my flight ticket and passport to the pick-up desk to collect the items I purchased earlier. This is all possible because the duty-free shops and the airport services are closely linked to each other.

The smartphone application provided by Incheon Airport is also very useful. It gives me information about a variety of services offered at the airport such as menus of the restaurants and the location of the parking lots. If I set my departure schedule in advance, it also reminds me of the time of flight with push alerts and helps me easily locate the departure gate through a navigation service.

On this trip, I tried to cut down my budget by having a layover in Frankfurt before arriving in Munich. The baggage I checked in at Seoul station before getting on the express train was directly transported to Munich without me having to pick it up in Frankfurt. This requires a well-connected, streamlined shipping process throughout the airports and airlines all over the world.

Incheon airport offers the right services at the right moment in an automated fashion. Each and every service is not only very useful and special on its own, but I was exceptionally pleased to find the services to be extremely well aligned and smoothly connected. I believe this is why Incheon airport has been ranked number one in the ASQ Global Ranking for the last nine consecutive years, and we are able to enjoy a harmonious experience at the airport.

7.3   Relational Cohesiveness

We have seen how the services within Incheon airport are tightly connected to each other: the express train transportation service, its WIFI service, the check-in service, the duty-free shopping service, and many other services. The degree to which people or systems are connected to each other is referred to as relational cohesiveness. As illustrated in the 3-D figure below, relationships among the services at Incheon airport can be seen as highly cohesive (Fig. 7.1).

As explained earlier in Chapter 2, the concept of relational cohesiveness was originally used in sociology to explain the relationship between people. The concept was later extended to further explain the human relationship with products or services (Moody and White 2003; Friedkin 2004). It measures the tightness of a relationship not only between people but also between people and systems, both products and services, as well as between the systems themselves.

So what are the important factors that determine relational cohesiveness in human experience? According to the networks theory, a group can be analyzed in terms of connectivity or distribution (Yamagishi et al. 1988). The former is

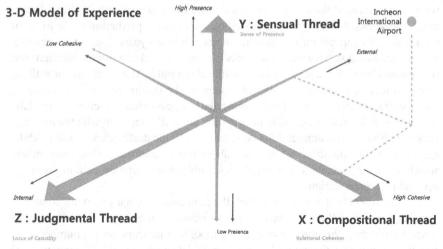

Fig. 7.1 A three dimensional model of the Incheon Airport experience

concerned with the one-to-one relationships between the members of a network, while the latter is concerned with the property of a network as a whole. When discussing the relational cohesiveness of a group, both connectivity and distribution have to be considered. If we put our focus only on connectivity, we can easily miss the characteristic of an entire network. Likewise, if we only consider the distribution, relationships between the individuals that compose the network can be overlooked.

Density is a property concerned with the connectivity of members of a network, and centrality is a property concerned with the distribution of an overall network structure. Let's take a deeper look into these two properties in the following section.

7.3.1   Density: A Key Lever of Connectivity

Most people know of the Swiss Army knife. A Swiss Army knife usually comes with a sharp blade along with various tools such as mini scissors, can opener, key holder, etc. It was named after the army knife manufactured by a Swiss company, Victorinox, but these became so popular that the term "Swiss Army knife" has now become a standard English noun that refers to most other multi-purpose knives with similar functions and shapes (http://www.victorinox.com/ch/content/swissarmy). One interesting thing about the tools in the Swiss Army knife is that they are not necessarily related to each other and each serves its unique purpose. For example, the scissors and the can opener are not meant to be used together, although they are placed next to each other in the Army knife.

On the other hand, let us think of a GPS navigation service on a smartphone (http://www.tmap.co.kr/tmap2/navigation/tmap40/tmap_introduce.jsp). GPS services recommend the shortest or fastest route based on real-time traffic information. Oftentimes, I find myself surprised by the accurate prediction made from the road data and temporal information aggregated over the years. It also features a real-time streaming service that broadcasts the current road conditions. Furthermore, the system also makes use of the information about public transportation or walking routes to recommend the best possible routes to the destination. It is important to note that these functions are closely connected to one another. Functions or modules that deal with the real-time traffic information are well integrated with the map data on smartphones to recommend the optimal route to the destination. These modules can also access and share information about bus or metro schedules and routes, which makes it possible to easily integrate public transportation data in providing optimal recommendations.

Density refers to the extent to which the members within a group are connected or related to each other (Friedkin 1981). In networks theory, density can be computed by dividing the number of existing links in a network by the number of all possible links within the network. For example, let us take a look at the two network structures in Fig. 7.2. Both structures have four nodes. In the figure on the right, all the nodes are linked to each other, so the density is one. The network structure on the left is only comprised of three links while there can be a total of six links. Therefore this structure has a density of 0.5.

The concept of density was first introduced in 1950. For the next 60 years and forth, density has been the most widely used property that describes a network (Kephart 1950). It is because density deals with two important aspects regarding the connectivity of a network (Wasserman 1994). The first important aspect is the connectivity between the nodes itself. As described earlier, density is concerned with whether the nodes are connected to each other or not, and it is measured based on all the possible connections that can take place within a network. The second important aspect is if the connections are unidirectional or bidirectional, for density

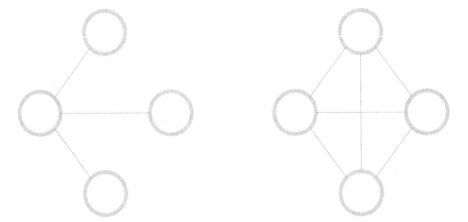

Fig. 7.2 Two network structures of different density

is generally computed based on bidirectional connections. Let us go back to the example of GPS navigation system. Public transportation related services and map services send and receive information with one another to recommend the optimal path. In other words, the relationship between the two modules is bidirectional and of a high density. In contrast, a Swiss Army knife is a low-density product because its components are not directly related to each other in terms of two-way communication. As such, density can explain connectivity and bi-directionality of the nodes in a network well (Friedkin 1981). In this way, density is a key lever that can control the level of relational cohesiveness.

7.3.2   Centrality: A Key Lever of Distribution

You can play audio or video content simultaneously on multiple devices such as TVs, tablet PCs, or smartphones. My 9th grade son likes to watch professional gaming competitions, known as e-Sports, on TV. While watching the e-Sports games on the TV, he also watches the gaming video clips on YouTube through his tablet. Meanwhile, he messages his friends about the games through the smartphone instant messaging service. Sometimes he even plays games on his laptop while watching TV and communicates with his friends. It is amazing to watch him multi-task through a variety of devices; his gaming experience revolves around multiple IT devices including TVs, tablets, smartphones, laptops, etc.

Let us now think of a hotel concierge service. Concierge provides professional secretarial services for the hotel guests. During my trip to Munich, I once had to come back to the hotel very late after a long day. I went to the concierge to ask for a decent restaurant to have a light dinner. After making a few calls, the concierge recommended several popular restaurants with reasonable prices. The one I went to was in fact very impressive, so I later suggested that place to my friends as well. Another memorable experience in Munich was watching the finals of the World Cup 2014. In hopes of enjoying the game together with the local Germans, I asked the concierge for a good place to watch the game. As expected, most restaurants were already fully booked on the finals day. Yet, the concierge introduced me to a local bar run by his friend who kindly pulled out an extra table for me to watch the game.

Centrality is a measure that shows the degree to which a person is in the center of a network (Freeman 1979). As illustrated in Fig. 7.3, my son who enjoys games through multiple channels is in the center of the content consumption network. He has direct relationships with all the devices. Thus, N-Screen service, further described below, is a high-centrality experience for my son. On the other hand, the concierge service is not a high-centrality experience for the hotel guests. The guests interact only through the concierge who takes care of the rest. The concierge is in the center of a network with various restaurants and tourist agents. I did not personally have to contact any restaurants or bars to ask for availabilities or prices.

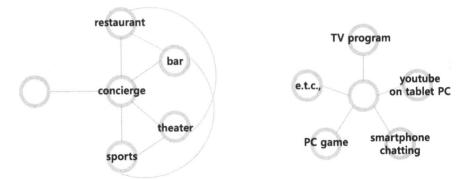

Fig. 7.3 Centrality in N-Screen and hotel concierge services

Centrality is an important measure that illustrates the distributive characteristic of a network. Centrality is closely related to the concept of "clusters" in a network. Clusters are groups of nodes in a network that are closely tied to each other (Opsahl and Panzarasa 2009). In the case of the hotel concierge service, the local restaurants together form a cluster of its own, and the tourist spots form another cluster. The hotel guests do not have any direct relationships with these clusters. Thereby the guests have low centrality within the whole network.

Another important distributive characteristic illustrated through centrality is the 'structural holes.' The hotel concierge acts as a bridge between the restaurant cluster and the hotel guests. Such nodes that fill in the gap, also known as structural holes, are likely to have high centrality (Burt 2009). It is because these nodes can influence a wide range of other nodes by interacting with multiple disconnected clusters (Burt 2001).

Clusters and structural holes are important concepts that describe the distributive characteristics of a network, and centrality can illustrate these characteristics. A node at the center can interact with diverse networks within a cluster, and it can also fill in the structural holes that exist between different clusters. Thereby, a user with high centrality is likely to be highly cohesive with the surrounding nodes. For instance, an N-Screen service user that accesses game content through multiple devices experiences high level of centrality, and accordingly high level cohesiveness. A concierge also has high centrality. On the other hand, centrality of the hotel guests is relatively low since they are only connected to the concierge, and the level of cohesiveness is also relatively low.

7.3.3 Density and Centrality

Density is a lever that represents the connectivity of a network, while centrality is a lever that represents the distributive property of a network. How are they related in terms of relational cohesiveness? Since both are related to the structure of a network, there is likely to be a synergy between the two levers. For instance, if a N-Screen service places the user at the center of the relationship and displays relevant content, the user possesses high centrality, and thereby, strong cohesiveness with the service. But if many services are well connected to each other so that the information received from the user through one service is automatically transmitted to another service for a later use, then the relational cohesiveness of the entire N-Screen experience would be even stronger. For example, if a computer understands my preferences through the interaction and sends this information to a TV so that the TV displays the channels based on this preference, my overall experience with the computer and the TV possesses strong cohesiveness. Of course, the opposite situation can arise as well. If both density and centrality are low, cohesiveness would also be perceived to be even lower. An interesting case is when density is high but centrality is low (e.g. the hotel concierge service) or when density is low but centrality is high (e.g. the Swiss Army knife). In these cases, cohesiveness would be higher than when both density and centrality are low. Likewise, in these cases cohesiveness would be lower than when both density and centrality are high.

What this tells us is that relational cohesiveness can be strategically controlled by considering both density and centrality. Since the two levers are independent yet closely related concepts, it is important that we understand the key UX factors and design features relevant to each lever.

7.4 Eight Case Studies on Density and Centrality

In the previous section, we reviewed the two important levers that affect relative cohesiveness: density and centrality. Let us take a look at four cases in which density is high/low and four cases in which centrality is high/low, as illustrated in Fig. 7.4. I have selected one exemplary product and a service that best suits each case. Through these eight examples, let us go deeper into the characteristics of both density and centrality. More details on each product and service can be found on the (http://extras.springer.com), as with other cases discussed in previous chapters.

	Density High	Density Low
Centrality High	**Product Samsung Galaxy S** Service: Facebook	**Product Google Glass** Service: Incheon International Airport
Centrality Low	**Product Samsung Smart TV** Service: SK Planet 11st	**Product Samsung Zipel Asak** Service: Favorite Store in Marketplace

Fig. 7.4 Eight cases to understand density and centrality in compositional experience

7.4.1   Google Glass

A product case of high density and high centrality. (https://www.google.com/glass/start/)

Google Glass is a wearable computer with an optical head-mounted display introduced by Google in February 2013. At the moment, Google Glass by itself cannot be a central computing device due to its limited computing capacity and speed. However it can be flexibly connected to other platforms and users can be in the center of these connections and have full control over the connected devices. Therefore, Google Glass users have high centrality. All the services linked to Google Glass are provided by Google. Since these services are closely connected to each other, the density is high as well. Google Glass is a representative example that provides an experience with high density and high centrality.

7.4.2   Incheon Airport

A Service case of high density and high centrality. (http://www.airport.kr/eng/)

As mentioned previously in this chapter, Incheon airport has been ranked number one for nine consecutive years for their quality service among over 1800 international airports on an airport service quality survey conducted by ACI (Airport Council International). This was possible because Incheon airport has diverse elements of experience that suit the needs of passengers. These services are located all over the airport, and the services are well integrated with one another to provide the best experience for its users. It is hard to find structural holes on the Incheon airport experience network. The services are tightly connected to one another, with the users in the center, which implies that the users have high centrality. The services at the airport are tightly connected to each other, leading to a high density within the service network.

7.4.3   Samsung Zipel Kimchi Refrigerator

A product case of low density and high centrality. (http://www.samsung.com/sec/consumer/kitchen-appliances/kimchi-refrigerator/)

A kimchi (a traditional Korean side dish that consist of fermented vegetables) refrigerator is a refrigerator designed to meet specific temperature and fermentation requirements to store kimchi in the best condition. Kimchi refrigerators are rarely related to other refrigerators or appliances in the kitchen. As can be inferred from the name, it is designed specifically to function for a specific type of food, kimchi. Thus, the density between other kitchen appliances and a kimchi refrigerator must be low. On the other hand, there is no central digital device that controls all the appliances in the kitchen. It is a user's role to take control of them, so the centrality of a kimchi refrigerator user is high.

7.4.4   Traditional Korean Market

A service case of low density and high centrality. (www.ddm-mall.co.kr)

In most countries with long history, traditional markets can be found, and most people have their favorite go-to stores in a market. My mother has been a regular customer of a fish store in the Dongdaemun Market for over 10 years. Whenever she visits the store, she comes back with a handful of fresh fish. The stores in the Dongdaemun Market are not directly related to each other, so the density is quite low. Furthermore, there is no system that fills in the structural hole that exists between these unrelated stores in the market. So when my mother visits the store, she has to visit separate stores to buy fruits, fish, meat, etc. She thus fills in the structural hole in her experience at the market and has a very high centrality.

7.4.5   Samsung Galaxy S Series

A product case of high density and low centrality. (http://www.samsung.com/sec/galaxys3/)

Digital convergence is a key characteristic of smartphones that distinguishes them from traditional feature phones. Present-day smartphones come with features of a phone with those of other digital devices such as cameras, MP3s, and GPS navigation units. A smartphone plays a central role in filling a structural hole among these digital devices. In other words, we only need the smartphone as it contains all the functions the other devices have and is able to connect to all of them. Since the phones are at the center of the experience, users have relatively low centrality in the smartphone experience. Meanwhile, the functions or modules within a smartphone are highly connected to each other. Data can be easily transferred between the modules. Therefore, smartphone experience has high density.

7.4.6   Facebook

A service case of high density and low centrality. (www.facebook.com)

Facebook is a major social networking service that lets people upload and share stories, photos, videos, and other information with their peers. The service acts as a hub that connects not only people but also many Facebook applications. Many of them allow people to easily log in to the service using their Facebook ID. Users become more and more connected to other people and/or services through Facebook, and their centrality becomes lower as a result. In contrast, friends and content on

Facebook are closely related to each other, and they interact frequently with each other. Thus, the density of a Facebook experience is high.

7.4.7   Smart TV

A product case of low density and low centrality. (http://kr.lgappstv.com/appspc/main/main/main.lge)

Smart TV is a multi-functional platform with the internet and Web 2.0 features. Besides the traditional functions of television sets, smart TVs also allow users to enjoy diverse functions using the internet, such as searching for products online, checking emails and exchanging messages. Smart TVs act as a gateway that connects diverse services including IPTV, games, shopping, and search modules. It connects the entertainment and network systems within homes, and fills in the structural hole on a network. Users only need to control the TV, so their centrality is low. Also, the functions and systems within the TV are not so closely related with each other. For instance, a home security system can be linked to a smart TV to display its recordings, but it is not yet linked with other internet-based functions in the TV. Thus, the density of a network composed of smart TV modules is also low.

7.4.8   11ST Online Shopping Mall

A service case of low density and low centrality. (www.11st.co.kr)

11ST is one of the biggest online marketplaces in Korea that manages and displays products sold by multiple retailers. An online marketplace is a unique form of e-commerce that allows individual retailers to put up products they want to sell on the virtual space. 11ST takes care of the major interaction with the customers, and the customers rarely come in contact with the individual retailers. From a customer's point of view, such shopping experience is of low centrality. Furthermore, there is no interaction between the retailers within the site. For instance, even if there are three retailers who sell the same product, there is likely to be no relationship between these retailers. Since most interactions occur solely within the 11ST platform, the experience network has low density.

To understand the important UX factors and design features that affect the compositional experience of users, an in-depth analysis on the above eight cases is conducted with respect to density and centrality. Details on case studies can be found on this book's website. The Table 7.1 below suggests important UX factors for the eight cases.

Table 7.1 Important UX factors and design features for four density and centrality categories

Density	Centrality	UX factor	Design features
High	High	Reciprocity	Omni-presence information architecture
			Pop-up alerts for synchronization
			Real-time update interfaces
High	Low	Complexity	Hub-type information architecture
			Multi-tasking bars
			Dashboards
Low	Low	Similarity	Gateway information architecture
			Customized filtering
			Standardized layout
Low	High	Salience	Intensified information architecture
			Skeuomorphism design

7.5   The Key UX Factor and Design Features for High Density

7.5.1   Reciprocity

Reciprocity is an important UX factor when it comes to experiences of high density and high centrality (e.g. Google Glass, Incheon Airport). Reciprocity is traditionally defined as the human inclination to give back what it has received (Blau 1964; Falk and Fischbacher 2006). When there is an equal reaction for every action among the elements of experience, we call it reciprocity. Let us assume that all the services at Incheon airport such as passport control, shopping, and airport guide are offered altogether as a single service. The size of the service would likely be too enormous to be maintained properly and it would be very complicated for users to use the system. Therefore the Incheon airport network is composed of multiple independent services that are tied to each other in a bidirectional and reciprocal manner.

Reciprocity can be either positive or negative, and it can be private or public (Chen and Li 2009; Whatley et al. 1999). When the elements of experience are compatible with one another to generate a synergy, there is a positive reciprocity. On the other hand, negative reciprocity can arise when elements of experience are not integrated with one another (Chen and Li 2009). For example, Google Glass integrates augmented reality technology for effective user interaction. By displaying computer-generated graphics on top of a real-world physical environment, the augmented reality technology allows the elements of experience to become denser. Furthermore, Google Glass is run on an Android-based OS, so that many services can easily be connected to each other. For such reasons, positive reciprocity occurs in a Google Glass experience.

HCI/UX communities have argued that increasing reciprocity can influence the perceived quality of a UX. Past studies about user cooperation and information exchange processes have argued that collaboration based on reciprocity affect the user satisfaction of services (Bootsma et al. 2004; Kimmerle et al. 2007). Also, reciprocity between computer systems and users has been shown to influence the work efficiency and satisfaction of users (Fogg and Nass 1997; Nass and Moon 2000).

Reciprocity is especially important for experiences with high density and high centrality. When the density among the elements of experience becomes higher, they become more related and dependent on each other. Such dependency can either generate synergy to yield positive effects or negatively impact the overall experience. But even if the elements are connected through the system, their high dependency could cause each element to lose its unique quality. A small change in the system can influence the entire system and result in inconvenience, and such small, partial changes can even cause a collapse to the whole system. Therefore, reciprocity that possesses a generally equal level of relationship between elements can be an important element of experience when density is high. Furthermore, the closer you are to the center of a network, the easier it becomes to access diverse elements of experience. This, in turn, enables better control of the usefulness of all the elements involved. Ultimately, it becomes more important to establish a relationship between the elements of experience. Therefore, as the relationships within a network become denser and the centrality increases, reciprocity becomes more important.

The compositional aspects of an experience are related to the information architecture of products or services. Information architecture can be thought of as drawing a blueprint for the overall UX. Therefore, I would like to first introduce the design features related to information architecture and describe some examples of interfaces and interaction mechanisms that can be implemented along with the information architecture.

For high density, high centrality cases, we need a design that can boost reciprocity. Effective design features for this include omni-presence information architecture for an immediate response, pop-up alerts for synchronization, and real-time update interfaces.

7.5.1.1 Omni-Presence Information Architecture

Omni-Presence Information Architecture is defined as the structure that helps a user access information at any time and from anywhere. In a highly dense experience network, we need a structure where elements of experience are easily accessible at any point. Thus, an omni-presence information architecture is a good option (Adkins et al. 2002; Jones and Jo 2004). In the case of Incheon Airport, the physical space itself is massive with thousands of passengers, so the services may not always be physically easy to access. However, as shown in Fig. 7.5, many services are

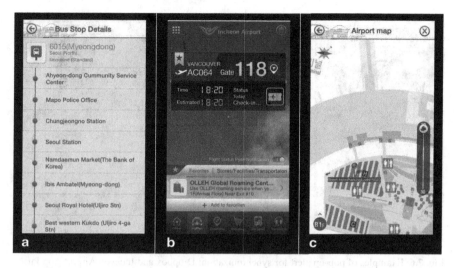

Fig. 7.5 Examples of Omni-presence information architecture: Incheon Airport Application allows one to check for information anywhere, anytime (**a** real-time location of airport shuttle bus, **b** airlines departure schedule, **c** location of my car at the airport parking lot). (Courtesy of Incheon Airport, used with permission)

easily accessible through the airport mobile application. For the case of Google Glass, we can access the information from the top to the bottom of an information hierarchy with a simple voice command. In general, if I want to send an email to a friend, I run an email service, open the contacts list, search for a friend's address, and then send an email. But when using Google Glass, I can simply speak out loud "send an email to my friend X saying that I will be late for lunch:" and the request is executed. This is one good example of a service with an omni-presence information architecture.

7.5.1.2 Pop-Up Alert for Synchronization

Real-time synchronization between a user and the elements is critical on a densely connected experience network. Users undoubtedly prefer to send and receive information at any point through a consistent interaction with products or services. It is thus important to instantly notify the users of any updates or changes on a system (Monaghan 2009). Let us take Dropbox for an example. When multiple collaborators are working together in the same project folder, the Dropbox system synchronizes the data and notifies the users of the updates in real-time. The Incheon Airport application is another example. If a passenger provides flight information, the app reminds him or her of the departure schedule and location with push alerts (Fig. 7.6). Google Glass displays certain information such as news or missed calls in one corner—without blocking the users' view.

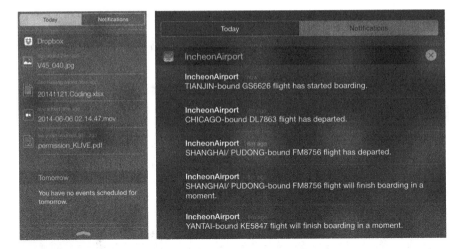

Fig. 7.6 Examples of pop-up alert for synchronization: Dropbox and Incheon Airport App Push-Alarms that notifies the user of any updates. (Courtesy of Dropbox, used with permission)

7.5.1.3 Real-Time Update Interface

In a product or a service where the elements of experience are highly connected to each other, it is important to update the users of any changes that occur to any of the elements. Users need to understand what changes were made to which part of the system. Real-time update interfaces takes the entire system as a single entity, and shows the updates that occurred within any of the embedded services or modules (Kopetz 2011). At Incheon Airport, real-time departure and landing information is displayed in multiple locations through diverse channels (Fig. 7.7). The information is also broadcasted through voice announcements. The airport is providing users with the necessary information through real-time update interfaces. Likewise, Google Glass responds promptly to the actions of its users. The elements of experience are well connected to each other so that the users can feel as if the launching of an application and changes in the environment are happening simultaneously.

7.5.2 Complexity

Complexity is an important factor in experiences of high density and low centrality, for example smartphones and Facebook.

Complexity is the extent to which a user feels that a system is composed of multiple elements related to each other (Campbell 1988; Earley 1985; Te'eni 1989; Wood 1986). For example, a user feels that there are multiple functions in a smartphone system, such as sending emails or listening to music, and that these functions

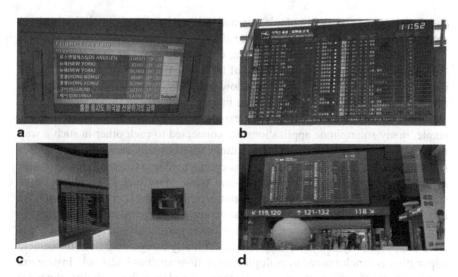

Fig. 7.7 Examples of real-time updates: flight information in Incheon Airport (**a** flight schedule screen in the airport express train, **b** and **d** screen at the airport lounge, **c** screen at the airport duty free shop). (Courtesy of Incheon Airport, used with permission)

are closely linked to one another. Complexity is the opposite of simplicity, since a UX can become simpler as complexity is reduced.

We generally experience three types of complexities (Nadkarni and Gupta 2007; Wood 1986). Firstly, there is component complexity which arises from the diversity of the components of a system. People feel that a system is complex if it is densely filled with diverse components. For example, if our Facebook feed is packed with assorted information from diverse sources, we would feel that the system is complex.

Secondly, there is coordinative complexity, which comes from the interaction between the components. If the components are engaged in a wide range of high-degree interaction, we would feel that a system is complex. Let us say a bunch of people are intricately woven into a network on Facebook. If I feel that my friendship network is affected by this human relationship, I am feeling coordinative complexity from this relationship.

Finally, there is dynamic complexity, which is derived from the uncertainty or ambiguity of relationships. If information from the same source is understood in different ways, or if the same action results in different outcomes, the experience is perceived to be complex. For instance, if a Facebook post leads to different interpretations, or if a photo upload brings different responses every time, a user would feel that their experience is complex.

Past studies claim that the quality of a UX can be enhanced when complexity is reduced (Chae and Kim 2004; Nadkarni and Gupta 2007; Tuch et al. 2009). A study on smartphone use shows that simplicity is increased by reducing component, coordinative, and dynamic complexity, and that an increased simplicity leads to increased user satisfaction (Choi and Lee 2012).

As illustrated in the examples above, complexity plays an important role in the overall satisfaction and experience of the users. Complexity is especially important for cases with high density and low centrality. The denser the relationship between the elements of experience, the higher the degree of interaction between them. As a result, users perceive their experience to be overly complex. For example, many smartphone applications are connected to each other in such a way that a change in a single part of the settings affects many services. This causes users to feel that their smartphone use is complex. When the centrality of a user is low, his/her experience is built upon some other entity such as Facebook or the smartphone itself and he/she is away from the center of an experience network. As a user is positioned further away from the center of an experience network, uncertainty and complexity increases. When I organize my photos on my smartphone, I am often not exactly sure how the photos are initially categorized since the camera application is synchronized to multiple applications such as Facebook, Instagram, and Evernote. Therefore, the higher the density and lower the centrality, the more likely to feel that an experience is complex. Such a complex experience needs to be simplified in order to become a better experience.

For cases with high density and low centrality, we need to simplify the experiences by reducing the complexity. Effective design features for this include hub-type information architecture, multitasking bars, and dashboard interfaces.

7.5.2.1   Hub-Type Information Architecture

Hub-type information architecture arranges information and functions based on relevance. Complex information and functions are thematically organized so that users can easily access a product or a service based on their needs (Kuby and Gray 1993; O'Kelly and Miller 1994). These information or functions are linked to each other so that they can be further expanded. Users can navigate through related content through these links, and execute the functions they need in sequence. Hub-type information architecture is a useful way of organizing and presenting the complex information. Facebook's Open Graph (Fig. 7.8) is a structure that connects friends, sites, and news content that are highly related to each other. Facebook users can place links on their photos or stories, so that this content can act as hubs to related news content or sites. Whenever a user breaks the record on a Facebook game, related information about the game, the records, and the user is displayed on the Facebook news feed. Similarly, a smartphone OS is also built upon hub-type information architecture in which related applications are grouped together. One example would be a photo album module on a smartphone. When a user selects photos from the album, the phone suggests applications or functions related to the photo and users can further process the photo, for example upload the photo on Facebook or set the photo as a profile picture.

Facebook Interface

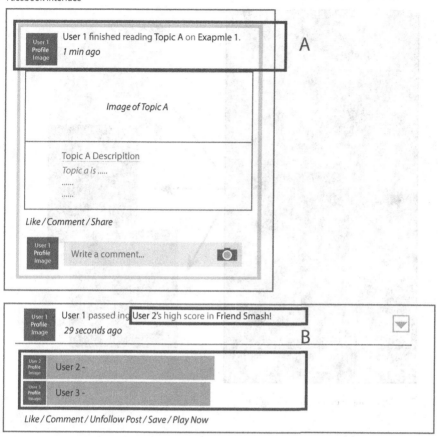

Fig. 7.8 Hub-type information architecture shown in open graph

7.5.2.2   Multi-Tasking Bar

A multi-tasking bar shows a list programs that are currently running, so that a user can easily check for the current status without having to navigate back and forth the screen (Wang and Chang 2010) (Fig. 7.9). A simple tap on the bar enables users to manage the active programs. If a user wants to quit the program, he or she can use a finger flicking gesture, and if he or she wants to move onto the next program, he or she can use a rolling gesture. We often find ourselves controlling other external devices through smartphones. During this process, it is difficult for users to control every component of other devices and functions, which leads to increased uncertainty. A multi-tasking bar can help users to be aware of these components without having to individually check the status of all the devices and functions. Multi-tasking

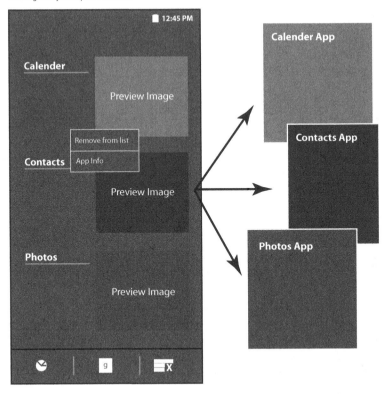

Fig. 7.9 An example of a multi-tasking bar

bars are therefore an effective mechanism to decrease users' uncertainty and reduce complexity of an experience.

7.5.2.3 Dashboard

A dashboard is a user interface that organizes and presents diverse information in one place in a way that is easy to read (Few 2006). Users can easily monitor, compare, and find information through this interface. The information is further summarized in a form of a widget. On a smartphone, we have control bars or notification bars that allows one to access or check the status of applications. Facebook offers a dashboard function where users can check the overall friendship status or system-related notifications. Through Facebook notification bars or news tickers, we can also check friends' statuses as well as our own, in real time, as demonstrated by (Fig. 7.10).

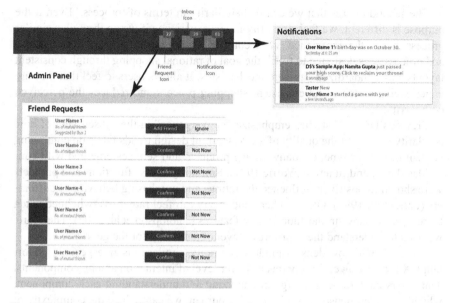

Fig. 7.10 An example of notification dashboard: showing news and various messages from friends

7.6   The Key UX factor and Design Features for Low Density

7.6.1   Similarity

Similarity is an important UX factor to consider in experiences of low density and low centrality (e.g. Samsung Smart TV, 11ST Open Market). Similarity is the construct that measures the extent to which users feel that the elements of experience are comparable to each other (Medin et al. 1993; Navarro and Lee 2004). For instance, the consistency in the way that products and retailers are displayed on the 11ST Open Market platform can affect a user's cognition of similarity of a system. It is a contrasting concept of diversity. In other words, reduced similarity results in increased diversity.

There are two items in which users can experience similarity (Estes 2003). The first one is that we can feel similarity with respect to 'purpose'. In trying to achieve a certain goal or a purpose, users feel that their elements of experience are similar when there is a consistent goal underlying these elements. For example, consumers of 11ST need a smart way of comparing and contrasting the characteristics of products, thus an effective way to group the products based on the purpose is necessary. Since the retailers are not directly connected to each other, it is difficult to measure the similarity between them from the customer's point of view. The 11ST Street Open Market groups the retailers that sell similar products and presents them in a way so users can easily make comparisons.

The second item is that we can feel similarity in terms of 'process.' Even if the purpose is different, we feel similarity in our experience if we go through a similar process during the experience. 11ST considers similarity in terms of both purpose and process; it is designed to fulfill the goal of rational shopping through consistent layouts and standardized payment mechanisms. It allows users to feel that they are experiencing a stable and consistent shopping process and reduces the perceived complexity.

Previous HCI/UX studies emphasize "convergence" in their discussion of how similarity can affect the quality of a UX. Current design trends focus on combining content of similar type, as many unique products and services emerged with consolidated data and function (Yoffie 1997). Similarity across functions and products were shown to positively influence the ratings and purchasing behavior of customers (Park et al. 1991). On the other hand, users can feel rather overwhelmed when there are too many similar functions or features (Thompson et al. 2005). Therefore, we need to understand the appropriate level of similarity for the good UX.

For cases with low density and low centrality, similarity is an especially important UX factor. Lower density means lower level of interaction among components. Thus users have to be in charge of analyzing and understanding each component, which can be burdensome. To lighten the burden, we can reduce the complexity of products and services through the designs that allow users to feel similarity among related features and functions. In the 11ST example, similarity of the retailers is considered in the system to help users to have a better shopping experience. It is especially important when there is a relatively weak relationship among the components, with low density and low centrality.

When centrality is low, users are not in the center of an experience. In such cases they tend to be involved in an indirect experience through another medium. This medium, or the center of a relationship, influences the users. 11ST or a smart TV act as a channel through which people can have an indirect experience. They can be thought of as some sort of 'helpers' that allow people to get in touch with other people, products, or services. In other words, 11ST or a smart TV can portray other in a similar way so that users can sense a high similarity from the experience.

For low density, low centrality cases, we need the design features that can boost a user's sense of similarity. Effective design features include the gateway information architecture, customized filtering, and standardized layout within a system.

7.6.1.1 Gateway Information Architecture

Let's think of popular online portal sites such as Google or Naver (a Korean portal site). To find certain information, we access the web site, type the search keyword/s in the search box, and browse through the results. If we want other results we again type keywords in the search box. As illustrated in this example, Gateway information architecture is structured in a way that users have to resume from the starting

Fig. 7.11 Examples of gateway information architecture: 11ST and Smart TV. (Image **a**: courtesy of 11ST, used with permission)

point every time they want to access information (Fig. 7.11). On the 11ST, we go through the same search process as on Google or Naver to find the products we are looking for. Same applies to Smart TVs. If we want to use a specific application, we always have to start from the home screen. Gateway information architecture eliminates the unnecessary process of comparing and contrasting the unrelated content. The search process on 11ST always follows the same gateway structure, so users can engage in a familiar process when making searches for different products or retailers.

Fig. 7.12 Advanced customized filtering function: 11ST (**a** category filtering function, **b** advanced category filtering function. Courtesy of 11ST, used with permission)

7.6.1.2 Customized Filtering

Interaction between a user and products or services can be either unidirectional or bidirectional. A recent trend is geared towards a bidirectional relationship where users are more active than passive in interacting with products or services. Customized filtering is one example of an active, bidirectional mechanism. Customized filtering lets users configure and define their needs and purposes. Customized filtering and gateway information architecture together create a synergy effect, for they allow users to take the lead in finding and selecting desired information. Advanced sorting configurations on 11ST is one example of customized filtering module (Fig. 7.12).

7.6.1.3 Standardized Layout

The very basics of presenting a large amount of information is to have unified and standardized layout scheme composed of consistently organized information. On the gateway information architecture, branches of experience are initiated at a starting point. We need a standardized rule to structure these diverse experiences in a systematized way. A starting point of a gateway information architecture functions as an emulator that links many experiences. Thus, a consistent and unified layout can bring about a heightened sense of similarity in the UX. Let's go back to 11ST (Fig. 7.13). While various retailers exist on the market, standardized interface is

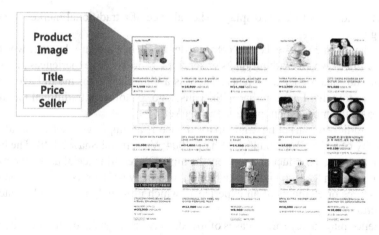

Fig. 7.13 An example of standardized layout: mini-shop list interface of 11ST. (Courtesy of 11ST, used with permission)

used all across to present the retailers and the products they sell. Standardized layout is necessary because the goal of users is to make a thorough comparison of products they want to purchase. The mini-shop list interface of 11ST is a good example with a standardized layout scheme. Same goes for smart TVs as well. Multiple functions and modules embedded within smart TVs are presented in a consistent, unified layout format.

7.6.2   Salience

Salience refers to the relative prominence of a product or a service (Alba and Chattopadhyay 1986). Similarly, brand salience is the extent to which a brand is thought of or noticed when a customer is in a buying situation (Ehrenberg et al. 1997; Gruber 1969; Lynch and Srull 1982). The degree to which I feel a kimchi refrigerator performs better than refrigerators in general is an example of salience. Kimchi refrigerators are clearly distinguishable from other refrigerators; they are specifically designed to store kimchi so that it does not freeze in cold temperatures and maintain its crisp taste and aroma for a long time. Salience is based on not only technological innovation, but also non-technical features such as its drawer-type ergonomic design that allows people to easily handle kimchi. Salience plays an important role for such experiences of low density and high centrality (Gruber 1969). People experience salience largely in two ways.

First of all, there is salience that comes from unique characteristics of the products or services themselves. Salience is about one or two characteristics of a product or a service that speaks out loud. For instance, all the stores in a traditional market are unique in their own ways. They are owned by different people, sell different products, and have different displays. The salience of a traditional market is therefore high.

The second one is salience that comes from frequent exposure. In other words, it is how familiar we are with products or services. More recent experiences are more familiar and thus higher in salience. There is a high chance for me to have recent visits to a store that I am familiar with. Thus, a go-to store at a traditional market is likely to be the most salient place in the market.

Past studies in marketing argue that salience is an important factor that affects the quality of a UX (Romaniuk and Sharp 2004; Vieceli and Shaw 2010). The higher the salience of a product or a service, the higher the confidence of users in making decisions, which leads to higher satisfaction. In other words, users can focus on specific features or elements of an experience, which ultimately results in heightened satisfaction.

Salience plays a key role in cases of low density and high centrality. Low density implied low level of interaction between the elements of an experience. As a result, users are likely to focus on individual elements of an experience than the entire experience as a whole. In the case of a traditional market, a user has to visit every store to find out the best option for him or her. If a store exhibits salient features, the shopping process of a user can become simpler and easier.

If a user has high centrality in an experience network, other elements of experience are likely to have relatively lower centrality. Then it becomes difficult to distinguish one element from another. In this case, we can increase salience through amplifying specific features of other elements or by letting users become familiar with these elements. For example, stores in the traditional market can make efforts to distinguish them from others through special offers or discounts. Storekeepers can also try to become friends with the customers by having small talks or giving useful cooking tips.

It is important to boost salience for low density, high centrality experiences. Some examples of effective design features are intensified architecture and skeuomorphism design.

7.6.2.1   Intensified Information Architecture

Unlike other hierarchical structures, intensified information architecture emphasizes certain functions or features. By focusing on a limited number of functions or features, we can draw users' attention to salient components of a product or a service. In a kimchi refrigerator, we have specific features solely for kimchi such as fermentation controls. With regular refrigerators in the past, it was difficult to keep kimchi in its best condition. But with the kimchi-specific features and information architecture, we are now able to have a functionally salient experience (Fig. 7.14).

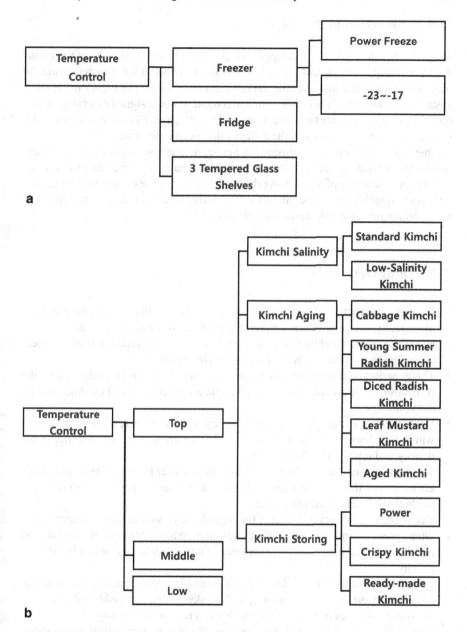

Fig. 7.14 A kimchi refrigerator's intensified architecture (**a** setting and controls for general refrigerators, **b** settings and controls for kimchi refrigerators)

7.6.2.2 Skeuomorphic Interface

Skeuomorphism is a design concept in which design cues are taken from their real-world counterparts (Hou and Ho 2013). The level of abstraction can determine the way users understand and evaluate the products or services. The higher the level of abstraction, the harder it is for users to understand. If not designed carefully, skeuomorphism can sometimes be unnecessary and unattractive. But when designed well, skeuomorphic design increases the salience that people perceive.

One example of skeuomorphism is the process of calibrating the compass function on the iPhone. To calibrate the compass, users have to tilt the screen to roll the ball around the shape of a circle. As the ball rolls around, users can see the red arc being drawn inside of a circle. Such specific design features that are taken from the real world experience help boost salience in a UX.

7.7 Summary

- From the perspective of compositional experience, it is important to keep harmonious relationships with the surrounding people, products, and services.
- Harmonious relationships can be achieved by controlling relational cohesiveness according to the changes in the external environment.
- The experiential dimension of relational cohesiveness can be controlled by the levers of density and centrality, which explain connectivity and distribution of a network.
- Density of an experience network is a key lever that represents the extent to which the elements are tied to each other. The stronger the tie, the higher the density and relational cohesiveness.
- The centrality of a user is higher as he or she is closer to the center of an experience network that fills the structural hole. The higher the key lever of centrality, the higher the relational cohesiveness.
- Reciprocity is the key UX factor for high-density, high-centrality experiences. Omni-presence information architectures, pop-up alerts for synchronization, and real-time update interfaces are examples of design features that can boost reciprocity.
- Complexity is the key UX factor for high-density, low-centrality experiences. Hub-type information architectures, multi-tasking bars, and dashboard interfaces are some examples of design features that can reduce complexity.
- Similarity is the key UX factor for low-density, low-centrality experiences. Gateway information architectures, customized filtering, and standardized layouts are some examples of design features that can boost similarity.
- Salience is the key UX factor for low-density, high-centrality experiences. Intensified information architectures and skeuomorphism are examples of design features that can boost salience.

7.8 Discussion Topics

- Think of a harmonious experience you recently had while using a product or a service.
- Analyze the relative cohesiveness of your experience network in terms of the levers of density and centrality.
- Which one of the four types of cases (i.e. high/low density, high/low centrality) does your experience fall in?
- Evaluate your experience in terms of salience, similarity, complexity, and reciprocity.
- Which part of the product or service led you to have a harmonious experience? Find the examples of design features introduced in this chapter.
- Can you think of other effective design features not introduced in this chapter?

References

Adkins M, Kruse J, Younger R (2002) Ubiquitous computing: omnipresent technology in support of network centric warfare. Paper presented at the System Sciences, 2002. HICSS. Proceedings of the 35th Annual Hawaii International Conference on System Sciences (HICSS'02), (pp. 551–559). IEEE

Alba JW, Chattopadhyay A (1986) Salience effects in brand recall. J Mark Res 23(4):363–369

Blau PM (1964). Exchange and power in social life. Transaction Publishers

Bootsma RJ, Fernandez L, Mottet D (2004) Behind Fitts' law: kinematic patterns in goal-directed movements. Int J Hum-Comput Stud 61(6):811–821

Burt RS (2001) Structural holes versus network closure as social capital. Social capital: theory and research. 31–56

Burt RS (2009) Structural holes: the social structure of competition. Harvard University Press

Campbell DJ (1988) Task complexity: a review and analysis. Acad Manage Rev 13(1):40–52

Chae M, Kim J (2004) Do size and structure matter to mobile users? An empirical study of the effects of screen size, information structure, and task complexity on user activities with standard web phones. Behav Inf Technol 23(3):165–181

Chen Y, Li SX (2009) Group identity and social preferences. Am Econ Rev 99(1):431–457

Choi JH, Lee H-J (2012) Facets of simplicity for the smartphone interface: a structural model. Int J Hum-Comput Stud 70(2):129–142

Earley PC (1985) Influence of information, choice and task complexity upon goal acceptance, performance, and personal goals. J Appl Psychol 70(3):481–491

Ehrenberg A, Barnard N, Scriven J (1997) Differentiation or salience. J Advert Res 37:7–14

Estes Z (2003) A tale of two similarities: comparison and integration in conceptual combination. Cognitive Sci 27(6):911–921

Falk A, Fischbacher U (2006) A theory of reciprocity. Games Econ Behav 54:293–315

Few S (2006) Information dashboard design: O'Reilly. pp 120–206

Fogg B, Nass C (1997) How users reciprocate to computers: an experiment that demonstrates behavior change. Paper presented at the CHI'97 extended abstracts on Human factors in computing systems

Freeman LC (1979) Centrality in social networks conceptual clarification. Soc Netw 1(3):215–239

Friedkin NE (1981) The development of structure in random networks: an analysis of the effects of increasing network density on five measures of structure. Soc Netw 3(1):41–52

Friedkin NE (2004) Social cohesion. Annu Rev Sociol 30:409–425

Gruber A (1969) Top-of-mind awareness and share of families: an observation. J Mark Res 6(2):227–231

Hou K-C, Ho C-H (2013) A preliminary study on aesthetic of apps icon design. IASDR 2013, pp. 3845–3856

Jones V, Jo JH (2004) Ubiquitous learning environment: an adaptive teaching system using ubiquitous technology. Beyond the comfort zone. Proceedings of the 21st ASCILITE Conference(s 468), 474

Kephart WM (1950) A quantitative analysis of intragroup relationships. Am J Sociol 55(6):544–549

Kimmerle J, Cress U, Hesse FW (2007) An interactional perspective on group awareness: alleviating the information-exchange dilemma (for everybody?). Int J Hum-Comput Stud 65(11):899–910

Kopetz H (2011) Real-time systems: design principles for distributed embedded applications. Springer

Kuby MJ, Gray RG (1993) The hub network design problem with stopovers and feeders: the case of Federal Express. Transp Res Part A Policy Pract 27(1):1–12

Lynch Jr JG, Srull TK (1982) Memory and attentional factors in consumer choice: concepts and research methods. J Consum Res 9(1):18–37

Medin DL, Goldstone RL, Gentner D (1993) Respects for similarity. Psychol Rev 100(2):254

Monaghan S (2009) Responsible gambling strategies for Internet gambling: the theoretical and empirical base of using pop-up messages to encourage self-awareness. Comput Hum Behav 25(1):202–207

Moody J, White DR (2003) Structural cohesion and embeddedness: a hierarchical concept of social groups. Am Sociol Rev 68(1):103–127

Nadkarni S, Gupta R (2007) A task-based model of perceived website complexity. MIS Q 31(3):501–524

Nass C, Moon Y (2000) Machines and mindlessness: social responses to computers. J Soc Issues 56(1):81–103

Navarro DJ, Lee MD (2004) Common and distinctive features in stimulus similarity: a modified version of the contrast model. Psychon Bull Rev 11(6):961–974

O'Kelly ME, Miller HJ (1994) The hub network design problem: a review and synthesis. J Transp Geogr 2(1):31–40

Opsahl T, Panzarasa P (2009) Clustering in weighted networks. Soc Netw 31(2):155–163

Park CW, Milberg S, Lawson R (1991) Evaluation of brand extensions: the role of product feature similarity and brand concept consistency. J Consum Res 18(2):185–193

Romaniuk J, Sharp B. (2004) Conceptualizing and measuring brand salience. Mark Theory 4(4):327–342

Te'eni D (1989) Determinants and consequences of perceived complexity in human–computer interaction*. Decis Sci 20(1):166–181

Thompson DV, Hamilton RW, Rust RT (2005) Feature fatigue: when product capabilities become too much of a good thing. J Mark Res 42(4):431–442

Tuch AN, Bargas-Avila JA, Opwis K, Wilhelm FH (2009) Visual complexity of websites: effects on users' experience, physiology, performance, and memory. Int J Hum-Comput Stud 67(9):703–715

Vieceli J, Shaw RN (2010) Brand salience for fast-moving consumer goods: an empirically based model. J Mark Manage 26(13–14):1218–1238

Wang Q, Chang H (2010) Multitasking bar: prototype and evaluation of introducing the task concept into a browser. Paper presented at the Proceedings of the SIGCHI Conference on Human Factors in Computing Systems, pp 103–112

Wasserman S (1994) Social network analysis: methods and applications, vol 8. Cambridge University Press

Whatley MA, Webster JM, Smith RH, Rhodes A (1999) The effect of a favor on public and private compliance: how internalized is the norm of reciprocity? Basic Appl Soc Psychol 21(3):251–259

Wood RE (1986) Task complexity: definition of the construct. Organ Behav Hum Decis Processes 37(1):60–82

Yamagishi T, Gillmore MR, Cook KS (1988) Network connections and the distribution of power in exchange networks. Am J Sociol 93(4):833–851

Yoffie DB (1997) Competing in the age of digital convergence. Harvard Business Press

.

Part IV
Summary

Chapter 8
Design for the Next Real Experience

8.1 Introduction

The ultimate purpose for all of us is to provide senseful, valuable, and harmonious experiences for users This book suggests a perspective of designing products or services based on experiences of users. Our experiences with products and services resemble an intertwined lump of threads. We need to be able to untangle this lump into useful strands of threads in order to effectively provide desired experiences for users. The sensual, judgmental, and compositional threads of experience are introduced in this book. Based on the three threads of experience, we looked into how we can analyze the experiences of users with current products and services and further examined how changes in sociocultural, economic, and technological environments influence our experiences. We then identified conflict and cognitive dissonance as the two factors that can cause an imbalance between experience and environment. We further propose a way to resolve these issues—designs that can provide new experiences for the users. What are the processes and organizations necessary for designing the next senseful, valuable, and harmonious experience?

8.2 The Internet: A Life-Changing Experience

My first internet experience was about 20 years ago, when I was finishing my Ph.D. thesis. I was busy working on C++ programming in the computer cluster on the 4th floor of the Computer Science building in Carnegie Mellon University. At that time, I used to pull all-nighters together with other students in the computer lab all the time. The funny thing is, as with most students, I spent more time chatting with friends than working. Once, a friend of mine came up to me and excitedly told me about a newly launched web browser application—Netscape. Then he installed the application on his workstation and showed us how it worked. Although the installation process was a bit complicated, I felt like there was so much you could do with it once the installation was complete. And the browser itself seemed really easy to

© Springer International Publishing Switzerland 2015
J. Kim, *Design for Experience*, Human-Computer Interaction Series,
DOI 10.1007/978-3-319-14304-0_8

work with (maybe because C++ was giving me headaches at the time). I could really picture everyone, not just the tech-savvies, using the internet on their computers.

Then after 5 or 6 years, I came back to Korea and had a chance to organize an event named "The Internet Survival Game" with a popular media company, Chosun Ilbo. Five contestants were given a million Korean won (approximately USD 1,000) to survive for 100 hours, only depending on the internet. Initially, the organizers were extremely worried; after all, the internet was at its beginning stages, and these people were only amateurs. So everyone was on their toes, and we even had ambulances on standby. The participants seemed to struggle a bit on the first and the second day, but on the third day and the final day they had no problems getting what they needed using the internet. In the end, all five were able to survive through the 4 days. Four days can seem too easy for us in the modern world living with smartphones and express shipping services, but it was a real challenge at the time when there wasn't even a single proper online shopping mall. After the game, I was convinced that the internet would one day become a part of everyone's lives.

From then on, businesses started to realize the potential of the internet as a marketing channel, and it was mainly used for commercial purposes. We have witnessed an explosive growth in online shopping and online stock trading. Newspaper businesses and radio broadcasting companies built their own homepages to provide diverse content through the web, and game companies started to distribute online network games packed with flashy graphics.

However, in the early 2000s, "the internet bubble" burst. Internet-based companies, both in and outside of Korea, went bankrupt one by one after a considerable hype by investors on their monetary worth. I was one of those who had to close down an internet startup company, which involved a local venture capital firm. At the time I sensed there was something unsound with investing millions of dollars in internet companies with unrealistic business plans that just seemed impossible to implement with existing internet technology. Nevertheless, I didn't quite expect them to suddenly plunge so fast into darkness.

After about 10 years of suffering, we entered the era of Web 2.0, where many online services that emphasized on the concept of social computing started to emerge. Social network services such as Facebook and social media services like YouTube are the typical examples. These services share at least three common characteristics. They allow users to be more deeply involved in creating and utilizing content through its service. The content is not just for creators and can be easily shared with a wide audience. And finally, that this act of creating and distributing content is not always driven by economic benefits but also by meaningfulness and fun. For example, many people enjoy the process of helping others through creating and sharing the content.

The internet will continue to penetrate deeply into every part of our lives. We can find the internet even at "Seodang," a traditional private village school in Korea that is separate from most of modern technologies. Farmers living in the countryside also use the internet to communicate with their clients in the cities. While waiting for a subway, I frequently spot people shopping for groceries through the virtual supermarket on LED screens installed in Seoul metro stations.

Imagine living in an interconnected world where all the objects and people have their own uniquely identifiable internet addresses. The internet will have an even greater impact in our lives once we start to communicate with literally every "thing" around us. High-speed trains will send me a message to inform of vacant seats and tiny devices, even smaller than smart watches, will fly around us to guide us in congested department stores. We might have pet robots replacing golden retrievers at home. Who knows? The internet might once again completely change our lives.

8.3 Why Does Experience Come First?

Most of us living in the modern world spend many hours of our lives experiencing products or services of some sort every day. The internet, which is not that old, has given us many opportunities to enhance the quality and quantity of our experiences. Let's take my daily routine as an example. I start my day experiencing the sound of my alarm from my smartphone. The alarm application is smart enough to read through my schedule from the online calendar. I have no other choice but to wake up when I hear, "You have 13 appointments today. At eight thirty, there is a research meeting with your students…" After getting out of bed, I spend a few minutes reading through the daily bible verse online, and then I share the scripture with my friends and peers through email. Then I go down to the gym and run while watching the TV installed on the treadmill. During breakfast, I check the weather and read the day's news headlines on my iPad. Then I get ready to go to work. I turn on the GPS in my car, which calculates the optimal route, considering road conditions and the traffic. After I get to school, I begin by replying to new emails that had arrived overnight. Then I try to spend the rest of my morning reading papers and other material related to my ongoing research projects. I read all the material using an iPad on which I also keep notes and jot down ideas using a stylus. I can later share these thoughts with students and researchers through email. Afternoons are usually spent on meetings or conferences. I always have my iPad at the meetings or conferences I attend, to scribble down my thoughts and to search for information. Everything I've written down is automatically saved on my cloud drive. On my way back home from work, I again turn on the GPS. At home, I video chat with my son, who's abroad at the moment. At the end of the day when I go to bed, I read through the current events on my iPad. While asleep, a wearable device monitors my sleeping pattern.

It may sound a bit like an exaggeration, but my day is mostly made up of experiences with products or services of some kind. In other words, my life is filled with experiencing products or services. The more meaningful, valuable, and harmonious, my experiences are of using a product or a service, the more meaningful, valuable, and harmonious my life becomes. In the end, this determines the quality of my life.

The ultimate goal of our lives is to make it meaningful, valuable, and harmonious. And that's why we, by instinct, prefer products or services that provide us with a meaningful, valuable, and harmonious experience. Of course it is possible to under or overestimate products or services at times. However, these misjudgments usually do not last long, as we keep experiencing in our daily lives. Thus, products or services that provide meaningful, valuable, and harmonious experiences for users tend to be long lasting and dominant in the market. Thereby, when designing a product or a service, we should focus on what the target users will experience. Not only is this a necessary element of success, but it also helps design our lives to become meaningful, valuable, and harmonious.

8.4   Design for the Next Experience, Under a Telescope

A design that focuses on human experience is composed of four main elements, as depicted in Fig. 8.1.

The first element is the experience that arises when people interact with products or services. It can be explained through the three threads of experience as discussed in Chapter 2 of this book. The sensual thread of experience is about how we perceive and react to things by seeing, hearing, feeling, smelling, and tasting. When playing social network games, for instance, we go through a sensual experience through the images, sounds, clicking, shaking, and so on. The judgmental thread of experience is concerned with how satisfied I am with getting what I wanted or needed through the experience. It's about my evaluation of whether an experience is valuable and meaningful—whether I enjoyed the process of playing a social network game, or whether I felt enjoyment thinking that I was getting better at the game, for instance. The compositional thread of experience comes from the relationships between the entities that make up an experience. It is about my connections and relationships with the friends playing the game with me and with the other objects or applications in the game as well. Analyzing the holistic experience of users based on these three threads of experience is the first important step in designing experience-oriented products or services.

The second element is to understand the external environments surrounding our experience, as explained in Chapter 3 of this book. Our everyday experience involves endless interactions with our surroundings. We need to examine the characteristics of the environment, what impact it has on our experience, as well as how our actions impact the environment. This book introduces three aspects of the environment: socio-cultural, economic, and technological aspects. The socio-cultural aspect is concerned with the awareness and behavior of a person who uses a product or a service. Let's take social network games once again as an example. In the modern world, we have smaller-sized families so we have fewer family members to talk with in our home. Furthermore, our online identities are often considered as important as our offline identities. In this culture, social network games are more than just a game; they can be interpreted as an important medium through which we build relationship with our peers. Elements of the economic environment impact our willingness to pay for the products or the services. When the economies stumble or interest rates rise, we naturally try to cut down our living expenses. As a result,

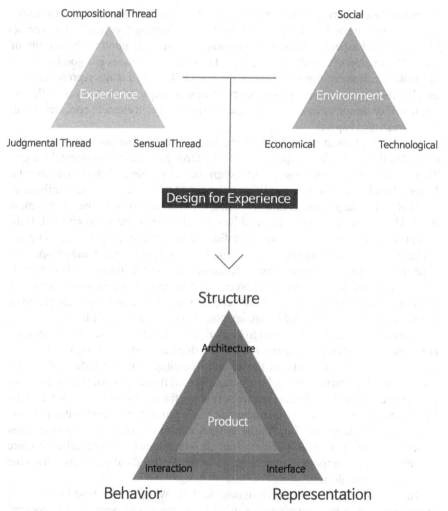

Fig. 8.1 Main framework for design for experience

people seek better prices on products or services, which leads to higher demand for social shopping services that offer group discounts and coupon codes. Elements of the technological environment include the maturity of the technology, its potential for further development, as well as every other environmental factor related to the technology. For example, the emergence of a new algorithm used to connect users in a social network game can influence the experience of the users.

The third element are the inherent characteristics of products or services. We discussed in Chapter 1 the three aspects of products or services: the structural, behavioral, and representational aspects. The structural aspect is concerned with the components of a product or a service, and how these components are assembled with one another. In cases of digital products or IT services such as smartphones or social network services, a good example of a structural element would be the information architectures, which we have described in Chapters 5, 6, and 7 of this book. The behavioral aspect reflects how products or services respond to the activity of users. The interaction mechanism of digital products or services is a good example of the design element from the behavioral aspect. The third is the representational aspect, which refers to how products or services are depicted in the eyes of the users. Interface design covered in this book is a typical design element concerned with the expressional aspect.

The fourth element of design for experience is to find the point of balance between the three threads of experience and the three external environmental factors. There is a strict tension between the experience of people and the environmental factors. In other words, being able to understand how the environment influences a UX is just as important as understanding the characteristics of the environment itself. Thereby we need to understand how the changes in the socio-cultural, technological, and economic environment influence the sensual, judgmental, and compositional aspects of our experience. At the same time, our current and prospective experience impacts the socio-cultural, technological, and economic environment. It is because a feedback loop exists between our experience and the environment. The balance between the two mutually influencing each other is what we referred to as the point of balance (dynamic balancing point) in Chapter 4 of this book.

There are two matters that need to be clarified at this point. The first matter concerns the three threads of experience and the three elements of design which may seem quite similar—the sensual thread corresponding to user interface, the judgmental thread to interaction, and the compositional thread to information architecture. However, the three threads are actually about the experience of users, while the three design elements are the characteristics of a product or a service itself. While user interfaces do greatly impact the sensual experience of users, the interaction features and information architectures can also contribute to the sensual experience as well. Thus, it is important to distinguish the three threads of experience from the three elements of design.

The second matter concerns designing for UX. We generally tend to start with analyzing, from a micro perspective, what users are experiencing at the moment, and what they are expecting in the future. A benefit from this method is that it is very user-centered, so we can focus on their needs and wants. The downside is that it is hard to exactly understand the reason behind their wants and needs. Also, it's often difficult to explain why certain interaction mechanisms and information architectures are effective in certain environments.

On the other hand, some existing products or services are designed based on the technological availability, economic reasons, or socio-cultural trends. The advantage of this approach is that we can predict whether a product or service will succeed as a business. However, we will not know for sure what experience it will result in for people and whether people will appreciate the experience or not. Therefore, as illustrated in Fig. 8.1, a UX design comes from understanding both the experience of users from a micro perspective and the impact of the surrounding environment from a macro perspective. The process of finding the point of balance between the two in considering the structural, behavioral, and expressional aspects of design is what we call an experience design.

8.5   Putting the Framework into Action

This book does not suggest detailed procedures for experience design. Rather, it is concerned with the components of human experience, the elements that build up these components, what type of UX is important for them, and which design factors are relevant in providing each type of experience. In that sense, this book explains the principles of design for experience. So what is the process for designing experience for those using certain products or services?

In explaining the principles covered in this book, I would like to use the example an on-going project on designing a wearable device. Wearable devices can be thought of as a "companion" in our lives, in a sense that they always stay with you and "share" many of your moments. Other typical examples of companions in life are spouses, friends, and/or companion animals, or pets. We are living in a world with a decreasing number of nuclear families, increasing number of single parents, a higher life expectancy than ever, and the availability of Internet of Things (IoT) technology where everything and everyone surrounding us is tagged with an Internet Protocol (IP) address. In this kind of environment, there have been many attempts to create small wearable devices that can function as life-long companions for people. Let's imagine a wearable device project aimed at providing users with an experience of having a lifetime companion. And let's try to think of how we can apply the principles discussed in the earlier chapters to this virtual project. Even though I cannot provide the results of the ongoing project, more up-to-date information will be shared with the readers on the book website.

8.5.1   Step 1: What is a Companion Experience?

The first step of designing the companion experience is to understand what people are experiencing with their current companions and what experiences they are looking forward to sharing together in the future. We will begin with interviewing middle- to old-aged married couples. We will also interview those who have recently lost their companions to find out what they miss most about their spouses. We will also be interviewing teenagers about the benefits and support they are getting from their best friends. Furthermore, we will interview those that live with companion animals, dogs in this case. Some questions that we will be asking include the following: What are the privileges and responsibilities of having a dog? What experiences do you go through together? Our intention is to include the dogs a representative companion, in the interviews when asking their owners for their thoughts and feelings.

Meanwhile, we will search in the humanities and social science research on companionship for the most widely accepted concept and definition of 'companionship.' For example, one scholar defined the concept as 'social involvement' in shared activities, recreational or non-recreational, which is pursued for the intrinsic goal of satisfaction or enjoyment (Rook 1987). The reason we search for the general concept and its definition is to clarify unclear or ambiguous ideas, and to use the common term in any of our future discussions. Based on the research, we will define a companion as a partner that shares every action and experience with another person, and apply that to the overall characteristics of a companion device, the product we are trying to develop. We will also be conducting a literature review, as well as a research into the concept of companionship, or other related concepts from relevant academic fields. Sociology or psychology is often interested in the relationship between the partners in marriage. (Altergott 1981; Edgell 1972; Haynes et al.1992). Through these studies, we will be able to understand that companions are those that fully understand each other's context, love each other, and go through hardship together. The topic of pets is dealt with in ethology and psychology (Zasloff 1996; Kidd and Feldmann 1981; Kidd and Kidd 1980), and studies on life-long friends will be covered in educational psychology and developmental psychology (Buhrmester and Furman 1987; Epstein 1990).

8.5.2 Step 2: What are the Environmental Factors Affecting Companion Experience?

The first question we must ask is: How have the socio-cultural, economic, and technological environments changed with respect to companion devices? A growing number of single people and older people in today's society has amplified the importance of companion devices. The role of companion devices can be critical for those coming back to an empty house after a day out, whether it be from working or studying. This does not only apply to people who live by themselves but also to children of parents who both work long hours. Senior citizens might also need companions to fill in up the empty space left behind by their children, especially if they spend much time home alone.

I come across many pet shops in the streets of Seoul, which is probably an indication of growing amount of disposable income. A higher amount of disposable income can lead to a higher willingness by people to spend part of it for a companion or a companion device. Furthermore, with increasing income, consumers are more likely to pursue their desires to be immersed in a senseful experience, which further stimulates the development in the technology to strengthen the sense of presence for users.

Wearables, IoT, and sensing technologies currently being developed will bring great technological advancements to the development of companion devices. Rechargeable batteries and motors are becoming more and more powerful, compact, and lightweight, allowing us to create devices that can perform for a long period of time. It will be possible to accumulate big volume of data, make computations based on this data, and make decisions on behalf of ourselves, leading to an external judgmental locus of causality. IoT technology will let us freely interact with people or things around us, and our experience, from a compositional aspect, will become denser as a result. Meanwhile, if the companion device itself becomes the center (hub) of the composition that fills the gap in the social network, people will as a result not be positioned in the center, and the relationship centrality will become smaller.

8.5.3 Step 3: Where is the Point of Balance of Companion Experience?

Our next question is: where is the point of balance for experience with a companion device? The most widely used companion device is the smartphone—which is often marketed as such currently. Smartphones can certainly be used for various purposes. Smartphones have evolved in a way that heightens our sense of their presence; they have become bigger in size, and stronger in computing powers. They are built in a way that satisfies both the hedonistic and the utilitarian purpose, with more automated built-in functions that contribute to the external locus of causality. Although we are becoming more densely connected than ever through the increased presence of smartphones, the human network has become less cohesive because the smartphones are often at the network hub, or the center.

We are facing a growing conflict with the smartphones as companion devices. While smartphones provide both internal and external values for many users, they have become quite bulky in size and overly expensive. The future direction of the smartphone will be something entirely different than it has been hereto.

Considering the development of smartphones and wearable devices, how do we picture our experience with a new companion device? It can be explained through the six levers of experience. Figure 8.2 summarizes the six levers of experience.

Presence is the most important dimension of the sensual thread of experience. The two most important factors that affect the sense of presence are the perceived vividness and interactivity from an experience. Vividness measures the richness of stimulation that comes from a certain medium. Interactivity shows the degree to which a user can transform a target. These two elements represent the representational and behavioral aspects of the sense of presence, so they can effectively enhance the sense of presence of users. In other words, an added degree of vividness and interactivity would lead to higher sense of presence for users, while a lower degree of the two would lead to a lower sense of presence. This is covered in more depth in Chapter 5.

Locus of causality is the most important dimension for the judgmental thread of experience. The two biggest elements that affect the locus of causality are the hedonistic and utilitarian values as the experience outcome and the level of automation associated with the experience process. The utilitarian value is concerned with the usefulness of effectiveness of an experience in achieving the goal, while the hedonistic value depends on the amount of pleasure from the experience. The

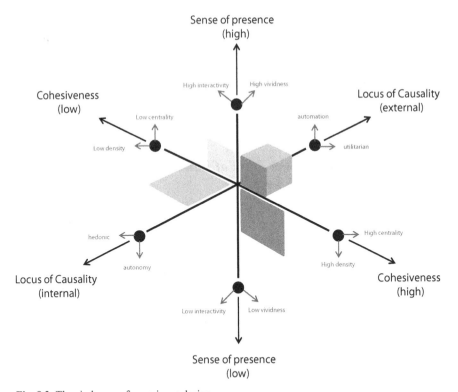

Fig. 8.2 The six levers of experience design

level of automation denotes the extent to which the devices or systems take care of the works of humans. The two components are related to the result and process of an experience, respectively, and have a high chance of creating an interaction effect with each other. If we have more control over a product or a service, and find hedonistic value from the process, we will perceive the locus of causality to be even more internal. On the other hand, if we achieve utilitarian goals through an automated process, we will find the locus of causality to be external. This is covered in more detail in Chapter 6.

Cohesiveness is the most important dimension for the compositional thread of experience. The two main elements that affect cohesiveness are density and centrality. Density shows the extent to which the members of a group are related to each other, and it is used to characterize the relationships within a network. Centrality is a concept that shows how close one is from the center of a network connecting people and objects, and it depends on the composition of a network as a whole. Density and centrality are the two representative elements describing the connectivity and distribution of a network that can greatly affect cohesiveness. The higher the density and centrality, the higher the cohesiveness. On the other hand, the lower the two, the lower the cohesiveness. The details are covered in Chapter 7.

An important thing to note is that the two elements of each thread of experience are pulling the thread together. We refer to this phenomenon as the "double lever effect." For example, if there was only one lever to pull on the thread, a thread would easily slip off the lever. If there are two levers attached to the thread, it would be less likely that the thread would slip off, since the two levers are supporting each other. Thus, it is important to keep in mind that the two elements jointly pull each thread.

Another important point is to understand the interaction between the levers across different threads of experience. For example, as the level of automation from the judgmental thread of experience becomes higher, we may need to lower the level of interactivity from the sensual thread of experience. Or, as the centrality of the network from the compositional thread of experience becomes higher, there may be a need to lower the level of automation from the judgmental thread of experience. There is no fixed rule for how we manage the interaction between the levers, since it depends on the characteristics of products or services. But, when the characteristic of each lever is defined and the product description given, we have to make sure the levers are well-balanced without contradicting each other. For example, let's say we aimed for an external locus of causality by increasing the level of automation. Let's say we also tried to heighten the sense of presence by enhancing the level of interactivity, leading to a conflict. To resolve this, we can increase the level of vividness instead of interactivity for a higher presence. Or we can lower the level of automation but instead add more functions of increased utilitarian value, which can contribute to external locus of causality. Likewise, we have to make sure to check for the balance and consistency among the levers at this point.

Let's go back to the discussion on the on-going project of a wearable device. From the sensual aspect, a new device is likely to be less vivid than existing ones. So far, hand-held devices have become fancier and more vivid, but are overly large and expensive as a result. A new device will have to be designed with strengthened level of interactivity in mind, because companion devices will be sharing every part of our life through interactions, and will also be interacting with other people and things. Companion devices will be mainly focused on hedonistic values, providing satisfaction and amusement for the users. Thus, the automated system can be in charge of most matters, while allowing people to take part in necessary decision-making processes. From the compositional perspective, the relationships will grow denser, where the center of a network is not the device, but the person wearing it. Taking into consideration the balance between the levers, there can possibly be a conflict between the high level of automation and the high level of interactivity. One possible way to balance out the two is to shift the locus of causality towards a more internal orientation by focusing on the fun factors of the UX.

8.5.4 Step 4: Which UX Factors Lead to a Point of Balance?

So far, we have set the levers for our experience design. Now, we must select the important UX factors that influence the levers we selected. Then, we need to decide the necessary design features that should be implemented into the product or service.

The two important levers for sensual experience are vividness and interactivity. However both are very abstract; in order to connect the levers with the imple-

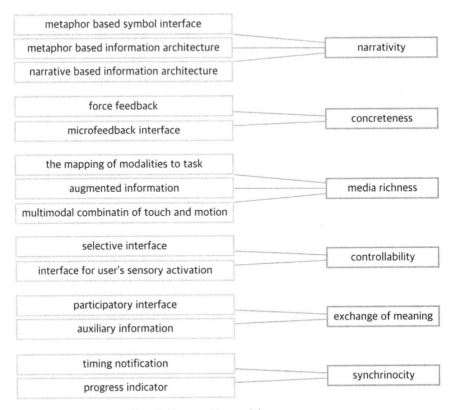

Fig. 8.3 UX factors that affect vividness and interactivity

mentable design elements, we have to describe specific UX factors that link the two. The three UX factors that affect vividness are narrativity and the concreteness of content, as well as the richness of a medium. As for interactivity, UX factors include controllability, exchangeability of meanings, and synchronicity. Figure 8.3 summarizes these factors, and the details are elaborated in Chapter 5 of this book.

The main dimension of the judgmental thread of experience is the locus of causality. The locus of causality can be controlled through the two levers: hedonistic/utilitarian values and automation/autonomy controls. The UX factors that can boost hedonistic values are serendipity and playability. Utilitarian value can be boosted through compatibility and consistency. Customizability and challenge contribute to the increased autonomy for users. Similarly, agent-awareness and adaptivity affect the level of automation of systems. Figure 8.4 shows the summary of these factors, and the details are covered in Chapter 6.

The main dimension for a compositional thread of experience is cohesiveness, which can be controlled with density and centrality. In cases of high density and high centrality, reciprocity is an important UX factor to consider. When density is high but centrality is low, complexity is an important UX factor, while for cases with low density and high centrality, similarity is the key UX factor. Finally, in case

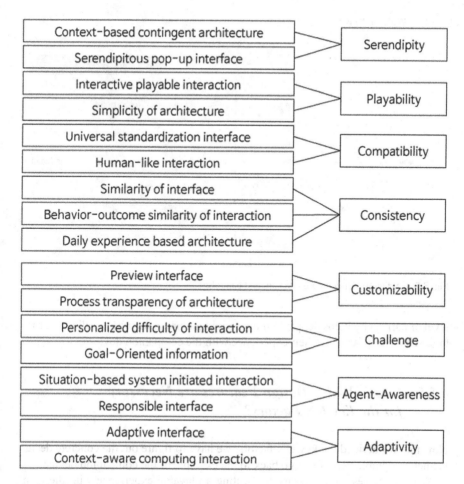

Fig. 8.4 UX factors that affect hedonistic/utilitarian values and autonomy/automation controls

of low density and low centrality, salience is an important UX factor to consider. The details on these factors are covered in Chapter 7, and the summary is illustrated in Fig. 8.5.

Then based on our prior analysis on the six levers of experience, what are the important UX factors for the companion device? Reciprocity would be an important factor in terms of the compositional thread of experience. The role of the device is to be a 'companion,' meaning there should be a mutually balanced interaction and feedback between the device and the people. From the perspective of a judgmental thread of experience, we need to focus on playability. People using the device will have to find the experience enjoyable. Companion devices should be something we can depend on to share our thoughts, thus we will also have to let users be agent-aware and increase the level of automation of the system. To increase the level of interactivity, we have to pay attention to how people can effectively exchange meanings with the devices. It can also be effective to increase narrativity. A high

Compositional Thread

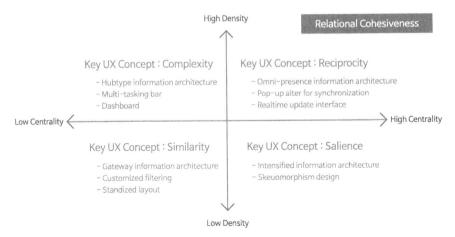

Fig. 8.5 UX factors depending on density and centrality

level of narrativity helps people to draw a vivid picture in their mind, allowing for a high sense of presence of their experience with the companion devices.

8.5.5   Step 5: Which Design Features are Necessary for the Key UX Factors?

Now that we derived the key UX factors, we have to figure out the concrete design elements to implement. Let's go back to the example of the companion device.

Which features are necessary in creating a playable experience with the companion device as an agent, where users can effectively exchange meanings with the device with a high level of reciprocity? For a high level of reciprocity, we need to design a ubiquitous information architecture that can be accessed anytime and anywhere, provide real-time updates to the related components, and be actively synchronized through methods such as pop ups. A more detailed description can be found in Chapter 7.

To enhance playability, an interface where users can directly manipulate the target will need to be installed. Users will need to be able to send and receive information through diverse modalities in real-time. For better agent-awareness, prospective actions or goals of users need to be predicted in advance, and the device will have to react accordingly based on the prediction. More details on this can be found in Chapter 6.

For an effective exchange of meanings, we need to provide a participatory interface through which users can voluntarily take part in information sharing process. Narrativity is highly related to metaphor designs. Symbol interfaces based on metaphors, operations based on metaphors, and sequential information architecture based on narratives are effective means of boosting narrativity. For more information about implementations of narrativity can be found in Chapter 5.

We have to be careful about a few things at this stage. The aforementioned descriptions may seem like a sequential, step-by-step instruction, but they are not. In fact, these "steps" should rather take place in parallel than in sequence. So please note that it was for the ease of explanation that they were organized that manner. Also, nothing is decided at once; we go through an iterative, gradual process of deciding the right elements. While thinking of new design features, we may happen to come up with new UX factors, or even shift the direction of "pulling" by the levers. Then, what kind of organizations do we need to effectively carry out this complex process of experience design?

8.6   The Characteristics of Organizations that Create Great Experiences

Our experiences are often subjective, change dynamically, and greatly depend on context. Experience design has to consider both the micro aspects of individual experiences and the macro aspects of environmental changes. Furthermore, we have to be able to think in terms of both the gradual evolution and disruptive innovation, through which we can derive specific experience factors and design features. Then how can organizations prepare themselves to implement a design for experience?

Firstly, an organization must possess a deep understanding of the theories of the humanities and social sciences. People are the ones who experience, not products or services. Thus, we have to be able to understand people first. Humanities and social sciences are studies that focus on people. These theories can help set the directions for seeking the appropriate UX factors. For example, the concept of playability has been studied for years and many theories have been established in the past (e.g., Huizinga 1938). They can guide us in understanding the different types of playability, as well as which factors are necessary for people to experience playability. In addition, these researches provide useful information for us in understanding the success factors of past designs, and help us with our decisions in incorporating certain structural, functional, or representational elements into our new designs.

However, it is often difficult, in the industry, to find the right people or organizations that have strong background in humanities and social sciences. Therefore, a collaboration between academia and industry is a must. Past academia-industry collaborations have mainly focused on students participating in qualitative user studies. This is not necessarily wrong, but without strong theoretical background, it may be inefficient to try to draw UX factors solely through user analysis. It can mistakenly lead to repeated conclusions already made by many social scientists who concentrated on this topic over the past hundreds of years. Thus, it is critical to study in advance the existing theories relevant to the project and spend time and efforts in transforming the relevant theories into key UX factors. Further, organizations will need to strengthen their employees' internal education programs to enhance their understanding of humans and knowledge of important social science theories.

Secondly, firms must build an interdisciplinary organization. There has been a recent hype of the term "interdisciplinary" in academia as well as in the industry. Although the word may seem ambiguous, there are many benefits in having an interdisciplinary organization within a firm. The HCI Lab at Yonsei University has maintained its interdisciplinary nature since it was founded 20 years ago. The lab is composed of members with diverse backgrounds: technical backgrounds such as computer science or electrical engineering, arts backgrounds such as design or music, as well as social science backgrounds. With such a diverse group, we are able to tackle problems and challenges from different perspectives. For example, when designing a companion device for the elderly, researchers with humanities and social science backgrounds study theories regarding the role of companions and how friendships are formed. Based on this research, we can apply important concepts to a companion device. Those who studied design can transform these abstract concepts into tangible features and functions of the device. They can catch additionally important properties that were not identified by the social scientists. Those with computing and development skills can implement the ideas and designs into an actual functioning system. During the implementation process, they can suggest supplementary functions, interfaces, or information architectures that can further enhance the device, based on up-to-date technological skills.

One way of running an interdisciplinary organization is to form a group composed of product planning/strategy team and HCI/UX team. In designing a new product or service, both teams are necessary. Thus, I strongly call for a need to integrate both teams together. The biggest benefit from this is the fact that a point of balance between individuals' experience and environment can be effectively reached. As explained in Chapter 3, the point of balance continues to change dynamically. Thus, there has to be an effective mechanism through which the changes in individual experiences and the changes in the environment can be aligned with the strategic goal of an organization. Keeping together the planning/strategy team with the HCI/UX team can be an effective means of finding this dynamic point of balance.

Thirdly, the organization that deals with an experience design should be like a "nickel-silver pot." Nickel-silver pots are kitchen utensils made of alloy of nickel, copper, and zinc. In this fast-changing digital society, properties of nickel-silver pots should be a virtue for organizations in charge of UX.

The first property of a nickel-silver pot is its fast speed. Because the pots are of high thermal conductivity, they heat up very fast. The pots also cool down really fast because the metal is very thin and can't conserve the heat energy well. The pots are excellent for cooking instant noodles, because they can be cooked really quickly without having to worry about the noodles being stuck at the bottom of the pot. This trait of a silver-nickel pot is a perfect trait for the organization dealing with UX since speed is the most critical factor for a successful incremental experience. Let's take as an example the Samsung Galaxy Note. The Galaxy Note was introduced right after the release of the iPhone4S. At first, there was a clear line between the groups that liked and disliked the product. Bigger screens were perceived as a merit to some people; it was easy to run multiple apps at the same time, and it was especially useful when watching videos or surfing the web. On the other hand, some people thought the phone was too bulky to grab, and the stylus pen was not precise. Usually, we do not see any upgrades for a certain period of time after phones' releases. However, the case of Galaxy Note was very unusual in that Samsung provided super-speed upgrades, a total of 15 upgrades in 1 year after its release, half of which transformed the experience of users. As a result, we observed a tremendous growth in the market share of the Galaxy Note after each upgrade was released, and it led to the successful release of a follow-up product, the Galaxy Tab. This example shows why speed is important, and why we need to have a nickel-silver pot-like organizations within firms.

The second property of a nickel-silver pot lies in its degree of conflict. Once the water in the pot starts boiling, it continues to boil ferociously. It is the reason why the noodles stay chewy. This trait is important for organizations dealing with UX. Fast-paced sustaining innovation is not always the solution to a successful experience design. If sustaining innovation develops too much towards one direction, people would perceive a greater level of cognitive dissonance from the incremental innovation. Then users would seek ways to resolve the conflict, while some companies will try to turn this conflict into opportunities to take over market share. The two will trigger a shift in the paradigm, creating a disruptive innovation in terms of UX. A strong level of conflict is an indication of a large number of people feeling cognitive dissonance from the current dominant design. With the increase in the cognitive dissonance of individuals, the discrepancy in the striving aspiration of the companies will become more distinct. That's how sharp conflicts, which can trigger a paradigm shift in products or services, become visible. Companies dealing with UX will have to be able to feel the conflicts and deal with them accordingly. In other words, they have to be able to forecast the opportunities for disruptive innovation before its competitors do. Interdisciplinary organizations in a firm can create this kind of conflicts and dissonance. Researchers from different backgrounds are likely to have different values and factors that they think of as important, leading to conflicts and dissonance within a group. This is why interdisciplinary groups go through many hardships. However, this is a good practice to experience conflict and dissonance. Therefore, evaluation of these groups should not be based on how harmoniously and consistently the members worked together, but rather on how they were able to close in on the gaps of conflict and dissonance in order to create and develop ideas for a new experience.

The third trait is flexibility. Nickel-silver pots are very cheap and easily bendable. When current design can no longer resolve the stitch up the cognitive dissonance felt by the users, organizations have to shift from the old design to a new design paradigm. There are of course the unsuccessful cases in which they have decided to take a hasty shift from the old to the new. Yet, clinging onto the old is way more riskier than a hasty paradigm shift. At first, the risk may seem smaller but the danger can gradually grow to a point where there is no turning back. Some examples include the fall of Nokia's cellphones, Sony's televisions, and Kodak's camera films. Therefore, teams and divisions within an organization that designs experience must be evaluated on how many meaningful exchanges took place between its members based on failures and lessons learned from those failures rather than through the scale of success of a project.

Lastly, for an effective design for experience, companies have to actively participate in HCI/UX conferences and research forums. By participating in these events, they can stay up to date with technological, socio-cultural, and economic changes. Also, the planning/strategy teams and HCI/UX teams can together think of products or services that can create new experiences for users. HCI Korea is one example. HCI Korea is distinguishable from many other conferences for the following reasons: first, the participants are from diverse backgrounds and participants represent in a balanced way both academia and industry, which allows for a fair amount of interaction between those two groups—it is truly magnificent to experience the dynamics in such a place where ideas are shared and challenged. Some people are interested in the technical aspects of new interfaces and modalities. Some people present their research findings on how to use a GPS navigation system in a car from an anthropological perspective. Most academic conferences are composed mainly of professors and students with their focus on theories, and most business events consist of people from the industry addressing their experiences. Lastly, HCI Korea is entertaining and relaxed. This is an annual conference held in the beginning of each year at the peak of the ski season—and is held at a top ski resort. When I first attended the conference more than 10 years ago, I was impressed that I got a discount on ski tickets from the conference. I could therefore participate in the conference during the daytime, and go skiing in the night. For many reasons, HCI Korea has grown into a gigantic conference with more than 2,000 participants attending for full three days, which has made HCI Korea the biggest specialized conference in Korea. The conference is attended by many non-Korean HCI specialists that are observing studies or projects going on in the Korean HCI community, now that Korea has become one of the leading nations that create products and services used by people all over the world.

Design for the next experience will become more important than ever in the future. We will have to be able to understand the theories and principles from humanities and social science, and organizations will have to be composed of people with diverse backgrounds and specialties working together in a speedy, flexible, and sensitive manner like the nickel-silver pots.

8.7 Summary

- Our lives are filled with experiences of products and services. The values and meaning of our lives are determined by our everyday experiences.
- A person's experience is composed of sensual, judgmental, and compositional threads of experience.
- Technological, socio/cultural, and economic environments impact our experiences, and our experiences impact our environments.
- Products and services are composed of structural, behavioral, and representational characteristics, and they are implemented through information architecture, interaction mechanism, and interface technology, respectively.

- Design for experience is about translating the point of balance achieved between the external environment and a person's experience, into the structural, behavioral, and representational aspects of a product or a service.
- Each thread of experience is tied onto two levers, which together pull the thread.
- For each lever, relevant UX factors and design features can be applied to products and services.
- An organization that designs for experience needs to understand the theories from humanities and social sciences.
- An organization that designs for experience needs to be composed of people from diverse background such as technology/development, design/arts, etc.
- An organization that designs for experience needs to be flexible and sensitive but yet deal with conflicts and dissonance with speed.

8.8 Discussion Topics

- Interdisciplinary units may be easy to form but hard to operate. Are they necessary for UX designs?
- Conflicts and dissonance are usually perceived as problems. How can they be utilized as opportunities instead?
- What are the traits of the 'nickel-silver pots' that are needed in companies that are designing for UX?

References

Altergott K (1981) Behavioral companionship in marriage: a cross-national analysis. J Comp Fam Stud 12(2):171–185

Buhrmester D, Furman W (1987) The development of companionship and intimacy. Child Dev 58(4):1101–1113

Edgell S (1972) Marriage and the concept companionship. Br J Sociol 23(4):452–461

Epstein SM (1990) The stability of victimisation in elementary school children. Unpublished master's thesis, Florida Atlantic University, Boca Raton

Haynes SN, Floyd FJ, Lemsky C, Rogers E, Winemiller D, Heilman N, Cardone L (1992) The marital satisfaction questionnaire for older persons. Psychol Assess 4(4):473–482

Huizinga J (1938). Homo Ludens. Amsterdam University Press, Amsterdam

Kidd AH, Feldmann BM (1981) Pet ownership and self-perceptions of older people. Psychol Rep 48(3):867–875

Kidd AH, Kidd RM (1980) Personality characteristics and preferences in pet ownership. Psychol Rep 46(3):939–949

Rook KS (1987) Social support versus companionship: effects on life stress, loneliness, and evaluations by others. J Pers Soc Psychol 52(6):1132–1147

Zasloff RL (1996) Measuring attachment to companion animals: a dog is not a cat is not a bird. Appl Anim Behav Sci 47(1):43–48

Epilogue

It has been more than 20 years since the HCI Lab at Yonsei University was founded. There has been a dramatic change in our surroundings over the last 20 years. The internet has become an inseparable part of our lives, and smartphones are now more important than PCs. I expect the changes in the next 20 years to be just as dramatic in speed and scale, if not more.

The HCI Lab has been, and still is, working extremely hard on its researches. We participate in numerous government-funded research projects, and we work together with the industry to seek solutions to its problems. I have been highly motivated to teach courses at the university, thanks to the wonderful students who have showed their diligence and enthusiasm towards the field of HCI. We work hard to develop the ideas that are brought up during classes and projects into research papers.

Yet sometimes, I feel like something is missing. Even great research papers become outdated in few years. This is especially true for HCI papers that are based on trendy IT technologies in this fast-paced world. In reality, journal papers in HCI field easily fall behind the trends during its review period.

So I began to think that we need to understand the fundamental principles in the field of HCI in order to devise design principles and processes that can last for decades. Moreover, it is more important to understand "why" than "how." So I initially began putting down my thoughts on my daily experiences with various IT products and services in small hopes of finding out the "why."

But the small hopes grew larger during the process of writing. As a president of the Korean HCI Society, I became ambitious to let the world know of the excellence of the HCI community in Korea. I also felt responsibility as a General Conference Chair of the organizing committee for the ACM SIGCHI conference, which is held in Korea for the first time in 2015. While writing, I was also appointed as Vice President of the Library and Information Services of Yonsei University.

However, such big hopes and ambitions were more of a hindrance than help for my writing as I became too stressed out and pressured to enjoy the process of the writing itself. I even thought about deserting the writing completely.

© Springer International Publishing Switzerland 2015
J. Kim, *Design for Experience*, Human-Computer Interaction Series,
DOI 10.1007/978-3-319-14304-0

The closer I drew to finishing my manuscript, the more stressed I became. At the most difficult time of my writing, a close friend of mine invited me to visit Dosan Seowon (a private Confucian academy) of Toegye Yi Hwang. He is a key figure of the Neo-Confucian literati, who is depicted on the Korean 1,000 won bill. Below is the very last poetry he wrote before his death titled "Self Epitaph" (自銘). Reading through this poetry, I realized how foolish I was in my thoughts of stress and pressure.

"Until the day a reigning scholar passes away, knowledge strays further the more I attempt to seek it,"

he wrote. I was ashamed of myself for being overly ambitious and conclusive about my merely 20 years of knowledge. There is no definite ending to learning.

With that altered mindset I became as open and candid as possible in my writing. I focused on writing with the purpose of yearning for more learning rather than try too hard to come up with something grandiose. "My layman clothes feel light on me and so I dance," Toegye Yi Hwang wrote. He further wrote, "I follow the natural path, what more shall I seek?" I therefore wrote about exactly what I saw, heard, and felt, which was based on his words.

This is how I wrote the book. I hope that this book, *Design for Experience*, can inspire its readers to start thinking about their experiences and learn more rather than to conclude on them. And with my sincere hope that all the forthcoming efforts to create a great experience for people will come together as "The Science for Experience" in the near future, I would like to wrap this book up with Toegye Yi Hwang's last poetry, Self Epitaph (自銘).

Self Epitaph (自銘)

Hwang Yi (Toegye)

生而大癡(생이대치): I was dull when I was born,

壯而多疾(장이다질): and riddled with disease when coming of age.

中何嗜學(중하기학): I somehow found to enjoy the pursuit of knowledge in middle age,

晚何叨爵(만하도작): and how did I end up to rise to a government post in my last years?

學求猶邈(학구유막): I seek knowledge but it becomes more distant the more I try,

爵辭愈嬰(작사유영): and I turn down my government post yet I am still attached to it

進行之路(진행지겁): When I head straight I falter,

退藏之貞(퇴장지정): but when I fall back I stand straight.

深慙國恩(심참국은): I was ashamed of the grace the country provide me with,

亶畏聖言(단외성언): and fearful of the words of the sages.

有山嶷嶷(유산억억): The mountains reach high

有水源源(유수원원): and the waters flows.

婆娑初服(파사초복): My layman clothes feel light on me and so I dance
脫略衆訕(탈략중산): The slanders are far away and so I feel lighthearted
我懷伊阻(아회이조): No one knows my heart
我佩誰玩(아패수완): so who is there to rejoice with me?
我思古人(아사고인): I miss a person of my past
實獲我心(실획아심): I keep a tight hold on my heart.
寧知來世(녕지래세): How can I guess the next life
不獲今兮(불획금혜): when I do not yet know of today
憂中有樂(우중유악): There is pleasure in worry
樂中有憂(악중유우): and there is worry in joy
乘化歸盡(승화귀진): I follow the natural path
復何求兮(부하구혜): what more shall I seek?

Printed in the United States
By Bookmasters